EVERYDAY ENCOUNTERS
WITH
STATE AND CAPITALISM

EVERYDAY ENCOUNTERS
WITH
STATE AND CAPITALISM

BHABANI SHANKAR NAYAK

ANTHEM PRESS

Anthem Press
An imprint of Wimbledon Publishing Company
www.anthempress.com

This edition first published in UK and USA 2025

by ANTHEM PRESS
75–76 Blackfriars Road, London SE1 8HA, UK
or PO Box 9779, London SW19 7ZG, UK
and
244 Madison Ave #116, New York, NY 10016, USA

British Library Cataloguing-in-Publication Data
A catalogue record for this book is available from the British Library.

Library of Congress Cataloging-in-Publication Data: 2024925197
A catalog record for this book has been requested.

ISBN-13: 978-1-83999-487-6 (Hbk) / 978-1-83999-488-3 (Pbk)
ISBN-10: 1-83999-487-8 (Hbk) / 1-83999-488-6 (Pbk)

Cover Credit: Author, Generated by ChatGPT

This title is also available as an e-book.

I dedicate this book to my comrade Bharath Kumar, who fed me, sheltered me in his room, and stood by me when I had nothing during my student days at the University of Hyderabad, India. The words in this book are political testaments and a personal tribute to your unwavering commitment. I value this bond, forged in hardship, continues to represent a rare camaraderie beyond compare.

ABOUT THE BOOK

This book, *Everyday Encounters with State and Capitalism*, illustrates how different forces shape ideas, knowledge traditions, policies, processes, institutions and everyday lives to domesticate both people and the planet in pursuit of profit. It examines the myriad ways in which contemporary ruling and non-ruling elites influence politics, culture, economy and religion, and shape our daily interactions, emphasising their impact on individuals, families, communities, democratic praxis, societal structures and nature. The book portrays power structures that are skewed in a manner that marginalises many while upholding the interests of a few. It depicts numerous contradictions inherent in capitalism and the state, while also presenting alternative ideas drawn from the everyday experiences of working people.

State and capitalism territorialise and deterritorialise lives and livelihoods. They destabilise social, cultural and economic relationships. Everyday crises are manufactured, and conflicts are designed to divert the masses from exploring alternatives to capitalism. This strategy aims to maintain the status quo by ensuring that attention and resources are consistently focused on the accumulation of wealth and prosperity for a few, thereby preventing widespread consideration of alternative and egalitarian systems and processes for mass welfare.

ABOUT THE AUTHOR

Bhabani Shankar Nayak is a political economist and works as Professor of Business Management at the Guildhall School of Business and Law, London Metropolitan University, UK. He is the author of twenty two books and numerous articles in different international journals.

ACKNOWLEDGEMENT

The journey of bringing this book to life has been a deeply rewarding experience both politically and personally. I reflect on the ways I encountered and experienced the state and capitalism in my everyday life, which I depicted in this book. It started with writing journalistic articles, commentaries and editorials on contemporary issues in the *South Asia Journal, Counter Currents, Mainstream Weekly, Eurasia Review, Morning Star* and many other news portals. I owe a debt of gratitude to many people whose support, encouragement and expertise have made this book possible.

First and foremost, I would like to thank my wife for her unwavering support and understanding throughout the many late nights and early mornings spent working on this project. Your patience and encouragement have been my greatest sources of strength.

A heartfelt thank you to all my editors whose keen insights and meticulous attention to detail have significantly shaped the final manuscript. Your guidance has been invaluable, and this book is much stronger for your involvement.

Special thanks to my comrades, friends and colleagues who offered their expertise, feedback and moral support. Geeta, Piyya, Suresh, Suhas, Seema, Oliver and Dr Gopabandhu Dash provided thoughtful critiques, supports and suggestions that were instrumental in refining my ideas.

To the many individuals who shared their stories, experiences and wisdom with me, thank you for your openness and generosity. Your contributions have enriched this book in ways I could never have achieved alone.

I hope this book serves as a valuable resource for alternative ideas and inspires you on your own journey to question the state and capitalism in your everyday life. All errors are mine.

With gratitude,
Bhabani

London,
23 August 2024

CONTENTS

INTRODUCTION

Everyday Encounters with State and Capitalism depicts how the modern state governs people, places, the planet and resources to uphold the interests of capital. Everyday governance by the state, through the use of laws, courts, police forces and armies, shapes, secures and sustains capitalism as a system, often at the expense of working people and the environment. Such tools of everyday governance create a cohesive culture of mass socialisation and acceptance, making it appear as if the state represents the interests of the people. This culture normalises capitalism as a system. Alternatives to capitalism have been undermined either by brute force or by propaganda against them.

Market-led democracies domesticate citizens as consumers, naturalising mass consumerism, where individual freedom is defined by the individualistic ideals of utility, pleasure and satisfaction, all of which depend on access to commodities and services provided by market forces. Such a narrow, illusive and utilitarian ideal of freedom has replaced the social foundations of collective culture, where freedom and happiness were interrelated. In African culture, this concept is called 'Ubuntu', which means 'I am because we are'. It emphasises the interconnectedness of our everyday lives. Similarly, in Indian philosophy, the collective foundation of health and happiness is expressed in the last verse of the Garuḍa Purā ṇa (2.35.51) and in the Bhavishya Purā ṇa (3.2.35.14), which states: 'Sarve Bhavantu Sukhinah, Sarve Santu Niramayāh' (May all be happy, may all be free from illness). Similarly, the collective values of Confucianism in Asia, along with the collective indigenous cultures in the Americas and working-class values of solidarity in Europe, reveal the foundational role of collective principles in shaping societies and lives.

These collective foundations of societies and human lives were dismantled with the rise of private property, feudalism and later the economic expansion of Western Europe led by mercantile capitalism during the sixteenth century. The Descartian philosophy, based on 'I think, therefore I am', shaped an individualistic 'self' that became concomitant with the requirements of Western capitalism that the world is experiencing today. The Descartian philosophy of the 'individual self', the moral philosophies of Adam Smith based on 'self-interest', David Ricardo's concept of 'rent-seeking revenue accumulation for profit' and John Locke's political justification for 'unlimited private accumulation of property' are some of the philosophical foundations of modern capitalism in all its forms.

The rampant individualism, consumerism and commodification of human beings and nature in the pursuit of material accumulation, under the guise of individual freedom and happiness, have diminished progress, prosperity and peace in societies governed by capitalism. *Everyday Encounters with State and Capitalism* reflects these ruinous transformations, while also offering hopes on human potentials to access and implement available alternatives for a better tomorrow.

CHAPTER 1

TERRITORIALISATION, DETERRITORIALISATION AND CAPITALISM

Introduction

The three processes of territorialisation, deterritorialisation and reterritorialisation of ideas, knowledge traditions, land, space, time, identities, labour and emancipatory struggles are integral to capitalism. These processes are embedded within various institutions and structures that extend beyond geographical boundaries (Deleuze & Guattari, 2009; Cocco, 2007).

Territorialisation refers to the establishment and consolidation of control not only over a particular area but also over knowledge, ideas and lives of labour, leading to the creation and reinforcement of boundaries in the name of security and national sovereignty that define ownership, power and influence. This process is evident in the way capitalist economies allocate resources, distribute labour and manage spaces to maximise productivity and profit while marginalising working people (Cox, 2024).

Deterritorialisation, on the other hand, involves the disruption and dismantling of these established territories as per the requirements of capitalism. It reflects the fluid and dynamic nature of capitalism, where boundaries and controls are constantly being reorganised and redefined for the mobility of capital. This can be seen in the global movement of capital, labour and information, which often transcends traditional national borders and regulations while upholding the interests of capitalist core (Hillier, 2023).

Reterritorialisation is not only the process of re-establishing control and creating new territories but also knowledge, ideas and labour. As capitalism evolves, new forms of organisation and governance emerge to adapt to changing conditions. This can involve the creation of new markets, the restructuring of industries and the reconfiguration of social and cultural identities which are concomitant with the requirements of capital expansion. The call for strong borders and immigration control are part of this project, which takes often reactionary cultural and nationalist turns (Elden, 2022; Skonieczny, 2023).

These processes are deeply interwoven with various institutions, such as governments, states, corporations and international organisations which operate on local, regional, national and global scales. The influence of these processes can be seen in economic policies, social norms and cultural practices that shape our world today. By understanding these dynamics, one can better grasp the complexities of capitalism and its ruinous impacts on individuals, families, communities and societies.

Privatisation and Territorialisation of Land

In the early seventh century in rural England, the process of territorialisation played a major role in the transformation of land into private property in its institutionalised form. This transformation was facilitated through the implementation of various practices such as surveying, husbandry and legal frameworks. The rise of territorialisation marked a profound shift in the relationship between communities and the land they inhabited. The transition from communal ownership, often associated with divine commons, to private property rights reshaped the dynamics of land usage and stewardship. Previously, land had been held collectively, with communities sharing rights and responsibilities for its collective usage and communitarian management (Sevilla-Buitrago, 2012).

However, as territorialisation advanced, individual ownership emerged as the predominant form of land tenure. Surveying techniques allowed for the precise delineation of property boundaries, facilitating the demarcation of individual land parcels. Concurrently, advancements in agricultural husbandry practices improved land productivity, incentivising individuals to assert control over specific tracts of land for personal gain. Moreover, legal systems began to recognise and enforce individual property rights, granting landowners exclusive authority over their holdings. This legal framework provided the foundation for the establishment of private property norms, further solidifying the concept of individual land ownership. As a result, the once-shared relationship between communities and the land gradually shifted towards one characterised by private individual rights. This transformation not only altered the economic landscape but also had profound social and cultural implications, fundamentally reshaping the way people interacted with and perceived their environment (Peluso & Lund, 2011).

The process of land privatisation in England did not begin solely in the early seventh century but rather unfolded over several centuries, with significant milestones marking its progression. While territorialisation laid the groundwork for the emergence of private property, it was the Norman Conquest of 1066 that initiated a more pronounced shift towards private ownership of land. The Norman Conquest brought about a restructuring of land ownership, as William the Conqueror redistributed vast tracts of land among his supporters, consolidating power and establishing a feudal system. This redistribution fundamentally altered the landscape of land tenure, with large estates granted to Norman nobles in exchange for military service, effectively privatising formerly communal land (Blomley, 2007).

However, it was not until the period of the Enclosures during the sixteenth century that land privatisation reached its zenith. Enclosure Acts were passed by the English Parliament, allowing landowners to convert common lands into private property by enclosing them with fences or hedges. This process, driven by economic and social factors, led to the displacement of rural communities and the concentration of land ownership in the hands of a wealthy elite. The Enclosure Acts not only solidified the concept of land as private property but also catalysed the transition to more intensive agricultural practices, contributing to the growth of capitalism and the emergence of a modern agricultural economy. Therefore, while territorialisation laid the foundation for land privatisation, it was the Norman Conquest and the Enclosure Acts of the sixteenth century that played pivotal roles in cementing the transformation of land into private property in England (Webster, 2023).

The process of territorialisation of land indeed played a crucial role in shaping the emergence of Westphalian nation-states in Europe. The Peace of Westphalia, signed in 1648, marked a significant turning point in European history, establishing the principles of state sovereignty and territorial integrity. Central to these principles was the idea of clearly defined borders and exclusive control over a defined territory, laying the groundwork for the modern nation-state system with feudal and rent-seeking characteristics (Blomley, 2019).

However, the territorialisation of land did not remain confined to Europe; it was also a central feature of European colonialism. European colonial powers embarked on vast imperial projects aimed at expanding their territorial control and extracting resources from colonised lands. This process involved the imposition of Western legal and administrative frameworks on indigenous societies, often resulting in the dispossession of traditional landowners and the establishment of colonial land tenure systems. Colonialism thus globalised the project of territorialisation of land, as European powers sought to assert control over vast territories in Africa, Asia, the Americas and Oceania. The primary objectives of colonial territorialisation were twofold: to facilitate revenue accumulation through the exploitation of natural resources and labour, and to extend political and economic dominance over colonised people (Herbst, 2014).

In pursuit of these goals, European colonial powers employed various tactics, including land expropriation, forced labour and the imposition of property laws favouring colonial settlers. These practices not only entrenched colonial control but also perpetuated patterns of land inequality and social injustice that continue to have lasting consequences in many parts of the world today. The imperialist wars, regional organisations, trading routes, geopolitical and military alliances and organisations are territorial by nature. Moreover, the legacy of colonial territorialisation continues to shape contemporary geopolitical dynamics, as post-colonial states grapple with issues of land rights, resource management and territorial disputes. The enduring legacy of colonialism underscores the complex interplay between land, power and identity in the modern world (Dube, 2002), highlighting the need for a critical understanding of the historical processes that have shaped our present-day realities, where real estate companies are reproducing landlessness (Issar, 2023).

The territorialisation of private property has historically accelerated the emergence of individualist and exclusionary societies. Within these societies, the ownership of landed properties has served as a crucial determinant of power and social status for individuals and families. Through their control over these properties, they have exerted influence over both people and natural resources. This phenomenon has laid the groundwork for the feudal system of governance, which has persisted in various iterations worldwide. Consequently, the legacy of private property rights continues to shape social structures and power dynamics in contemporary societies. In the age of technofeudalism, major private and public corporations continue to control vast amounts of land in the world today.

Enclosers of Space

The territorialisation of land has not only resulted in a world structured around the concept of land as private property but has also facilitated the formation of territories at various levels, leading to the segregation of private spaces based on gender, property ownership and subsequently on the grounds of class, race, caste, tribe and other forms of marginalisation. This process has unfolded through the establishment of private and public spheres, a dynamic that emerged with the advent of agricultural societies based on land as private property. In such societies, the private sphere was predominantly designated for women, while the public sphere was created for men. Remarkably, this societal framework still reverberates across different regions of the globe today. Examples abound to illustrate the enduring impact of this phenomenon (Klein, 1995; Sevilla-Buitrago, 2015).

In Western Europe and America, racialised ghettos stand as stark reminders of spatial segregation (Matlin, 2018). Likewise, in the United Kingdom, the phenomenon of postcode poverty underscores how territorialisation manifests even within relatively affluent nations (Melamed, 2015; Rogaly, 2020). In India, the division of geographical space and residential properties along caste and religious lines vividly demonstrates how the territorialisation of land and private property intertwines with broader societal and economic divisions. In this interconnected narrative, the territorialisation of land, private property and space evolves in tandem. The higher classes, castes and propertied individuals wield significant influence over various spheres of life, controlling resources (Beteille, 2012) and shaping the very fabric of our planet.

The gendered division of labour and discrimination, racialised capitalism, caste-based ghettos and class-based shanty towns and slums all stem directly from the territorialisation of space predicated on property ownership, with land retaining a pivotal role in these dynamics. The gendered division of labour, for instance, is deeply entrenched in societies where land ownership dictates social norms and economic structures. Women often find themselves relegated to domestic roles, constrained by traditional expectations rooted in property ownership patterns. Similarly, racialised capitalism perpetuates inequalities by exploiting marginalised communities, relegating them to inferior living conditions and limited economic opportunities, all within the framework of property ownership delineated by historic racial boundaries (Elias, 2024).

Caste-based ghettos and class-based shanty towns and slums further illustrate how territorialisation perpetuates social stratification. In these contexts, land ownership serves as a stark marker of privilege, with marginalised groups relegated to marginalised spaces, perpetuating cycles of poverty and exclusion. In essence, the territorialisation of space based on property ownership creates and perpetuates systems of inequality (Anthias, 2021), where access to resources, opportunities and basic rights is intricately linked to one's position within the property ownership hierarchy. Until these underlying structures are addressed, the consequences of territorialisation will continue to shape and perpetuate societal divisions, political marginalisation and economic injustices.

The territorialisation of space poses significant challenges for working people, affecting their accessibility to, availability of, and distribution networks for essential resources. These challenges are often shaped by the principles of purchasing power within the market. All kinds of markets themselves are stratified based on the purchasing power of individuals, delineating who frequents which streets for shopping and thereby defining their social status, economic influence and political standing within society. In this paradigm, individuals become characterised by the commodities they consume, leading to a society where material possessions serve as markers of individualistic identity (Crompton, 2008).

In commodity-conscious societies, where dead commodity defines people with life and consumerism reigns supreme, there is a heightened sense of orderliness and a culture of compliance. In such a society, human beings behave like orderly objects in the markets (Slater, 1987). Individuals conform to market-led societal norms dictated by consumption patterns, making such societies easier to govern. Consequently, the territorialisation of space emerges as both a strategy and a tool of governance (Gualini, 2016) wielded without necessarily instigating revolutionary consciousness or significant social and political upheavals. These dynamics underscore the intricate relationship between space, consumption and governance, wherein the organisation of physical space and access to resources serve as mechanisms of control and social stratification (ibid). Until there is a shift away from the commodification of human existence and a re-evaluation of societal values, the territorialisation of space will continue to perpetuate systems of inequality and reinforce existing exploitative power structures dominated by the propertied class (Rasmussen & Lund, 2018).

The territorialisation of space fosters a regressive consciousness rooted in the ideals of 'me', 'mine' and 'mine' only. This mindset, entrenched in notions of individual ownership and exclusive possession, promotes a narrow worldview focused solely on personal gain and the preservation of one's territory. At its core, this regressive consciousness prioritises the protection of individual interests above collective well-being (Upreti, 2023), leading to a fragmentation of communities and a breakdown of social cohesion. Rather than fostering collaboration and mutual support, it breeds competition and distrust among individuals and groups vying for control over limited resources and spaces.

Moreover, this mindset perpetuates a cycle of scarcity mentality, wherein individuals perceive resources as finite and hoard them out of fear of scarcity, further exacerbating inequalities and depriving others of access to essential goods and opportunities. Ultimately, the regressive consciousness spawned by the territorialisation of space impedes progress towards a more inclusive and equitable society, as it reinforces divisions and hampers efforts to address systemic injustices. To counteract this, it is imperative to cultivate a collective consciousness that prioritises cooperation, solidarity, empathy and shared responsibility for the well-being of all members of society and the planet (Maistry, 2008).

The fencing of space driven by territorialisation has a profound effect on human consciousness, narrowing its scope and eroding the inherent and integral relationship between individuals and both their fellow human beings and the natural world. This separation is not incidental but rather central to the survival of capitalism as a system, which thrives on the principles of private property and profit (Harvey, 2014). By delineating boundaries, destroying the collective foundations of society and human lives and enclosing spaces, territorialisation reinforces a sense of individualism and isolation, severing the ties that bind communities together and disconnecting individuals from the ecosystems in which they exist. This isolation serves the interests of capitalism by atomising society, making it easier to exploit human beings and nature for profit.

The emphasis on private property inherent in territorialisation perpetuates a mindset of ownership and control, where the accumulation of wealth and possessions becomes the primary measure of success and status. This mindset fosters competition rather than cooperation, exacerbating inequalities and undermining collective efforts to address pressing social and environmental challenges. In this way, the fencing of space and the separation it engenders not only diminish human consciousness but also perpetuate the conditions that sustain capitalism (Jansson, 2024).

In search of alternatives, it is essential to challenge the notion of private property as sacrosanct and foster a deeper sense of connection and interdependence among individuals and with the natural world. Only by transcending the boundaries imposed by territorialisation can we cultivate a more just, equitable and sustainable society.

Ghettoisation of Ideas and Knowledge

The development and dissemination of ideas and knowledge are deeply rooted in collective efforts and shared experiences. Every form of knowledge, whether it be scientific discoveries, philosophical insights, ethnographic experiences, or cultural traditions, is shaped by the contributions of countless individuals and communities. Throughout history, human societies have engaged in the exchange of ideas through various means, including oral traditions, written texts, artistic expressions and interpersonal communication. These interactions serve as the foundation upon which knowledge is built, refined and transmitted across generations. At its core, knowledge emerges from the collective endeavour of sharing experiences from everyday life. Observations, reflections and innovations stemming from individual experiences are shared within communities, sparking dialogue, debate and collaboration. Through this collaborative process, ideas are tested, challenged and enriched, leading to the advancement of understanding in diverse fields of inquiry.

The collective nature and foundation of knowledge extend beyond individual communities to encompass global networks of communication and collaboration (Watson & Levin, 2023). In an interconnected world, ideas and knowledge flow across geographical and cultural boundaries, fostering cross-cultural exchange and enriching intellectual discourse. Recognising the collective foundations of knowledge underscores the importance of inclusivity, diversity and collaboration in the pursuit of understanding. By valuing and incorporating diverse perspectives and experiences, societies can foster innovation, creativity and social progress. All forms of knowledge are a testament to the collective endeavours of humanity, reflecting our shared quest for understanding and enlightenment. The acceptance of a collective ethos not only enriches our intellectual pursuits but also strengthens the bonds that unite us as members of a global community.

The territorialisation of knowledge traditions and ideas, whether they be Arabic, African, Asian, British, Chinese, Indian, American or European, has not only undermined individual excellence rooted in collective foundations of knowledge production and dissemination, but it has also commodified knowledge as mere skills, reducing it to essentialist aspects while neglecting the emancipatory potential of knowledge (Escobar et al., 2020). Throughout history, diverse cultures and civilisations have developed rich and multifaceted knowledge systems, each reflecting the unique perspectives, experiences and values of its creators. However, the process of territorialisation has often led to the imposition of artificial boundaries and hierarchies, which limit the exchange and integration of ideas across cultural and geographical divides.

In this context, knowledge becomes commodified, stripped of its context and reduced to marketable skills or products. This narrow focus on the utilitarian aspects of knowledge overlooks its transformative power and its capacity to challenge and reshape social norms and structures. Additionally, by emphasising certain knowledge traditions over others, territorialisation perpetuates hierarchies of power and privilege, marginalising voices and perspectives that fall outside dominant paradigms (Ince, 2012). This not only stifles creativity and innovation but also reinforces inequalities and injustices within society.

European colonialism and its associated racialised capitalist systems played a significant role in dismantling collective foundations of knowledge traditions by propagating a narrative that European knowledge was synonymous with 'science', while relegating Asian, African, Arabic and American knowledge traditions to the status of mere 'ethnographies'. This myopic, false and racialised distinction was actively promoted by European colonisers to assert their cultural and intellectual superiority while undermining indigenous knowledge systems and their emancipatory potentials. Under colonial rule, European powers imposed their own systems of education, governance and language upon colonised peoples, often at the expense of local traditions and ways of knowing. Indigenous knowledge, which had developed over generations through close observation of nature, community practices and cultural rituals, was systematically devalued and marginalised (Bhambra, 2014; Seth, 2009; Taiwo, 1993).

By portraying European knowledge as the epitome of scientific rigour and progress, colonial authorities justified their domination and exploitation of colonised territories, natural resources and labour. This narrative not only served to legitimise colonial rule but also reinforced racial hierarchies and stereotypes, portraying colonised peoples as primitive and backward compared to their European counterparts. So, the promotion of European knowledge as the sole arbiter of truth and progress perpetuated a legacy of epistemic violence, in which indigenous knowledge traditions were denigrated and erased, leaving lasting scars on communities and cultures around the world (Buchowski, 2004; Tilley & Gordon, 2017).

The processes of colonial rule and its strategies of territorialisation of knowledge undermine both the essentialist and emancipatory aspects of knowledge traditions, ultimately eroding the very foundations of knowledge itself. By imposing artificial boundaries and hierarchies, territorialisation restricts the free flow of ideas, inhibiting the exchange and integration of diverse perspectives and insights. On one hand, territorialisation tends to essentialise knowledge, reducing it to static, commodified forms that prioritise practical utility over broader understandings of truth and meaning. This reductionist approach limits the richness and complexity of knowledge traditions, stripping them of their dynamic and evolving nature. On the other hand, territorialisation also undermines the emancipatory potential of knowledge by reinforcing existing power structures and marginalising voices and perspectives that challenge dominant narratives. By privileging certain knowledge traditions over others, territorialisation perpetuates inequalities and injustices within society, stifling creativity, innovation and critical thinking. Ultimately, the process of territorialisation threatens to fragment and homogenise knowledge, erasing the diverse cultural, historical and social contexts from which it emerges (Cooper, 2005; Patel, 2022).

Therefore, it is imperative to acknowledge and challenge the colonial legacy of territorialisation of knowledge production and dissemination for decolonising our understanding of the world and fostering genuine dialogue and exchange among diverse knowledge traditions. This requires acknowledging the inherent value and questioning the authenticity and validity of all knowledge systems, regardless of their cultural or geographic origins and working towards a more inclusive and equitable approach to knowledge creation and sharing. It is also essential to recognise the interconnectedness of knowledge across cultures and to create spaces for dialogue, collaboration and mutual learning. By embracing the diversity of human experience and valuing the contributions of all knowledge traditions, societies can harness the full potential of knowledge as a tool of empowerment, liberation and social change. It is time to reclaim decolonial, diverse and emancipatory knowledge traditions and work towards a more just, equitable and sustainable future based on science and secularism.

Territorialisation of Identity

The concept of identity, as a reflection of one's own self as an individual, is intricately intertwined with various factors such as birth, sex and a myriad of social, political, cultural and economic determinants. These determinants, ranging from class and race to region, religion, gender and nationality, wield significant influence in the formation of one's identity. Moreover, this identity is not static; it evolves over time and adapts to different environments because of experiences, beliefs and activities. Individual identities are as diverse as the people who possess them, each characterised by personal traits and uniqueness. However, individuals are not solely defined by their individuality; they also belong to various social, cultural, political and economic groups based on shared similarities with others. These group identities, too, exhibit their own nuances and distinctions (Nayak, 2021a).

The process of identity formation is dynamic, shaped by the interplay of time, place and various processes. Individuals share aspects of their sense of self with others, leading to the emergence of distinct identities based on the context of when, where and how these interactions occur. Both individual and group identities are subject to change, influenced by shifting circumstances and evolving societal norms. However, the complexity and diversity inherent in these identities pose challenges for institutions and processes of governance, which often struggle to accommodate the multifaceted nature of human identity (ibid).

The territorialisation of identity formation, shaped by Westphalian ideology, remains heavily influenced by factors such as birthplace or the possession of an official passport issued by a specific nation-state. This process involves the state's official assignment of identity, a procedure largely beyond an individual's control, often dictated by bureaucratic and geopolitical boundaries. However, this rigid framework overlooks the diverse nature of identities and their multifaceted material and non-material manifestations. Identity is not solely defined by territorial borders or legal documentation but encompasses a rich and diverse landscape of cultural, linguistic and experiential elements. Moreover, the rigid territorialisation of identity fails to account for the fluidity and complexity inherent in contemporary global, regional, national and local societies, where individuals often navigate multiple identities simultaneously (Johansen, 2008).

The diverse conditions of multiple identity formation pose a significant challenge to the construction of a monolithic society and compliant individuals, as required by various forms of capitalism in the age of technofeudalism. In this era, characterised by a blend of advanced technology and feudal-like power structures within the platform economy, the expectation of a homogeneous societal fabric becomes increasingly untenable. Capitalist systems, particularly in their contemporary manifestations, often prioritise conformity and uniformity to streamline consumption patterns and maintain control over labour forces. Ghettoisation of people and their multiple natural and flexible identities is a cultural and political project of capitalism opposed to diversity (Vincze, 2019).

The reality of multiple identity formations disrupts the idealised vision within capitalist frameworks, where a culture of compliance shapes autonomous individual identities. In traditional capitalist narratives, there's often an expectation of a singular, dominant cultural paradigm that facilitates compliance with the prevailing economic system. This narrative assumes that individuals will conform to societal norms and expectations, aligning their identities with the values and behaviours conducive to capitalist productivity and consumption for the accumulation of profit. However, the existence of multiple identity formations challenges this assumption. Individuals possess complex, layered identities that are shaped by a myriad of personal, cultural and social factors. These identities may intersect and diverge in ways that resist assimilation into a singular cultural narrative. As such, attempts to enforce a homogeneous cultural identity for the sake of capitalist compliance are met with resistance and often fail to account for the diverse realities of human experience (Gibson-Graham, 1995).

Moreover, the autonomy of individual identities is compromised when subjected to pressure to conform to a standardised cultural framework. Rather than freely expressing and exploring their multifaceted identities, individuals may feel compelled to suppress aspects of themselves that do not align with the dominant cultural narrative. This suppression can lead to feelings of alienation, disconnection and even internal conflict as individuals navigate the tension between their authentic selves and the expectations imposed upon them by capitalist ideology. In essence, the existence of multiple identity formations highlights the limitations of the idealised vision of capitalism, revealing the complexities and multiplicities of human identity that cannot be neatly contained within a single cultural paradigm (Leong, 2021).

Individuals and their identities exist within intersecting webs of multiple identities shaped by factors such as ethnicity, gender, sexuality, class and more. These multifaceted identities resist reduction into a singular, standardised mould. Consequently, the capitalist pursuit of a monolithic society encounters resistance from the complexities of human diversity. Moreover, in the age of technofeudalism, where power dynamics echo feudal structures with technology magnifying inequalities, the pressure for compliance intensifies. Yet, individuals with diverse identities bring with them diverse perspectives, needs and desires, challenging the hegemony of a singular narrative or set of norms. In this context, the tension between the demands of capitalism for compliance and the reality of multiple identity formations becomes stark. The attempts to homogenise society risk marginalising and oppressing those whose identities deviate from the prescribed norm.

Capitalism leverages both the territorialisation and deterritorialisation processes of identity assignment to undermine collective, communitarian and diverse forms of individual and societal identities (Nayak, 2021a). By emphasising the primacy of national borders and the identities associated with them, capitalism perpetuates a framework that prioritises individualism over collectivism and homogenises diverse identities into a singular, market-friendly narrative. This approach is evident in the reactionary politics of dominant identities mobilised by capitalist systems to sustain their processes of identity formation. By promoting and privileging certain identities deemed advantageous within the capitalist framework, such as those aligned with the interests of the ruling class or dominant cultural norms, capitalism perpetuates systems of oppression and marginalisation. These dominant identities serve to consolidate power and control, maintaining the status quo by marginalising and subjugating those whose identities do not conform to the prescribed norm (Bohrer, 2018).

In contrast, the identity politics of marginalised masses emerges as a form of emancipatory politics, seeking to challenge and disrupt the hegemony of dominant identities perpetuated by capitalism. By focussing on the experiences and perspectives of marginalised communities, identity politics serves as a catalyst for social change and progress rooted in diversity and inclusion. It provides a platform for amplifying voices that have been historically silenced and advocating for the recognition and affirmation of all identities, regardless of their alignment with dominant narratives. In essence, while dominant identity politics seeks to preserve the existing power structures and resist change, the identity politics of marginalised masses represents a transformative force that challenges the status quo and paves the way for a more equitable and just society.

By embracing diversity and advocating for the rights and dignity of all individuals, emancipatory identity politics holds the potential to foster genuine social progress and collective liberation. Recognising and embracing this diversity is essential for the growth of a more inclusive and equitable society that honours the autonomy and dignity of all individuals. Thus, a more inclusive and equitable approach to social, political, economic and cultural organisation becomes imperative, one that recognises and celebrates the richness of diverse identities while challenging the oppressive structures that seek to erase them within the processes of territorialisation

It is time to reclaim our identities as global citizens, based on solidarity beyond the boundaries of nation-states and their narrow colonial political, cultural and economic projects of capitalist territorialisation.

Territorialisation of Citizenship Rights

Working people have historically fought against various forms of oppression, including feudalism, capitalism, colonialism, imperialism and religious fundamentalism, to advance democracy and secure citizenship rights. The anti-colonial and anti-imperialist struggles in Asia, Africa, the Americas and the Arab world significantly contributed to the realisation and expansion of citizenship rights beyond the narrow ideology of the Westphalian framework, while also strengthening democratic systems of governance within Western Europe.

These movements not only challenged the political and economic dominance of imperial powers but also inspired global solidarity among oppressed people across continents. The successes of these struggles underscored the interconnectedness of global movements for justice and highlighted the importance of collective action in achieving democratic ideals beyond narrow territorial borders (Howard, 1995; Navarro, 2017). Consequently, the influence of these liberation movements extended beyond their regions, prompting reforms and progressive changes in political systems worldwide. This global ripple effect emphasised the universal quest for equality, justice and democratic governance, reshaping political landscapes and encouraging a more inclusive approach to citizenship and human rights (Kabeer, 2005).

However, in recent times, democratic and citizenship rights are under threat from reactionary and anti-democratic forces who wish to continue and revive their hegemony over people, to control resources by expanding the project of territorialisation. These forces aim to roll back the progress made by previous generations in securing democratic freedoms and rights. By undermining democratic institutions and spreading disinformation, the reactionary ruling classes seek to weaken public trust and erode the foundations of participatory and democratic governance. The resurgence of these authoritarian tendencies poses a significant challenge to the principles of equality, justice and freedom that underpin democratic societies (Bruff, 2014; Inglehart & Norris, 2017).

There are consistent attempts to spread the venom of territorial nationalism to weaken the universal approach to citizenship rights (Argun, 1999) in the name of the national question or in the name of Eurocentric cultural relativism. These efforts aim to divide people along narrow sectarian lines, categorising them as natives or foreigners, Hindus, Christians, Muslims, rich, poor, urban, rural, educated, illiterate, skilled, unskilled, migrants and various racial and territorial nationalities. This strategy seeks to weaken unity and solidarity among the working masses. By promoting these divisions, reactionary forces create an environment of distrust and conflict, undermining collective efforts to achieve social and economic justice.

The division among and between people on territorial grounds weakens the collective and democratic foundations of citizenship rights. Our citizenship rights are interconnected, meaning that the weakening of one person's citizenship rights inherently weakens everyone's citizenship rights. When individuals are divided along territorial, racial, religious, or economic lines, the unity and solidarity necessary for a strong, democratic society are undermined. This fragmentation makes it easier for reactionary forces to erode democratic institutions and infringe upon individual freedoms. Therefore, it is crucial to recognise and protect the interconnected nature of our rights, ensuring that all citizens, regardless of their background, are afforded the same protections and opportunities beyond territorial lines (Sassen, 2002; Teune, 2009).

Furthermore, territorialisation often aligns with the interests of those in power, who use it as a tool to maintain control over resources and populations. Both the processes of territorialisation and deterritorialisation of citizenship rights are exclusionary and detrimental. Both processes follow the requirements of capitalism and its various forms. They not only weaken citizenship rights but also dismantle people's abilities to reclaim these rights by fostering divisions along narrow, reactionary lines. Territorialisation imposes rigid boundaries that prioritise the rights of certain groups over others, leading to discrimination and inequality. On the other hand, deterritorialisation can create a sense of statelessness and disenfranchisement, leaving many without a clear claim to rights or protections. These processes spread division by categorising people based on arbitrary distinctions, such as nationality, ethnicity, religion, or socioeconomic status. This fragmentation undermines collective action and solidarity, essential components for defending and advancing citizenship rights (ibid).

It is time to reclaim the legacies of various mass movements throughout history to reassert our citizenship rights beyond narrow and reactionary frameworks of the Westphalian ideology. By doing so, we can put an end to so-called nationalist wars that primarily serve to protect the power and interests of corporate capital. Historical mass movements have shown that collective action and solidarity can achieve significant advancements in democracy, equality and justice. These movements have fought against various forms of oppression, from feudalism to imperialism and their successes offer valuable lessons for today's struggles to reclaim the inalienability and universality of citizenship rights. By learning from these historical examples, we can work towards the deepening of global democracy based on the interests of people and the planet.

The triumphs of past movements demonstrate the power of collective action and solidarity in overcoming systemic injustices. These movements have shown that it is possible to challenge and dismantle oppressive structures through unified efforts. In the contemporary context, this means advocating for citizenship rights that are inclusive and universal, transcending narrow, reactionary frameworks that divide us. Reclaiming these rights involves resisting the forces that seek to undermine democratic principles and promoting policies that prioritise human well-being over corporate interests. By fostering global solidarity and inclusivity, masses can build a democratic system that reflects the interconnectedness of our world and addresses the needs of all people, regardless of their background. Ultimately, the lessons from historical mass movements remind us that the fight for citizenship rights and global democracy is ongoing. It requires continuous effort, vigilance and a commitment to justice and equality for all. By embracing these principles, people can create a more equitable and sustainable future for generations to come.

Territorialisation of Emancipatory Struggles

In an age of digital revolution, capital and its markets continue to be highly mobile, while human beings and their struggles against exploitation and inequalities remain territorialised in the name of nation-states. This disparity highlights a significant imbalance: financial resources and economic opportunities can flow freely across borders, yet the efforts of people fighting against exploitation and inequality are often confined to specific regions or communities. This territorialisation limits the potential for widespread solidarity and collective action, perpetuating the challenges faced by those striving for social justice and equitable treatment (Stavrides, 2020).

Emancipatory struggles against feudalism, patriarchy, colonialism, imperialism and capitalism were not confined within national territories. The English, Scottish and Welsh working people actively opposed apartheid and led numerous anti-colonial struggles across the globe. One notable example is John Harris, a white anti-apartheid activist and leader, who was perhaps the only white man executed in South Africa for his steadfast commitment to anti-colonial and anti-apartheid struggles. In all these movements, the working classes played a crucial role in driving social and political transformation in their societies worldwide (Yates, 2018).

The involvement of working people and groups transcended geographical boundaries, demonstrating solidarity with oppressed people in different parts of the world. Their efforts were not merely local but were part of a global resistance against various forms of oppression. The sacrifices and contributions of freedom fighters like John Harris highlight the interconnected nature of these struggles and the universal desire for justice and equality. Through strikes, protests and other forms of resistance, the working classes have consistently pushed for significant changes, challenging the status quo and advocating for a fairer, more equitable world. Their legacy continues to inspire contemporary movements for social justice and human rights (Lewin, 2011).

American students and youth have historically struggled against American imperialist wars, such as the wars in Vietnam, Iraq, Afghanistan and many other conflicts. Similarly, the British people have opposed their government's involvement in the wars in Iraq and Afghanistan. Israeli students and youth continue to challenge their Zionist government in defence of Palestinian citizenship rights. These examples illustrate how citizens often fight against their own state and government in the pursuit of justice and solidarity beyond territories (Nine, 2012; Johnston & Laxer, 2003).

Protests, teach-ins and demonstrations became common as young people voiced their opposition to what they saw as an unjust and imperialist conflict. This opposition was fuelled by a desire to promote peace, justice and an end to unnecessary loss of life. These anti-war movements were driven by a belief in the principles of international law, peace and universal human rights, as well as a desire to prevent further destabilisation of people's lives, livelihoods and the planet. These struggles are motivated by a commitment to equality, human rights and the vision of a just society where all citizens, regardless of ethnicity, have equal rights. These examples highlight a broader trend of citizens actively engaging in political and social movements to hold their governments accountable. Whether it's opposing wars, advocating for human rights or fighting for social justice, these movements demonstrate the power of collective action and the enduring spirit of solidarity beyond reactionary ideals of territoriality (Scholz, 2008).

In recent years, despite numerous attempts to contain and territorialise emancipatory struggles in different parts of the world, working people have shown remarkable unity in opposing imperialist wars across Europe, Africa, Asia and the Middle East. This reveals the profound power of people to rise above their immediate territorial, cultural, social and political identities, extending solidarity with the struggles of others in distant lands. This collective resistance underscores the universal desire for justice and peace, highlighting the interconnectedness of global struggles against oppression and exploitation (Ehsan, 2024).

The territorialisation of emancipatory struggles is a strategy designed to weaken these movements and undermine people's abilities to overcome crises in their everyday lives. By confining struggles to specific regions or communities, those in power aim to isolate and fragment efforts for social justice, making it harder for people to unite and address broader systemic issues. This tactic not only hinders the effectiveness of emancipatory movements but also diminishes the collective power needed to address and resolve ongoing crises.

In the name of stabilisation and the acknowledgement of cultural identities and unity, territorialisation in the context of nation-states becomes a tool for majoritarian mobilisation. This is the foundation of majoritarian dominance over politics, resources and culture (Mohanty, 2024). This approach often serves to consolidate power by promoting a singular national identity, marginalising minority groups and suppressing diverse voices. By framing cultural and territorial unity as essential for stability, those in power can mobilise the majority population to support policies that entrench their dominance and maintain the status quo, often at the expense of social justice and inclusivity.

In order to accelerate solidarity and minimise conflicts, it is crucial to uphold and celebrate working people's natural ability to live harmonious lives, free from the individual and institutional parasites created and sustained by colonial boundaries that territorialise, exploit and dominate. By recognising and fostering this inherent capacity for unity and cooperation, people can better resist the divisive forces that seek to maintain control through territorialisation and oppression. Global emancipatory struggles play a vital role in this process, helping to unite disparate movements and amplify their collective power against exploitation and inequality sustained by colonial, capitalist and imperialist power structures (Otero & Gürcan, 2024).

Global and universal citizenship rights, grounded in science, secularism and collective ownership of natural resources, along with egalitarian distribution mechanisms, can guide the world towards a peaceful and prosperous future. By embracing these principles, societies can ensure that all individuals have equal access to resources and opportunities, fostering social justice and reducing inequalities. This approach promotes a sense of shared responsibility and cooperation, essential for addressing global challenges and building a peaceful, prosperous, sustainable and harmonious world.

Conclusion

Capitalism sustains itself through its inherent contradictions by imposing the processes of territorialisation, deterritorialisation and reterritorialisation. These processes destabilise lives, relationships and livelihoods, and they weaken the collective consciousness necessary for unified struggles against the exploitative capitalist system.

Territorialisation involves the establishment of defined spaces and boundaries that capitalism uses to control resources, labour and markets. This process can lead to significant changes in land use, urban development and the organisation of economic activities and human relationships with each other and nature, often prioritising profit over community well-being. Deterritorialisation disrupts these established boundaries, reflecting the constant flux within capitalist economies. This results in job displacement, the erosion of local cultures and the rapid movement of capital to areas with more favourable economic conditions, often at the expense of local populations. Reterritorialisation is the subsequent re-establishment of control in new forms and areas, adapting to changing economic and social conditions. This can involve the creation of new economic zones, the introduction of new regulatory frameworks and the reshaping of societal norms to fit the evolving needs of capitalism.

These processes collectively contribute to the instability of lives and livelihoods, as they continually alter the social, cultural and economic landscapes. Relationships and communities are often strained or broken as people are forced to adapt to new conditions. Additionally, these processes weaken the collective consciousness required for unified resistance against capitalist exploitation, as the constant change and instability make it difficult for people to organise and maintain cohesive movements for emancipation. It is important to understand these dynamics to comprehend the mechanisms through which capitalism perpetuates itself and explore more effective strategies for collective resistance and the pursuit of equitable and sustainable alternatives.

CHAPTER 2

CULTURES OF CAPITALISM

Introduction

Capitalism is not merely an economic system; it comes with a distinct culture that has profound impacts on society, economy, culture and politics. This culture systematically erodes traditional collective foundations, paving the way for an expansive mass consumerism that, in turn, alters existing consumption habits and cultural practices. The culture of mass consumerism is essential for sustaining the mechanisms of mass production. As mass production increases, it fuels consumerism by creating a cycle where people are encouraged to constantly buy more products, leading to the perpetuation and deepening of consumerist values in society. Such a consumerist culture promotes individualism over collectivism, as personal success and happiness become increasingly measured by material possessions and consumption patterns. The cultural shift emphasises the importance of acquiring goods as a symbol of status and identity, which can undermine communal values and traditional cultural practices that prioritise shared experiences and collective well-being (Rutherford, 2008).

Moreover, the culture of capitalism often leads to the homogenisation of global cultures. As multinational corporations expand their reach, local cultures and traditions can be overshadowed by global consumer trends. This results in a loss of cultural diversity as unique practices and customs are replaced by standardised products and lifestyles promoted by global marketing strategies. The McDonaldisation of culture, consumption and everyday lives forms the foundation of the culture of capitalism. McDonaldisation is characterised by efficiency, calculability, predictability and control through non-human technology (Featherstone, 1990; Dirlik, 2003).

In the context of capitalism, McDonaldisation represents the broader trend of commodifying and standardising cultural practices and everyday activities. Efficiency prioritises streamlined processes and quick results, often at the expense of individuality and quality. Calculability emphasises quantifiable objectives, such as sales numbers and profit margins, rather than qualitative aspects like customer satisfaction or the cultural significance of production and consumption. Predictability ensures uniformity and consistency, reducing diversity and uniqueness in cultural expressions. Finally, control through technology minimises human involvement, potentially eroding personal connections and traditional skills (Lee, 2007).

The culture of capitalism, driven by these principles, encourages a homogenised global culture where local traditions and individual preferences are overshadowed by standardised, mass-produced experiences. This shift not only transforms consumption patterns but also reshapes social interactions, work environments and personal identities, aligning them with the capitalist ideals of productivity and profit.

The cultural dimension of capitalism not only supports its economic framework but also reshapes societal values and norms. The relentless pursuit of profit and growth drives the production and consumption cycles, altering the very fabric of culture and community. It is important to understand McDonaldisation to explain the pervasive influence of capitalism on contemporary culture and underscore the need to critically examine and address its implications for cultural diversity, community well-being and individual autonomy.

The distorted culture of capitalism promotes alienated lives within society, fostering an environment where forces of patriarchal parasites thrive. These forces glorify capitalism and its exploitative systems by spreading misinformation, aiming to undermine any potential alternatives. In this perverted capitalist culture, individuals often experience a sense of alienation in their everyday lives. The relentless pursuit of profit prioritises individual success and material wealth over communal well-being and human connections. This alienation manifests in various aspects of life, from workplaces that prioritise productivity over employee welfare to consumer practices that emphasise ownership over shared experiences (Leal, 2018).

Patriarchal parasites, entrenched in this capitalist framework, perpetuate these conditions by championing the status quo. They leverage their influence to propagate narratives that depict capitalism as the only viable economic system, often resorting to misinformation and propaganda. This deliberate spread of falsehoods serves to delegitimise alternative economic models and social structures that prioritise equity, cooperation and sustainability. By glorifying capitalist achievements and obscuring its inherent injustices, these patriarchal forces maintain control and reinforce systemic inequalities. They benefit from the existing power dynamics, which often marginalise women, minorities and other vulnerable groups, perpetuating a cycle of oppression and exploitation.

Loneliness and Capitalism

The epidemic of loneliness is spreading rapidly in our hyper-connected world of social media. Studies by the World Health Organization suggest that '20–34 per cent of older people in China, India, the United States and regions of Europe and Latin America experience loneliness'. Similarly, there is a crisis of friendship and meaningful connections among young people. Research by the *Campaign to End Loneliness* in the United Kingdom has revealed that '49.63 per cent of adults (25.99 million people) are lonely, and approximately 7.1 per cent of people in Britain (3.83 million) experience chronic loneliness, meaning they feel lonely "often or always" in 2022'. In 2017, the *Jo Cox National Commission on Loneliness* estimated the cost of loneliness to employers at £2.5 billion a year in the United Kingdom. It is impossible to calculate the social and emotional cost of loneliness. According to the report *The State of Loneliness 2023: Office of National Statistics data on loneliness in Britain, June 2023*, published by the *Campaign to End Loneliness*, there is an alarming rise in loneliness among all age groups. The growing crisis of loneliness leads to deaths, destitution, depression, ill health, mental health crises, crime and other forms of unsocial and antisocial behaviour in society. Loneliness is a global social and health crisis.

In modern capitalist societies, the notion of loneliness is not solely a product of individual disposition but rather a consequence of broader capitalist structures and processes shaped by new forms of digital capitalism. The ideals and culture of solitude can be a deliberate personal choice, but loneliness often emerges as a result of systemic factors deeply ingrained in capitalist culture. Within this framework, the emphasis on individual success and self-promotion can lead to a pervasive sense of isolation, as people prioritise their own advancement over collective well-being. This narcissistic culture perpetuates a cycle of alienation, where individuals become increasingly disconnected from one another and their communities. The very fabric of capitalist societies, with its emphasis on competition and material gain, cultivates environments that prioritise profit over the social bonds essential for human fulfilment. Thus, loneliness emerges not as an inherent trait but as a by-product of the alienating conditions fostered by capitalist society (Vighi, 2019).

Capitalism thrives on alienation, perpetuating and reproducing all forms of alienating conditions. In the *Economic and Philosophic Manuscripts*, Marx discussed four types of alienation: (i) alienation from one's own product and labour, (ii) alienation from the process of labour, (iii) alienation from one's own self and (iv) alienation from other fellow human beings/workers. These four forms of alienation continue to be the foundation of modern capitalism in the age of digitalisation. The technological advancements have accelerated all these forms of alienation. These alienating conditions generate helpless and lonely individuals who lack control over themselves. Their lives and freedoms are dictated by those who control capital and organisations.

Alienation is not an isolated condition; it is an integral part of the capitalist system, where the destruction of meaningful human and social connections is central to the creation of an insidious economy at the expense of society. Society is dismantled to promote a profit-driven economic system based on the exploitation of labour and nature. Such an exploitative system can only sustain itself by fostering disconnected and atomised individuals, thus promoting the growth of a 'loneliness economy' where capitalism becomes the only available alternative (Pratt, Johnston, & Johnson, 2023).

Capitalism, with its relentless pursuit of profit, often comes at the expense of the collective spirit and innate social nature of humanity. It champions ideals such as individual space, freedom, happiness, utility, pleasure and satisfaction, which are often portrayed as attainable through material wealth and consumption. However, the pursuit of these ideals within a capitalist framework can be insatiable, leading individuals into a perpetual cycle of labour and consumption, where fulfilment remains elusive. This is because the essence of these aspirations inherently lies in collective experiences and relationships rather than in the accumulation of material possessions or individual success. In a collectivist society that prioritises sharing, cooperation and empathy, these ideals find fertile ground for realisation, as they are inherently intertwined with the well-being of the community as a whole. Thus, there exists a fundamental misalignment between the individualistic ethos perpetuated by capitalism and the communal nature of human fulfilment and contentment (Fernandez, 2008).

Capitalism has eroded the collective foundations of society to such an extent that even the hyper-connected world of social media cannot change it. It is central to the production of insecure, lonely, powerless, fearful and disconnected individuals who grapple with depression and anxiety in their everyday lives. These weakened individuals are unlikely to question the exploitative and unnatural underpinnings of capitalism. There is no threat to capitalism in a society populated by lonely and alienated individuals. The notion of a free, happy and prosperous capitalism is nothing more than a myth (Torre, 2014).

Capitalism, in all its forms, breeds loneliness. The digital fantasies of capitalism can't end loneliness. Therefore, the struggle to end loneliness is a struggle against the very foundations of capitalism. A society liberated from exploitation and inequality, one founded upon principles of solidarity, compassion and collective sharing, stands as the sole alternative to the pervasive isolation endemic to capitalist societies.

Capitalism and Mental Health Issues

Capitalism, once hailed as the harbinger of peace, prosperity and happiness in its quest for global dominance as the sole available alternative, now faces a stark revelation. The recently published *Mental State of the World Report*, an annual publication by the Global Mind Project conducted by Sapien Labs, exposes a troubling reality: citizens of capitalist nations are grappling with the most severe mental health challenges. Surprisingly, it's amidst the affluence of these capitalist societies where the most profound discontent resides. The rise of capitalism is intrinsically linked to the erosion of mental well-being, forming an inseparable bond between economic structure and psychological health. The pandemic of mental health crises emerges as a direct consequence of the alienation fostered by capitalist systems.

According to the World Health Organization (WHO), over 700,000 lives are lost to suicide annually, with a staggering 77 per cent occurring in low- and middle-income countries. This tragic toll is exacerbated by the systemic exploitation and various forms of marginalisation inherent in capitalist societies, which contribute to these preventable deaths and the cycle of destitution they perpetuate. The WHO's data further reveals that a staggering 280 million individuals worldwide battle depression, with western capitalist nations emerging as the epicentres of this mental health crisis. Over the past two decades, the United Kingdom, in particular, has witnessed a concerning surge in poor mental health outcomes, marking it as a focal point for this growing epidemic. Moreover, schizophrenia, a severe mental disorder, is proliferating at an unprecedented rate within capitalist nations, highlighting the deep-seated challenges within these societies. Factors such as the privatisation of healthcare, economic instability, social upheaval, religious tensions and the perpetuation of capitalist-driven conflicts only serve to exacerbate this global mental health pandemic, further underscoring the urgent need for systemic change to address these pressing issues.

The resolution of the global mental health crisis extends far beyond the realm of medical science alone. Beneath the surface of individual diagnoses lies a complex web of societal factors that fuel the rise of poor mental health. The pervasive productivist culture, where worth is measured by productivity, coupled with the relentless marketisation of society, perpetuates an environment of constant pressure and competition. Within this framework, the exploitative economic system thrives, fostering inequality and marginalisation. Meanwhile, oppressive political structures and the erosion of democratic citizenship further compound the sense of helplessness and disempowerment among the populace. Capitalism, with its inherent drive for profit maximisation at the expense of both labour and nature, stands as a central figure in this narrative. Its mechanisms of exploitation and alienation lay the groundwork for the proliferation of mental illness on a global scale (Matthews, 2019).

The coexistence of capitalism with notions of peace, physical well-being and mental happiness becomes increasingly untenable as its very survival hinges on the perpetuation of exploitation and alienation. In essence, all forms of alienation, be it from labour, nature or society, serve as the bedrock upon which poor mental health thrives – a product of the capitalist system itself. Addressing the mental health pandemic necessitates a holistic re-evaluation of these capitalist, feudal and patriarchal societal structures and a fundamental shift away from the inherent mechanisms of capitalism (ibid).

Capitalism's relentless pursuit of individualist consumerism often comes at a profound cost to the fabric of societies, families and communities. In this paradigm, individuals are reduced to mere customers within a capitalist market society, where their worth is measured by their utility, purchasing power and satisfaction as consumers. This narrow focus on competition and consumption undermines the essence of solidarity and collective well-being. The capitalist ethos, rooted in profit maximisation and individual gain, stands in stark contrast to the principles that foster healthy development within individuals and societies. Instead of nurturing environments that prioritise human flourishing and social cohesion, capitalism breeds a culture of cutthroat competition and relentless pressure to consume (Jackson, 2021).

At its core, the capitalist system thrives on maintaining and perpetuating exploitative structures and unequal processes. A healthy mind, capable of critical thinking and empathy, naturally questions these dominant systems of capitalism, recognising their inherent injustices and inequalities. Thus, capitalism's fundamental opposition to the healthy development of individuals and societies becomes increasingly evident. By prioritising profit over people, it erodes the very foundations of community, solidarity and human dignity. In its place, it fosters a culture of individualism and materialism that corrodes the social bonds essential for collective well-being (Hanlon & Carlisle, 2009).

The collective spirit of society serves as the bedrock for fulfilling the basic and meaningful libidinal requirements of individuals – necessities such as hunger, shelter, healthcare, love, romance, friendships and connections. Within the framework of a thriving society, these needs are met through communal support, mutual aid and shared resources, fostering a sense of belonging and dignity for all. However, capitalism disrupts this natural order by commodifying these fundamental human needs, subjecting them to the whims of market forces (Roberts, 2021).

In the capitalist model, essentials like food, housing, healthcare and even emotional fulfilment are transformed into commodities, available to those who can afford them. This commodification process reduces individuals to solitary consumers, disconnected from the collective fabric of society and reliant solely on their purchasing power to meet their needs. The result is an environment marked by isolation, loneliness and alienation – a breeding ground for mental health issues that afflict individuals, families and entire societies worldwide. In this context, mental health problems are not merely personal afflictions but are deeply intertwined with the conditions created by capitalism. By turning human necessities into profit-driven commodities, capitalism perpetuates a cycle of individualism and disconnection that undermines the collective well-being of society. In doing so, it intensifies the very mental health crises it claims to address, highlighting the inherent contradictions between capitalist values and the human need for social connection and belonging (Matthews, 2019).

The decadent culture nurtured by capitalism perpetuates a form of domesticated consumerism, wherein individuals are defined by the possessions they acquire – branded clothing, cars, houses and fashion items – rather than by their authentic selves, intricately connected to the world around them. This commodification of individual identity and consciousness serves capitalism's agenda by masking its exploitation with the guise of individual freedom. Within capitalist societies, individual freedom becomes subjugated to the pursuit of profit, leading individuals to conform to a predetermined notion of orderliness and consumption. The illusion of personal autonomy is maintained, yet it is constrained within the confines of capitalist goals (Young, 2017).

As a result, individuals within capitalist systems often lead lives marked by loneliness and isolation, despite the semblance of personal space and freedom. This detachment from authentic social connections and meaningful interactions divorces individuals from their inherent nature as social beings, leading to a profound sense of disconnection from themselves and the world around them. This artificial schism between individuals and their true social essence lays the groundwork for the widespread mental health crisis gripping societies across the globe. By prioritising profit over people and reducing human experiences to marketable commodities, capitalism perpetuates a cycle of alienation and disillusionment that erodes the collective well-being of humanity (Iqbal, Gul, & Rashid, 2023).

The narrow silo of the pervasive culture of materialistic consumerism, with its focus on acquiring possessions and external validation, has engendered a profound sense of loneliness on an unprecedented scale. In this era, individuals are increasingly compelled to seek solace and connection to reclaim their social identities as human beings. However, capitalism's relentless pursuit of profit has come at the expense of the collective foundations of society. In its insatiable drive to expand its pyramid of wealth, capitalism has dismantled the communal bonds and social structures that once provided a sense of belonging and support for individuals. In this vacuum, loneliness festers and spreads, giving rise to a mental health crisis of staggering proportions (Swan, 2018).

Faced with the consequences of its own creation, capitalism offers a superficial solution: the commodification of mental health care. Medical practitioners, mental health hospitals and even prisons become lucrative markets, generating profits for the capitalist system while individuals, families and entire societies grapple with the devastating effects of mental illness. In this cycle of exploitation and suffering, capitalism perpetuates its own existence at the expense of human well-being. As long as capitalism and its profit-driven system remains the driving force behind societal organisation, the epidemic of mental health will continue to thrive, leaving a trail of devastation in its wake (Matthews, 2019).

Capitalism is not an alternative and can never be. Its very nature cannot serve as a viable solution to the mental health crisis plaguing societies worldwide. Instead, it perpetuates a cycle of oppression, exploitation, inequality and alienation that undermines the very foundations of meaningful individual existence. The structural and everyday injustices inherent in capitalist systems breed a pervasive sense of loneliness, eroding the social fabric and psychological well-being of individuals. The dehumanising effects of capitalism extend far beyond material deprivation; they encompass the profound psychological toll of living in a society where human worth is measured by productivity and consumption (Steed, 2016). The inhumane nature of capitalism stands as the root cause of mental illness on a global scale. As such, the struggle against capitalism emerges as the first step towards establishing a society free from the grip of mental health issues.

In place of the individualistic ethos promoted by capitalism, the cultivation of social solidarity and collective spirit offers a path towards collective mental well-being. By fostering connections, empathy and mutual support among individuals, societies can create environments that nurture the holistic health of all members, transcending the alienation and isolation perpetuated by capitalist systems. Ultimately, the fight against capitalism represents not only a struggle for economic justice but also a quest for human dignity and psychological liberation. Only through collective action and solidarity can societies hope to build a future where mental well-being is valued as a fundamental aspect of human flourishing sans capitalism.

Rising Tide of Social Parasitism

Social parasites are capable individuals who live off the values, products, services, donations and sacrifices resulting from the labour of others. These individuals are like the priestly class who remain in their comfort zones, refraining from engaging in any meaningful work, and they consider this parasitic lifestyle as normal and natural. Such social parasites neither contribute to the meaningful growth of their own lives nor to the well-being of their families, societies or states in any significant way. They often serve as the foundations for reactionary social, political, economic, cultural and religious trends within society. These parasites produce reactionary politics and social lumpens based on their reactionary ideals of dependency for survival (Shelby, 2002).

Social parasites exhibit a concerning pattern of behaviour where they exploit the efforts and resources of others while offering little to no meaningful input themselves. Their ability to thrive without meaningful contribution creates a cycle of dependency and complacency. These individuals often rationalise their lifestyle, seeing it as an acceptable norm rather than recognising it as a detrimental social issue. Their lack of contribution extends beyond personal growth to impact broader societal structures. By not participating actively in the economy or community development, they place additional burdens on those who are socially productive. Families often bear the weight of supporting these individuals, which can lead to strained relationships and reduced quality of life for those who are working hard to provide (Pfohl, 1993).

Social parasites are escapists who outsource their predicaments to the very individuals or institutions that sustain their lazy and parasitic lifestyles. Social parasites, by outsourcing their responsibilities and challenges, create a dependency loop that not only affects their personal development but also places undue strain on those who support them. These escapists avoid facing the difficulties and realities of life, preferring instead to rely on the efforts and resources of others. This behaviour erodes their own potential for growth and self-improvement, leaving them stagnant and unfulfilled. For the individuals supporting social parasites, the impact can be significant. Family members, friends, or institutions that provide for these individuals often experience increased stress and financial burden. The constant need to support someone who contributes little in return can lead to resentment and strained relationships. Over time, this dynamic can erode the quality of life for those who are productive and responsible, as they are forced to allocate resources and energy to sustain the parasites. The consequences of the growth of social parasites are far-reaching for both individuals and societies (Cockburn, 2018).

On a societal level, social parasites can perpetuate and reinforce reactionary trends. Their detachment from meaningful work and community involvement often aligns them with conservative or regressive movements that resist progress and change. This alignment can manifest in various ways, including supporting political ideologies that favour maintaining the status quo or opposing reforms that could benefit the greater good. The proliferation of social parasites can lead to broader economic and social issues. When a sizable portion of the population opts out of contributing meaningfully to their lives and society, it reduces overall meaningful contributions. This can stifle economic growth and limit opportunities for advancement and prosperity. Additionally, the presence of social parasites can exacerbate social inequality, as resources are diverted to support those who do not contribute, widening the gap between the meaningfully engaged and socially unproductive segments of society (Kramer, 2021).

Economically, their lack of participation stifles innovation and growth. When a significant portion of the population opts out of contributing meaningfully, it hinders the potential for collective advancement (Fitzpatrick, 2006). This economic stagnation can lead to increased inequality and social unrest, as the gap between contributors and non-contributors widens. Moreover, the reliance of social parasites on external support systems can drain resources. Social welfare programmes and charitable organisations that are designed to help those in genuine need can become overwhelmed by individuals who exploit these systems without making any effort to improve their circumstances. This misuse of resources can detract from the support available to those who truly need it, diminishing the overall effectiveness of social safety nets (Kramer, 2021).

Culturally and religiously, social parasites can become bastions of traditionalism as a safe haven for survival, resisting cultural evolution and clinging to outdated practices. Their influence can slow the progression of societal values, making it difficult for communities to adapt to changing times and embrace more inclusive, progressive ideals. Social parasites often embody and perpetuate a culture of complacency and entitlement, which can undermine the values of meaningful work, responsibility and mutual support that are essential for a healthy, functioning society. This culture can spread, influencing others to adopt similar attitudes and behaviours, further entrenching the problem.

The advent of the digital revolution has reshaped the very fabric of capitalism, speeding up its processes and expanding its reach. At the heart of this transformation are the so-called techno-feudals, the powerful entities that dominate the rent-seeking platform economy. The dominant platform companies like Amazon, Google and Facebook have become modern-day landlords, controlling vast digital territories and extracting profit from the activities within their unproductive domains, where producers, consumers and sellers alike are exploited. These techno-feudals have created ecosystems that promote a culture of relentless growth and consumption. In this environment, the concept of social parasitism emerges, where certain entities thrive at the expense of broader societal well-being. These social parasites can be seen as those who benefit disproportionately from the digital economy while contributing little to the common good. This includes not only the platform owners themselves but also the practices that encourage the exploitation of gig workers, the erosion of privacy and the manipulation of consumer behaviours (Shelby, 2002).

The normalisation of these practices is facilitated by the pervasive influence of digital platforms. They shape our perceptions, behaviours and even our social structures, making it increasingly difficult to imagine alternatives to the current system. As a result, the digital revolution not only accelerates capitalist culture but also entrenches the power of those who control the platforms, creating a new form of digital feudalism. The digital revolution has turbocharged the culture of capitalism by empowering techno-feudals within the platform economy, who normalise and perpetuate a growth culture that resembles social parasitism. This shift has profound implications for society, requiring critical examination and potential reimagining of how digital technologies and economic systems intersect and evolve a culture of social parasites (Maseland, 2013).

In this way, social parasites are capable individuals who, by living off the labour of others and avoiding meaningful work, hinder the growth and development of themselves and their communities. Their lifestyle not only burdens families and societies but also supports reactionary trends that resist necessary progress in various aspects of life. Subsequently, social parasites are escapists who outsource their challenges to those who sustain their lifestyles, resulting in personal stagnation and widespread societal consequences. The growth of social parasites imposes significant burdens on individuals, families and institutions, while also hindering meaningful contributions and fostering a culture of entitlement detrimental to progress, peace and prosperity.

Capitalism and its culture breed all forms of social parasitism and normalise lumpen culture. Social parasitism was criminalised in Soviet Russia to ensure the growth of meaningful and honest work. However, criminalisation is not a solution. Social parasitism can only end with the growth of socially meaningful individual consciousness, where individuals develop a need and desire to engage in socially meaningful life and activities.

Misinformation Undermines Life in the Age of Digital Revolution

In this era of an Artificial Intelligence-fuelled digital revolution, misinformation has emerged as a potent weapon wielded by both ruling and non-ruling elites. Their aim is often to undermine truth, dismantle democracy, sow division among people and exert control over various aspects of life and resources on the planet. The reach of Deep Fakes extends far beyond celebrities, politicians and industrialists; they now infiltrate everyday services and commodities that are consumed by the masses. This pervasive spread of deceptive information threatens not only public figures but also the trust and reliability of the information we rely on in our daily lives. As technology continues to advance, the challenge lies in distinguishing fact from fiction and ensuring that our digital landscape and society remain a trustworthy source of information for everyone (Jack, 2019).

Misinformation is not merely an accidental mistake; it is a meticulously crafted strategy designed to exploit the masses (Tripodi, 2022). This deliberate dissemination of false information serves to divert attention from the harsh material realities of capitalism, steering people towards a culture fuelled by emotion and falsehoods. In such an environment, it becomes increasingly challenging to engage with fact-based information that has a tangible impact on everyday human lives. This shift towards an emotional and misleading narrative undermines the foundation of informed decision-making, making it crucial for individuals to be vigilant and discerning in their consumption of information. As societies navigate this complex landscape, the importance of promoting critical thinking and media literacy cannot be overstated, empowering individuals to distinguish between reliable information and deliberate deception.

Misinformation is disseminated widely across all mediums of communication, intentionally blurring the lines between fact and fraud. This strategy serves to amplify deception, foster misgovernance and create a climate where accountability is sidelined. The pervasive nature of this misinformation campaign contributes to shaping a narrative where individuals are constantly confronted with false challenges and distorted realities. By muddying the waters of truth, those behind these campaigns aim to sow confusion, manipulate public opinion and undermine the foundations of a well-informed society. This deliberate strategy to disengage with accountability not only erodes trust in institutions but also hampers the ability of individuals to make informed decisions that affect their lives. It adopts a culture where misinformation thrives, making it increasingly difficult to distinguish between genuine information and deliberate falsehoods (Soon & Goh, 2018).

In such a deceptive environment, tobacco companies exploit the narrative of smoking being associated with smartness, while alcohol companies promote the supposed health benefits of drinking. Similarly, pharmaceutical companies market numerous unnecessary drugs under the guise of securing a healthy life. This false propaganda follows in the tradition of Goebbels, who famously stated, 'If you tell a lie big enough and keep repeating it, people will eventually come to believe it'. The fraudulent and misinformation campaigns orchestrated by these industries have little regard for truth; their primary objective is to weaken the foundation of truth and undermine the realities of life. By perpetuating falsehoods and manipulating public perception, these entities prioritise profit over the well-being of individuals and society as a whole. This insidious manipulation not only distorts public understanding but also erodes trust in legitimate sources of information. As a result, it becomes increasingly challenging for individuals to make informed choices about their health, contributing to a cycle of misinformation and exploitation.

Misinformation fuels all forms of authoritarianism by undermining democracy and leaving citizens ill-informed or misinformed. This deliberate spread of false information serves the interests of both ruling and non-ruling elites, enabling them to govern the masses without facing democratic accountability. In this context, misinformation acts as an escape route for the elites, allowing them to manipulate public opinion and maintain control over societal narratives. By controlling the flow of information and shaping public perception through misinformation, these elites can influence elections, suppress dissent and consolidate power without the checks and balances that a well-informed citizenry would demand. This erosion of democratic principles and practices poses a significant threat to the fabric of democratic societies, as it undermines the fundamental rights of citizens to make informed decisions and hold their leaders accountable (Tripodi, 2022). So, combating misinformation is not just a matter of correcting false information; it is a crucial step in safeguarding democracy and ensuring that governance remains transparent, accountable and responsive to the needs and wishes of the people. By promoting media literacy, fostering critical thinking and holding purveyors of misinformation accountable, people can work towards creating a more informed and resilient democratic society.

Misinformation serves as a tool for demagogues and dictators alike, exploiting the trust of ordinary people who often lack the means to verify the authenticity of information shared on digital platforms. In an age where information is readily accessible but not always reliable, the hard-working masses find themselves at the mercy of false narratives propagated by those with ulterior motives. Meanwhile, some intellectuals lazily label this era as one of 'post-truth', suggesting that truth and realities have become obsolete concepts. However, post-truth has little to do with truth; instead, it is a deliberate strategy employed by both governing and non-governing elites to shape public opinion and delegitimise factual information. By manipulating the narrative and spreading misinformation, these elites seek to maintain their grip on power without facing scrutiny or accountability (Tripodi, 2022).

This deliberate distortion of truth not only undermines the public's ability to make informed decisions but also erodes the foundations of democratic society. It is essential to recognise the dangers posed by the deliberate spread of false information and to actively work towards promoting a culture of transparency, accountability and factual integrity. By doing so, we can help safeguard democracy and ensure that the voices of ordinary people are not drowned out by the cacophony of falsehoods propagated by those who seek to manipulate public opinion for their interests. The power of misinformation campaigns based on fake news is undeniably potent in today's digital age, capable of undermining both life and truth. However, it's crucial to remember that this influence is not insurmountable nor permanent. While misinformation and fake news may obscure the truth, they cannot ultimately destroy it.

History stands as a silent yet steadfast witness to the ebb and flow of power and the enduring nature of truth. Time and again, the inherent resilience of truth has prevailed over deception and the efforts of those who sought to manipulate public opinion have been exposed and defeated.

Patriarchal Capitalism and Women

From dawn till dusk and dusk till dawn, she toils within the confines of an unjust patriarchal framework as a grandmother, mother, sister, lover, girlfriend, wife, partner, professional, worker and relationships of any other name. When misfortune strikes or accountability evades a man's actions, the burden of blame often unjustly falls upon her shoulders. This societal phenomenon perpetuates the cycle of inequality, relegating women to the role of scapegoats for the failings of a system that thrives on their oppression. Whether it's a trivial mishap or a grave error, the default response is to point fingers at the woman rather than addressing the root cause of the issue. This ingrained behaviour reflects not only a systemic imbalance of power but also a deep-seated reluctance to confront the inherent flaws within the patriarchal social, economic, political, religious, cultural and family structure itself (Capezza & Arriaga, 2008).

It becomes evident that the scapegoating of women worldwide serves to uphold the status quo, enabling men to avoid responsibility and perpetuate their dominance over women both in public and private spheres. This pattern of domestication of women is deeply entrenched in societal norms and expectations, making it challenging to dismantle without concerted effort and awareness. Furthermore, the consequences of this blame-shifting extend beyond individual interactions, shaping broader cultural attitudes and reinforcing gender stereotypes (Meyers, 1996; Tabassum & Nayak, 2021).

Blaming a woman's cooking skills for a man's stomach upset, faulting her attire and lifestyle for instances of rape or holding her responsible for a man's diminished libido based on her dress – all these instances underscore a disturbing pattern of shifting blame onto women for the shortcomings and misdeeds of men in society. This reflexive inclination to attribute fault to women, regardless of the circumstances, reflects a deep-seated bias ingrained within patriarchal structures (Taylor, 2020).

When familial bonds falter due to the irresponsible and unaccountable behaviours of lazy, irresponsible men, it's often she who bears the brunt of the blame, despite her potential role as a victim of such behaviours. This societal norm not only perpetuates injustice but also absolves men of their responsibility to introspect and address their actions. While she works tirelessly to sustain the household and support her family, the ingrained societal norm is to hold her accountable for any perceived failures or inadequacies, regardless of her actual culpability. This systemic bias not only undermines her efforts but also perpetuates a cycle of exploitation, inequality and injustice (Alur, 2007).

Despite shouldering the heavy burden of financial responsibility – paying utility bills, covering medical expenses and managing the day-to-day costs of family life – it's often she who bears the blame when things go awry in the lives of idle men. This unfair dynamic reflects a troubling imbalance in societal expectations and reinforces harmful gender stereotypes. Her contributions to the household are substantial and crucial for its functioning, yet they are often taken for granted or overshadowed by the pervasive tendency to attribute blame to women for any perceived shortcomings. This discrepancy highlights not only the undervaluation of her labour but also the persistent devaluation of women's contributions within the family dynamic. This systemic tendency to blame women for various aspects of men's lives is a manifestation of broader gender inequalities and power imbalances. It reinforces harmful stereotypes and undermines women's agency, relegating them to the role of perpetual scapegoats (Tabassum & Nayak, 2021).

In patriarchal societies, women face multifaceted challenges that permeate various aspects of their lives, ranging from entrenched customs like dowry to the insidious prevalence of domestic violence. Dowry, a tradition deeply rooted in many cultures, often becomes a financial burden for women and their families, perpetuating inequalities and reinforcing the notion of women as commodities to be traded in marriage. This system not only undermines women's autonomy but also contributes to their economic dependence on men, limiting their opportunities for independence and self-determination. Everyday violence in different forms defines women's life under patriarchal capitalism in contemporary society (ibid).

Moreover, various forms of domestic violence and public display of violence against women manifest in myriad forms, including physical, emotional, sexual and economic abuse, exerting control and power over women within their own homes. The pervasive nature of domestic violence creates a pervasive atmosphere of fear and intimidation, trapping women in cycles of abuse and preventing them from seeking help or escaping their situations. The lack of adequate support systems and legal protections further accelerates their vulnerability, leaving many women feeling isolated and powerless to break free from abusive relationships (Douglas, 2021).

These issues require a multifaceted approach that tackles both the systemic roots of gender inequality and the immediate needs of women experiencing crisis. It involves challenging patriarchal norms and attitudes, promoting gender-sensitive education and awareness programmes and implementing comprehensive legal frameworks that protect women's rights and hold perpetrators of violence accountable for their actions. Additionally, providing accessible resources such as shelters, counselling services, and economic empowerment programmes can offer women the support they need to rebuild their lives and break free from cycles of violence and oppression. By empowering women and challenging the structures that uphold patriarchal dominance, societies can create more equitable and safe environments where women can thrive free from the daily crises imposed by patriarchal systems (Van Niekerk et al., 2024).

The so-called public and private spheres were created to justify the domestication of women as a desirable commodity within the culture of private property. Women can't question such an unfair and unjust division of space dominated by men and their patriarchal power structure. The emancipation of women depends on their ability to break free from this cycle of unjust blame and inequality; we must challenge the very foundations of patriarchal thinking. People need to foster empathy, accountability and mutual respect within our communities, acknowledging that individuals – regardless of gender – are accountable for their actions. By dismantling these ingrained biases and promoting gender equity, people can strive towards a society where blame is not assigned based on gender, but on individual responsibility and accountability.

The freedom of women from patriarchy and capitalism is central to realising women's lives in the true sense. Non-cooperation, disobedience and non-tolerance are three immediate strategies to implement in personal, public and political life to regain control over women's lives. It is better to dismantle an exploitative and disrespectful family than to preserve the values of patriarchy in the name of family lineages, culture, tradition, society and blood relationships.

Roots of Rape

The World Population Review's *Rape Statistics by Country (2024)* highlights the widespread scope and severity of issues of rape and sexual violence against women, revealing the alarming frequency and nature of this global crisis. According to the report, while Botswana holds the hopeless title of the 'rape capital of the world', the so-called two largest democracies are not far behind. In the United States, the frequency of rape varies by state, but it averages out to one incident every one to two minutes. Similarly, the *National Crime Records Bureau of India* reports a disturbing rise in rape cases, with 31,000 cases recorded in 2022 alone. This statistic translates to nearly 85 women being raped every day in India. Rape culture is rampant in many countries, turning it into a global epidemic that disproportionately affects women.

However, the media, policymakers, political leaders and legal luminaries often portray incidents of rape as isolated events, focusing on specific criminal acts tied to specific times, places and people (Benedict, 1993). In many cases, women are unjustly blamed and shamed, accused of being the seducer or criticised for their choice of clothing, wrong company or the timing of their actions in terms of going out. The failure of law enforcement, the breakdown of order, ineffective policing, lack of education, exposure and consciousness are frequently cited as significant factors contributing to the increasing number of rape cases worldwide. The use of alcohol and other drugs is often employed as a smokescreen to obscure the collective social, political and legal accountability for the heinous and inhumane crime of rape (Bancroft, 2009).

There is no doubt that all the above reasons are contributing factors of rape and sexual violence. However, these incidents are not merely isolated aberrations; they are the result of a systemic condition that perpetuates rape and dehumanises women. Rape is a product of patriarchal culture that seeks to control women's bodies and labour. This is further exacerbated by capitalist culture, which commodifies women's bodies as objects of sexual pleasure and reduces them to mere reproducers of labour power and pleasure. Both patriarchy and capitalism create an unequal power structure where men control, dominate, discriminate and disenfranchise women at every stage of life. Rape and all forms of sexual violence are integral tools of patriarchal and capitalist control perpetuated by men (Goldberg, 2015; Bannerji, 2016).

Historically, rape has existed both in ancient and medieval periods, and there are also religious roots associated with it. In *Sacred Witness: Rape in the Hebrew Bible* (2021), Susanne Scholz provides redemptive reflections on rape in the troubling texts of the Hebrew Bible. However, most religions are inherently misogynistic, where everyday sexism is normalised and naturalised. Religious culture domesticates men and women with a patriarchal consciousness, where the subjugation of women is normalised as a natural state. Women are worshipped as mothers, loved as sisters and celebrated as friends, partners and wives, but within a culture that simultaneously undermines them in their everyday lives.

Many patriarchal cultures consider women as repositories of honour and family dignity, defining their character by what they do with their bodies, as if their genitals symbolise the cultural pride of patriarchy. Men kill women to protect, humiliate or assert each other's cultural pride and honour. Such patriarchal cultures normalise violence against women. This double standard is a strategy to justify subjugation in real life while celebrating women in predatory cultural and religious performances. The culture of 'hate the sin and not the sinner' is part of this religious discourse, where women are treated as if they are the repository of all sin, impurity and other devilish qualities, necessitating the intervention of male saints for the purification of their bodies and minds.

Many commentators, policymakers and political leaders have dismissed 'rape culture' as a myth since the term was coined by the *New York Radical Feminists Collective* in the 1970s. 'Rape culture' is no longer a myth (Sibley, 2021). Men are socialised into this culture on an everyday basis, which contributes to rape and sexual assault against women. Popular cultures that originate from religions create and nurture vulnerable conditions for women, where rape culture is normalised and patriarchal capitalism sustains it. Religion, patriarchy and capitalism are the three pillars of 'rape culture' where victims are blamed for their own assaults. Therefore, conviction rates in rape cases worldwide are very low. Such a legal culture of impunity encourages rape culture where rapists and perpetrators of sexual violence roam free while survivors endure various forms of mental, physical, social, sexual, cultural, economic and professional trauma. As a result, many rape victims even commit suicide (Ullman, 2004). The death does not end the slander, character assassination, blame and shame directed at the victims of rape.

The legal frameworks addressing rape and sexual violence, from the *Code of Hammurabi*, the *Code of Ur-Nammu*, the *Laws of Eshnunna*, the *Middle Assyrian Laws* and the *Hittite laws* within the *Code of the Nesilim* to modern-day courts and legal infrastructures, have failed to end rape and sexual violence against women (Smith, 1974; Pistono, 1987). Laws, courts and institutions of governance have not adequately protected women from the predatory influences of religion, patriarchy and capitalism. This failure is partly because these laws, courts and institutions of governance are predominantly led by men and shaped by religious and patriarchal capitalist systems.

Therefore, it is essential to integrate the struggle against rape and sexual violence (Alcoff, 2018) with the wider struggles against religion, patriarchy and capitalism. These struggles are intertwined; women cannot be safe as long as religion, patriarchy and capitalism continue to exist and influence everyday life. Women who are free from religion, patriarchy and capitalism are truly free from men to pursue and realise their dreams.

Origin of Abuse and Its Ramifications in the Age of Digital Revolution

Etymologically, the term 'abuse' has its roots in both French (*abus*) and Latin (*abūsus*). Historically, 'abuse' has been employed as both a noun and a verb since the Middle English period (1150–1500). Its multifaceted usage throughout history offers insight into the evolving landscape of societal norms and individual behaviours. Throughout the centuries, the term 'abuse' has transcended linguistic and cultural boundaries to encapsulate a spectrum of harmful actions and attitudes. Its etymology underscores the pervasive nature of such behaviours across cultures and epochs. From its earliest recorded usage, 'abuse' has served as a poignant marker of societal degeneration, reflecting the erosion of moral and ethical standards.

The historical evolution of the term 'abuse' mirrors broader shifts in societal attitudes towards power dynamics, consent and human rights. From its early associations with tyrannical rule and misuse of authority to its contemporary connotations encompassing domestic violence, individual misbehaviour and abuse in the name of relationships, substance abuse and institutional misconduct, the semantic trajectory of 'abuse' offers profound insights into the complexities of human interactions in a world of consumerism. In examining the myriad contexts in which 'abuse' manifests, one can discern a troubling narrative of exploitation, manipulation and cruelty. Whether wielded as a noun to denote physical or psychological maltreatment or deployed as a verb to describe the act of misusing power or trust, 'abuse' serves as a stark reminder of humanity's capacity for both benevolence and malevolence (Burris, 2022; Giles, 2020).

Abuse represents not only forms of self-degeneration but also serves as a tool wielded by reactionary individuals and failed institutions to thwart progressive transformations in the everyday lives of people and the planet. Individuals perpetrate abuse against each other, while capitalism, in its pursuit of profit, exacerbates this exploitation by monetising and commodifying lives and relationships in various forms. At its core, abuse embodies a regressive force, impeding the advancement of societies and hindering the realisation of collective well-being. Whether manifested through interpersonal violence, economic exploitation or systemic injustices, abuse undermines the fabric of social cohesion and erodes trust in institutions meant to safeguard the rights and dignity of individuals (Charron & Rothstein, 2018).

The nexus between abuse and capitalism underscores the insidious nature of exploitation within contemporary socio-economic systems. By commodifying human lives, relationships and natural resources, capitalism perpetuates a culture of exploitation wherein individuals and ecosystems are reduced to mere instruments of profit generation. In the process, human beings treat each other as commodities under capitalism. The false claims of ideological purity and individual integrity, devoid of any sense of accountability, honesty and responsibility, have become prevailing norms in the world of capitalist consumerism. The digital revolution has merely served to accelerate the perpetuation of abuse across various stages and steps of everyday life. Within the realm of capitalist consumerism, there exists a pervasive illusion of righteousness and moral superiority, often divorced from tangible actions and ethical considerations. This narrative of ideological purity not only shields individuals and institutions from scrutiny but also perpetuates a culture of impunity wherein exploitation and wrongdoing thrive unchecked (Doshi & Ranganathan, 2019).

The advent of the digital age has ushered in new avenues for abuse, expanding its reach and impact across diverse spheres of existence. From online harassment and cyberbullying to data privacy breaches and algorithmic discrimination, the digital revolution has provided fertile ground for the proliferation of abusive practices. Emails and social media platforms, while ostensibly designed to foster connectivity and community, have increasingly become breeding grounds for abusive behaviours. The anonymity afforded by digital interfaces, coupled with the rapid dissemination of information, has facilitated the spread of misinformation, hate speech and online vitriol. The digitalisation of various aspects of life, from education and employment to healthcare and governance, has introduced new vulnerabilities and challenges.

In essence, the term 'abuse' serves as a tool of ignoramusly ignorant, uncivilised and failed individuals, customs, traditions and institutions, encapsulating centuries of human experience, societal evolution and moral reflection. Its enduring relevance underscores the imperative of fostering empathy, promoting justice and combating the pervasive scourge of exploitation in all its forms. In confronting the intertwined phenomena of ideological hypocrisy and abuse in all its forms, it is imperative to re-evaluate societal norms and values. Rather than prioritising superficial displays of virtue, societies and individuals must cultivate a culture of accountability and responsibility, wherein individuals and institutions are held to task for their actions and decisions. Moreover, addressing digital abuse necessitates concerted efforts to promote digital literacy, raise civic consciousness, foster ethical technological development and establish robust regulatory frameworks to safeguard against online harm.

By recognising the complexities of the digital age and actively working to mitigate its negative consequences, societies can strive towards a more equitable and just future for all. The end of abuse, whether at the hands of individuals or systemic forces, is imperative to recognise its broader implications for social justice and environmental sustainability. Addressing abuse requires not only holding perpetrators accountable but also challenging the systemic conditions that enable and perpetuate such exploitation. Ultimately, combating abuse necessitates a holistic approach that prioritises the well-being of both people and the planet. By fostering solidarity, promoting equitable distribution of resources and advocating for systemic reforms, societies can work towards creating a world where abuse has no place and where all individuals and ecosystems can thrive.

Digital Capitalism and Technofeudalism

Feudalism managed to survive in different stages of its history. As a social, economic, political and cultural system that emerged in the Middle Ages, it has shown remarkable resilience by adapting and transforming throughout history. In contemporary times, it has reinvented itself in the form of technofeudalism. This modern iteration is dominated by platform companies that control various aspects of the economic activities of producers, consumers and distributors. These companies extract rent from producers, consumers and distributors, influencing the economic activities of individuals, societies, states and governments. The pervasive reach of these online platforms underscores the enduring nature of feudal structures, albeit in a new, technologically driven context (Gilbert, 2024).

Like medieval feudalism, technological feudalism does not produce tangible goods and services but instead survives through the accumulation of rent. While medieval feudal lords extracted agricultural produce and labour from serfs, techno-feudal lords extract value through data and user engagement on digital platforms. Both systems thrive by leveraging their control over resources and populations to generate wealth, not by producing anything themselves, but by appropriating the productivity and creative abilities of the working masses (Varoufakis, 2023).

The owners of tech corporations and online platform companies have become the new landlords of the digital age. They exert significant control over individuals, societies and political systems, effectively enslaving them. By fostering a culture that controls the creative abilities of working people, these tech giants ensure their dominance. Moreover, they actively reshape legal systems to maintain their influence and control over every sphere of life and the planet. This modern form of feudalism underscores the power and reach of these corporate entities in the contemporary world (ibid).

The accumulation of rent has been a central feature of feudalism throughout all stages of its history. This principle, which originally manifested through the collection of agricultural produce and labour from serfs, has evolved over time. In modern iterations, such as technofeudalism, rent accumulation is evident in the control and monetisation of digital spaces by tech corporations. Whether in medieval manors or contemporary online platforms, the core mechanism remains the same: extracting rent from dependent or subordinate groups to enhance the wealth and power of the feudal ruling and non-ruling entities (Geddes, 2019).

Techno-consumers of social media are akin to free slaves, labouring for the rental profits of social media company owners. Despite the perception of freedom and choice, these users are, in reality, contributing to the wealth of the digital platform owners through their engagement and data generation. This dynamic reflects a modern form of exploitation, where the users' activities and personal information are commodified for corporate gain (Charitsis, Zwick & Bradshaw, 2018).

Technofeudalism is designed to subjugate working people and manipulate their consciousness to serve the interests of techno-feudal lords, all under the guise of technological progress (Geddes, 2019). This system thrives without fostering genuine technological education, skills and consciousness among the masses, primarily due to digital divides and the lack of availability and accessibility of technology for all. The technological barriers are intentionally crafted to create an army of unemployed workforce that remains perpetually available to work for low wages and under unfavourable working conditions imposed by the techno-feudals. This dynamic perpetuates inequality and exploitation, reinforcing the dominance of the tech elites (Torabian, 2022).

Digital capitalism in all its forms, along with technofeudalism in all its iterations, complement each other to survive and thrive together, often at the expense of people and their planet. This symbiotic relationship enables these systems to exploit resources, labour and data, prioritising rental profit over the well-being of individuals and the environment. As they reinforce each other's structures and practices, they create a landscape where the interests of the few dominate, leading to increasing inequality, exploitation and environmental degradation (Thomas, 2024).

The working-class control over technology, the democratisation of digital platforms and technological infrastructure, the availability and accessibility of technological education and skills for all and the prioritisation of technology for people rather than profit are some of the immediate alternatives to ensure technological progress that upholds the interests of the masses. Through these concerted efforts, working people can harness technology as a tool for societal advancement and empowerment, ensuring that its benefits are accessible to all members of society, regardless of their socioeconomic status.

The cessation of the rent-seeking culture inherent in digital capitalism and technofeudalism stands as a pivotal factor in fostering the development of technology for the benefit of all, thereby ensuring the cultivation of a progressive technological consciousness. By dismantling the barriers erected by rent-seeking behaviours within these systems, working people can pave the way for equitable access to technological advancements. This inclusivity not only democratises innovation but also nurtures a collective awareness of the transformative power of technology, empowering individuals and communities alike to actively engage with and shape the trajectory of technological progress and future.

Perverted Society under Global Capitalism

Capitalism has managed to establish a perverted society where the individuals who construct homes often endure homelessness, those who produce food often go to bed hungry and those who build roads frequently lack a footpath to walk on themselves. Moreover, individuals involved in constructing schools, colleges and universities find that their own children lack access to quality education. Similarly, the workers who build hospitals often die without access to health services. The most meaningful workers live in slums often branded as bastions of crime. These stark narratives and disparities underscore the profound inequalities inherent in capitalist society, where access to basic necessities like housing, health, education and food is not guaranteed, despite the abundance of resources and wealth generated by the very people who face crises and live in a marginalised condition while few enjoy the privileges of capitalism (Armitstead, 2020).

The perverted capitalist society and its everyday realities illustrate how essential contributors to societal infrastructure and services often face deprivation and exclusion from the very benefits they help create. The disparity between labour and its rewards underscores the profound injustices ingrained within capitalist systems, where the distribution of resources and opportunities remains skewed. In such a society, the disconnect between labour and its fruits raises fundamental questions about fairness and human dignity. It calls into question the sustainability of an economic model that prioritises profit over people, leaving workers vulnerable to the harsh realities of poverty, hunger and inadequate access to essential services like education and healthcare.

In this capitalist society, the labour of individuals engaged in constructing homes is often undervalued and inadequately compensated, leaving many of them unable to afford stable housing for themselves and their families. Meanwhile, agricultural workers, responsible for cultivating and harvesting the food that sustains communities, may struggle to put food on their own tables due to low wages and precarious employment conditions (Scott-Villiers et al., 2016).

The marketisation and commodification of society within capitalism have played a significant role in creating the conditions of everyday alienation for the masses. In a capitalist system driven by market forces, almost everything, from housing and food to education and healthcare, becomes commodified – that is, turned into goods or services that can be bought and sold for profit. This commodification extends beyond material goods to essential aspects of human life and dignity. Housing is treated as a commodity to be bought and sold for profit, leading to inflated prices and housing insecurity for many. Similarly, food production becomes geared towards maximising profit rather than ensuring universal access to nutrition, leaving many to suffer from hunger and malnutrition (Weiler et al., 2016).

The basic services like education and healthcare, which are vital for personal development and well-being, become subject to market forces. The privatisation and commercialisation of education and healthcare often result in unequal access, with those who can afford to pay receiving better quality services while others are left underserved or excluded altogether. The marketisation and commodification of society exacerbate inequalities and prioritise the accumulation of wealth over the fulfilment of basic human needs. In such a system, the value of goods and services is determined by their market price rather than their inherent social or human value, leading to a distorted and often unjust distribution of resources and opportunities. These issues are not normal but created by the capitalist system. It requires questioning the underlying assumptions of capitalism and reimagining economic and social systems that prioritise human well-being and equity over profit maximisation (Alamad, 2024).

The growth of capitalism since its inception has profoundly reshaped society, giving rise to various forms that have left lasting impacts on individuals, families, states and societies across the globe. From its early stages to its contemporary manifestations, capitalism has wielded significant influence, moulding social structures and cultural norms in ways both profound and complex. These transformations have not only altered economic landscapes concomitant with the requirements of capitalism but also engendered shifts in cultural values, political ideologies and interpersonal relationships shaped by the values of mass consumerism for the growth of market for profit (Lunt & Livingstone, 1992).

The global trajectory of capitalism has led to the establishment of what some perceive as a distorted or perverted version of society. As wealth disparities widen and power becomes concentrated in the hands of a few, critiques of capitalism argue that it has engendered inequalities, exploitation and alienation among individuals and communities. This distorted societal framework challenges notions of fairness, justice and human flourishing, prompting calls for alternative economic models and social arrangements that prioritise equity, sustainability and collective well-being (Kothari, 2019).

These troubling realities of everyday marginalisation of masses highlight the fundamental flaws of a capitalist system that prioritises profit over human well-being and perpetuates cycles of poverty and deprivation. It underscores the urgent need for systemic change to address the root causes of inequality and ensure that all members of society have access to the essentials for a dignified and fulfilling life. As people confront these injustices in their everyday lives, it becomes imperative to advocate for systemic change that prioritises the well-being of all individuals and ensures that the benefits of labour are shared equitably. This necessitates a re-evaluation of economic priorities and a commitment to building a society where everyone could thrive and access the resources they need for a dignified and fulfilling life. This may involve basic reforms to regulate markets, promote social welfare and ensure universal access to essential goods and services, ultimately striving towards a more just and equitable society (Reinert, 2018).

Such a perverted capitalist society, moulded by a profit-driven capitalist market, systematically erodes the very fabric of social cohesion, rendering individuals as isolated and atomised beings, bereft of meaningful connection. This societal structure not only diminishes communal bonds but also engenders a pervasive sense of loneliness, exacerbating the fragmentation of human relationships and weakening the collective foundations upon which capitalist society thrives (Lebowitz, 2021).

In such a perverted capitalist society, shaped by alienation, the very 'social' foundations of society are undermined, leading to atomised individuals as 'lonely beings'. Therefore, capitalism can never offer any form of alternatives or platforms to reform itself. The struggle to end capitalism is the only alternative to reclaim the social foundations of society, economy, culture and life.

Capitalism as a Criminal Enterprise

Capitalism operates as a system that many argue is akin to a criminal enterprise, one that exploits both labour and nature in pursuit of ever-increasing profits. This economic model thrives on a hierarchical structure, resembling a pyramid, where those at the top reap the most benefits while those at the bottom bear the heaviest burdens. Laborers often find themselves subjected to low wages, precarious working conditions and limited rights, all to fuel the relentless capitalist pursuit of profit. Similarly, nature is treated merely as a monetised commodity or resource to be exploited for financial gain, leading to environmental degradation and ecological imbalance. The insatiable demand for profit drives this capitalist cycle of exploitation, creating a perpetual cycle of inequality and environmental destruction (Glasbeek, 2018).

Capitalism fosters various forms of criminal behaviour to establish a securitised state that primarily safeguards property interests. Under this system, there exists a legal framework that disproportionately criminalises individuals for minor acts of survival, such as shoplifting, while simultaneously shielding systematic crimes, such as wars justified under the guise of exporting democracy or combating terrorism. The real intentions are to capture natural resources for corporate plunder. This dichotomy underscores a fundamental injustice within the legal system, where the pursuit of profit and the protection of property rights take precedence over the well-being and survival strategies of marginalised individuals. In essence, capitalism perpetuates a skewed notion of justice that serves to reinforce existing power structures and inequalities, further entrenching the cycle of exploitation and oppression (Wang, 2018).

Capitalism has not only given rise to crime syndicates but has also legitimised them under the guise of credit-led banking systems and insurance industries. These sectors, which are integral to the capitalist economy, often wield significant power and influence, shaping the economic landscape to their advantage. In doing so, they effectively domesticate labour and control the distribution of wages. The banking system, through mechanisms like predatory lending and debt bondage, exploits individuals and communities, trapping them in cycles of financial dependence and vulnerability. Similarly, insurance industries capitalise on fear and uncertainty, profiting from the misfortunes of others while offering limited protection to those in need. This intertwining of capitalism with criminal enterprises not only perpetuates inequality but also erodes the fabric of social trust and solidarity, further entrenching the dominance of corporate interests over the well-being of individuals and communities (Schuilenburg, 2015).

The privatisation of healthcare services has led to the emergence of what can be characterised as a crime syndicate, consisting of pharmaceutical corporations, private healthcare providers and health insurance companies. Under this system, the pursuit of profit takes precedence over the provision of quality care, resulting in a business model that thrives on the business of sickness rather than wellness. Pharmaceutical companies, driven by profit motives, often prioritise the development and marketing of profitable drugs over addressing genuine health needs. This pursuit of profit can lead to practices such as price gouging and the suppression of cheaper, generic alternatives, further exacerbating healthcare inequalities. Private healthcare corporations, similarly, motivated by financial gain, prioritise treatments and procedures that yield the highest returns, sometimes at the expense of patient well-being. This profit-driven approach can result in overdiagnosis, overtreatment and unnecessary medical interventions, all of which contribute to rising healthcare costs and patient harm (Benson, 1998).

Health insurance businesses, operating within this framework, seek to maximise profits by minimising payouts and restricting access to care. This can manifest in practices such as denying coverage for pre-existing conditions, imposing high deductibles and co-payments and excluding certain treatments or providers from coverage. As a result, many individuals are left underinsured or uninsured, unable to afford necessary medical care, while others face financial ruin due to exorbitant medical bills. Together, these agencies, processes, institutions and structures form a powerful alliance that perpetuates a system of healthcare injustice, prioritising corporate profits over the health and well-being of individuals and communities. This arrangement not only exacerbates existing health disparities but also undermines the fundamental principles of healthcare as a human right (Leys, 2010).

The military-industrial complex led by defence corporations is undeniably intertwined with the criminal enterprises of capitalism and its securitised state, as they often promote and perpetuate conflicts in pursuit of accumulating wealth, regardless of the human cost (Gibbs, 2012). These industries thrive on the production and sale of weapons and military equipment, which are utilised in conflicts around the world. In the pursuit of profit, defence contractors frequently lobby governments to engage in military interventions and wars, sometimes fabricating or exaggerating threats to justify increased defence spending. The consequences of these actions are dire, as conflicts fuelled by the defence industry result in immense human suffering, loss of life and displacement of populations. Civilians bear the brunt of these conflicts, facing violence, destruction of infrastructure and the breakdown of societal systems. Meanwhile, the defence contractors responsible for supplying weapons often profit handsomely from these conflicts, further incentivising their continuation. Furthermore, the defence industry's influence extends beyond direct conflict, as it also plays a role in shaping foreign policy and perpetuating geopolitical tensions. Arms sales to authoritarian regimes and conflict zones perpetuate instability and human rights abuses, all in the pursuit of profit. In essence, the defence industry represents a particularly egregious example of capitalism's capacity to prioritise financial gain over human lives and global stability. It underscores the urgent need to reassess our priorities and advocate for a world where peace and diplomacy, rather than war and violence, are the primary means of resolving conflicts (ibid).

The pursuit of peace, cooperation, solidarity, the recognition of health as a universal and fundamental human right, the role of states and governments, the importance of just laws, impartial courts and ethical banking systems for the benefit of people, as well as the utilisation of science for the welfare of humanity and the planet, all constitute a collective struggle against capitalism. Anti-capitalist struggles based on scientific and secular consciousness can only ensure peace and prosperity in the world.

Capitalism and Its Narcissist Culture of Entitlement

Capitalism, with its inherent culture of psychopathic narcissism (Adams, 2016), nurtures a pervasive consumerist mindset of entitlement. This parasitic mentality enables capitalist entities to thrive off the value generated by the labour of working individuals. These chronic attitudes, processes and structural norms are ingrained within society to perpetuate a culture of entitlement unique to capitalist systems based on unearned incomes and profits. Today, this epidemic of entitlement manifests broadly across various societies, shaping the economic, political, cultural and social landscapes.

In capitalist societies, the notion of entitlement extends beyond mere economic gain. It permeates social interactions, influencing how individuals perceive their rights and privileges. The normalisation of this entitlement is evident in the way wealth and resources are disproportionately allocated, consumed and controlled often justifying the exploitation of labour for personal or corporate gain. The entitlement epidemic is not limited to the upper echelons of society. It trickles down, affecting interpersonal relationships, family and community dynamics. The constant pursuit of self-interest, driven by the culture of narcissism, undermines collective well-being and encourages social fragmentation (Golec de Zavala & Lantos, 2020).

The personality traits of narcissism and entitlement are not organically innate; they are products of capitalist socialisation, which instils and perpetuates such values and practices. In a capitalist society, individuals are often encouraged to prioritise self-interest, competition and material success over communal well-being and cooperation. This environment fosters a sense of entitlement and narcissism, as people are conditioned to view themselves as superior and deserving of special treatment. The focus on personal gain and achievement at the expense of others erodes collective values and promotes a culture where these traits are normalised and even rewarded. The understanding of the social roots of narcissism and entitlement is essential for addressing their pervasive influence (Adams, 2014).

The narcissistic culture of entitlement cultivates chronic laziness, selfishness, extreme individualism and various forms of exploitative behaviour in everyday life. In this environment, individuals believe they are entitled to reap the benefits of others' labour without contributing anything themselves. They operate under the assumption that everyone owes them everything, yet they owe nothing to anyone. Limitless self-indulgence continues to be the lifeblood of narcissism and entitlement (Piff, 2014; Twenge & Campbell, 2009).

This unchecked pursuit of personal gratification fuels these traits, reinforcing a cycle of selfishness and disregard for others. Narcissistic individuals prioritise their own desires and needs above all else, often at the expense of those around them. Their sense of entitlement drives them to seek constant validation and special treatment, perpetuating a mindset that justifies their actions and attitudes. This relentless focus on self-indulgence not only harms relationships and community dynamics but also undermines the potential for genuine personal growth and fulfilment (Roberts, 2014).

These narcissistic and entitled individuals, groups and cultures manifest in various forms of delusional self-confidence, often devoid of any real substance in their personal or professional lives. Despite their lack of genuine achievement or merit, they maintain an inflated sense of self-worth, ethics and entitlement. A common thread among all entitled and narcissistic individuals is their parasitic nature. They consistently seek to exploit the efforts and resources of others, displaying a profound lack of empathy and communal responsibility.

This parasitism undermines the very fabric of social cohesion, creating an environment where mutual respect and cooperation are eroded.

From grandiose narcissism to vulnerable narcissism and all other forms, these traits persist by projecting either superiority or inferiority. Grandiose narcissists assert their dominance and self-importance, often exhibiting arrogance and an inflated sense of self-worth. In contrast, vulnerable narcissists mask their insecurities and fragility by seeking excessive validation and attention. Both types, along with other variations of narcissism, rely on externalising their self-perception to manipulate how others view them. This projection not only reinforces their self-image but also serves as a defence mechanism against self-reflection and personal growth (Malesza & Kaczmarek, 2018).

Narcissists and entitled individuals consistently project their ignorance, incompetence, vulnerabilities and failures onto others, avoiding any form of self-reflection. They engage in relentless blaming, defaming, gaslighting and manipulation, constantly redirecting every situation back to themselves. Their lack of accountability is coupled with a deep-seated need to control the narrative through falsehoods, making it difficult for others to realise the realities. Such behaviours not only erode trust but also undermines the potential for genuine relationships. It is important to understand these patterns of behaviour for recognising and protecting oneself from such toxic dynamics of capitalist culture (Haller, 2015).

Narcissists and their culture of entitlement erode the collective foundations of society, promoting individualism in a way that enables capitalism to thrive without resistance. This shift undermines communal bonds and fosters an environment where personal gain is prioritised over the common good. The resulting fragmentation weakens societal cohesion, making it easier for exploitative systems to perpetuate themselves (Brown, 2006).

Moreover, this culture of narcissistic entitlement has broader implications for society. It promotes a mentality where success is measured not by one's contributions or achievements, but by one's ability to manipulate and exploit. This distorts social values, prioritising self-interest over collective well-being and eroding trust within communities.

It is crucial to foster a culture that values genuine contributions and reciprocal relationships based on truth. The growth of accountability, empathy and community engagement can help mitigate the negative impacts of narcissistic entitlement, promoting a more equitable and cohesive society. It is possible to cultivate a culture of resilience that values collective prosperity over individual gain by challenging the capitalist norms of narcissistic entitlement.

Conclusion

In the broader social and collective conception, ideals such as human happiness, freedom, democracy, peace, equality, justice, solidarity and prosperity
have been either totally neglected or pushed aside as irrelevant in the pursuit of
economic growth and development to establish and expand capitalism. Under
the dominant capitalist paradigm, economic indicators like GDP growth and
market expansion are prioritised over social well-being and equitable development. This focus on economic metrics overlooks the importance of comprehensive human development, which encompasses more than just economic growth.

In terms of human happiness and freedom, the ruling class often equates
these with consumerism and individual liberties, overshadowing the importance of collective well-being and social justice. Mass consumerism expands
the commodity market for profit by commodifying lives, labour and society.
Democracy is presented as a hallmark of free societies, yet the ruling class
influences electoral processes and policymaking to ensure that their interests
are preserved. The deepening of democracy is delayed in the pursuit of market interests. Human happiness, for example, is often reduced to consumer
satisfaction, ignoring the deeper aspects of well-being such as mental health,
community bonds and a sense of purpose. Freedom is frequently equated with
purchasing power and market freedoms, overshadowing the significance of
political and social liberties. Democracy, instead of being a genuine participatory process, becomes a facade where economic elites exert significant influence over political decisions.

Peace, equality and justice are similarly compromised. In many cases, economic growth is pursued at the expense of social harmony, leading to increased
inequality and social unrest. The environmental degradation that accompa-
nies unchecked economic development further exacerbates social inequalities
and threatens long-term sustainability. Solidarity and collective well-being are
often undermined in a capitalist society that champions individualism and
competition. The social fabric weakens as people are pitted against each other
in the race for economic success, leading to a fragmented society where the
vulnerable are left behind. In pursuit of prosperity defined by material wealth,
the richer segments of society accumulate more resources, while the poorer
segments face growing hardships. This disparity is rationalised by the ruling
class as a natural outcome of economic growth, sidelining the moral and ethical imperatives of justice and equality.

The skewed conceptions of peace, nationalism, wars, markets, human
happiness, freedom, democracy and everyday governance in contemporary

discourses are shaped by the ideas of the ruling class. These ideas are normalised and naturalised to strengthen the ruling class's grip on individuals, societies, cultures, politics, religions, states and governments. The ruling class uses its influence to propagate specific ideologies, presenting them as the standard and most rational approach to organising society and individual lives. This manipulation ensures that humanistic and alternative perspectives are marginalised, making it difficult for opposing views to gain traction. By controlling the narrative around crucial concepts such as peace and democracy, the ruling class maintains its power and ensures that societal structures remain favourable to their interests.

For instance, the notion of nationalism is often framed in a way that promotes unity and pride among the populace, but it can also serve to divert attention from internal issues and justify external conflicts to manipulate the masses and ensure their hegemony over people and resources. Similarly, the market is frequently portrayed as the most efficient means of resource distribution, despite evidence that it leads to significant inequality and exploitation. Everyday governance, from local municipalities to national governments, is also subject to the ruling class's influence. Through lobbying, campaign financing and control over media, they shape public opinion and policy decisions to align with their objectives. This pervasive influence underscores the importance of critical thinking and awareness among the populace to challenge and dismantle these entrenched power structures to reclaim freedom, democracy and citizenship rights.

The ruling class continues to propagate their ideas as the only viable alternatives, presenting these ideas and projects as their own initiatives. However, they also make working people believe in these ideas and projects as if they are universally beneficial. By dominating educational systems, media and public discourse, the ruling class frames their ideologies as common sense or the natural order of things. This manipulation is strategic, ensuring that the working class internalise these beliefs and support policies that ultimately serve the interests of the elite. The ruling class employs various means to achieve this, including cultural narratives that glorify individualism, meritocracy and free-market capitalism.

For example, in many societies, the concept of success is often tied to hard work and individual effort, overshadowing the structural barriers that impede equal opportunity for the majority of working people in society. This narrative convinces working people that their socio-economic status is a result of their own actions, rather than systemic inequalities. As a result, they may resist collective actions or policies aimed at redistributing wealth and power. Moreover, the ruling class utilises political rhetoric to align their interests with national interests, often invoking patriotism and fear of external threats to justify their agendas. This tactic diverts attention from domestic issues and frames dissenting voices as unpatriotic or radical.

Through the normalisation of ruling class ideologies, the elites ensure that any alternative viewpoints are perceived as unrealistic or impractical. This control over societal values and beliefs effectively marginalises revolutionary ideas and maintains the status quo. The ruling class's ability to propagate their ideas as the only alternatives, while making working people believe in them, is a testament to their control over societal institutions and narratives. Recognising and challenging these manipulative tactics is essential for fostering a more equitable and just society. It is essential to challenge the capitalist narrative and advocate for a holistic approach to collective human development. It is also important to prioritise human happiness, freedom, democracy, peace, equality, justice, solidarity and prosperity alongside economic growth to build a more equitable society and sustainable planet, where people are free to pursue their dreams and happiness.

The mass rejection of ruling class ideas and the end of the celebration of ruling class ideals are the first steps towards collective consciousness and the mass emancipation of human lives from the clutches of capitalism and its multiple variants in every aspect of our lives. To achieve true liberation, it is crucial for people to become aware of how deeply embedded ruling class ideologies are in our daily existence. These ideologies shape our perceptions of success, happiness and progress, often in ways that serve the interests of the elite while marginalising the needs and rights of the majority. By rejecting these ideas, individuals and communities can begin to envision alternative ways of organising society that prioritise human well-being over profit.

Developing collective consciousness involves understanding the interconnectedness of various social, economic and political issues. It requires recognising that the struggles of different groups – whether they be workers, marginalised communities, or environmental activists – are linked by a common thread: the pervasive influence of capitalist exploitation and oppression. This awareness fosters solidarity and encourages unified action against the forces that perpetuate inequality and injustice.

Ending the celebration of ruling class ideals means challenging the narratives that glorify wealth accumulation, competitive individualism and consumerism. It involves promoting values such as cooperation, community, sustainability and equity. Educational systems, media and cultural institutions play a critical role in this transformation by fostering critical thinking and providing platforms for diverse voices and perspectives. As people begin to reject the dominance of capitalist ideologies, they can start to explore and implement alternative economic and social models. These might include cooperative enterprises, community-based resource management and policies that prioritise social welfare and environmental stewardship over corporate profits. Such models offer practical examples of how society can be organised around principles of fairness, inclusivity and sustainability.

Ultimately, the mass rejection of ruling class ideas and the cessation of their celebration pave the way for a more just and equitable world. This process is not only about dismantling the existing structures of power but also about building new systems that genuinely reflect the collective aspirations and needs of humanity. It is a journey towards true emancipation, where the potential and dreams of every individual can be realised, free from the constraints of a capitalist framework that domesticates lives, love, liberties and livelihoods in pursuit of profit at the cost of people and planet. It is time to reject capitalism and its values in all its forms to rejoice in life.

CHAPTER 3

POLITICS OF CAPITALISM IN COLONIAL AND POSTCOLONIAL COUNTRIES

Introduction

Capitalism has profoundly altered the dynamics of everyday politics as a tool of social change, shifting the focus towards a market-driven politics of economic development. In such a condition, market forces control society and politics. In this new configuration between capitalism and politics, citizens are increasingly viewed and treated as customers (Leys, 2001). Therefore, democracy is no longer primarily about empowering citizens and ensuring their active participation in governance. Instead, it has become a mechanism for creating and facilitating conditions for the growth and expansion of profit-driven markets. This transformation impacts various aspects of politics. Public policies and government initiatives are often designed to attract investments and stimulate economic growth, sometimes at the expense of social welfare and equity. The needs and rights of individuals become secondary to the interests of corporations and market expansion (Holmwood, 2014).

Moreover, the role of the citizen is diminished as democratic engagement is replaced by consumer choices. Political participation, which should be about shaping the direction of the community and holding leaders accountable, is reduced to market transactions. This shift undermines the foundational principles of democracy, such as equality, justice and collective decision-making. In this way, capitalism's influence has redefined democracy to support and sustain economic agendas, prioritising market profitability over the empowerment and well-being of the working people. This raises critical questions about the future of democratic values and the true meaning of citizenship in a market-oriented world of capitalism (Alex-Assensoh, 2005).

Moreover, capitalism undermines the foundations of democratic politics and encourages the rise of right-wing and reactionary forces that prioritise the interests of large corporations over the welfare of people and the planet (Giroux, 2014). This erosion of democratic values manifests in several ways. First, the political influence of corporations grows, often leading to policies that favour deregulation, tax cuts for the wealthy and diminished social protections. These policies can exacerbate inequality and limit the government's ability to address social and environmental issues effectively. Second, the focus on profit maximisation often comes at the expense of sustainable practices, leading to environmental degradation. Corporations, driven by short-term gains, exploit natural resources and contribute to climate change without sufficient accountability (Wright & Nyberg, 2015). This disregard for ecological balance threatens the planet's health and the well-being of future generations. Additionally, the promotion of right-wing and reactionary ideologies can polarise societies and undermine social cohesion. These forces often capitalise on economic insecurities and cultural anxieties, diverting attention from systemic issues and scapegoating marginalised groups (Looney, 2017). This divisive rhetoric can erode trust in democratic institutions and weaken the collective resolve needed to address complex societal challenges.

Finally, the intertwining of capitalism and right-wing politics creates a feedback loop that perpetuates corporate dominance and diminishes the power of democratic governance. This dynamic poses significant risks to social justice, environmental sustainability and the integrity of democratic systems. It calls for a critical reassessment of the relationship between economic systems and political values to ensure that democracy serves the interests of all people and the planet.

British Electoral Irony

British prime minister Rishi Sunak was considered one of the most unpopular political figures in the United Kingdom after the electoral defeat of the Conservatives in the 4 July 2024 election. According to a YouGov Westminster Voting Intention survey conducted on May 30, the Labour Party was leading by 25 per cent over the Conservative Party, which led to the replacement of Mr Sunak by the most unpopular opposition leader, Sir Keir Starmer. Both Sunak and Starmer are representatives of two sides of the same ideological spectrum, which prioritises the interests of the wealthy, large corporations and both British and international elites, often at the expense of the working class.

This has led to significant disillusionment among voters, who feel that neither party genuinely addresses their concerns and needs (Grant & Evans, 2024).

The dominance of these two parties in British politics has undermined the conditions necessary for the deepening of democracy and the implementation of robust welfare policies. Leadership within both the Conservative and Labour parties is committed to policies that ultimately weaken the working masses, exacerbating exploitative working conditions and socio-economic inequalities. It often appears as though these two parties are in a contest to see who can be more ruthless in their treatment of the populace and follow legacies of Conservative politics (Williams, 2024).

Once upon a time, the Labour Party played a historic role in shaping progressive welfare policies, institutions, and laws such as the Equal Pay Act, the Minimum Wage, and key health and education policies including the establishment of the National Health Service (NHS). These contributions significantly advanced social justice and improved the lives of countless individuals. However, the current Labour Party seems to be undermining its own legacy. By adopting policies and stances that echo those of the Conservative Party (the Tories), it risks dismantling the very achievements that once defined it. This shift raises concerns among supporters who believe the party is straying from its foundational principles of equality, fairness and social welfare. The current trajectory of the Labour Party under Sir Keir Starmer's leadership has raised significant concerns about its adherence to traditional Labour values (Elhefnawy, 2024).

Ideologically, the Labour Party has traditionally been a broad church, encompassing a wide range of perspectives and beliefs. This diversity has included social democrats, democratic socialists, leftists, trade unionists, more centrist members and liberals who advocate for market-friendly policies within a minimalist framework of social justice. This ideological plurality has been both a strength and a challenge for the party, allowing it to appeal to a broad spectrum of voters while also navigating internal tensions. However, the Sir Keir Starmer-led Labour Party is moving into a reactionary political landscape sans labour values. From day one of his leadership, he has been busy suspending progressive, left-wing, trade unionist and democratic leaders within the party, as if he is on a mission to cleanse the Labour Party of its progressive character (Callaghan, 2024).

Similarly, the Conservative Party is dedicated to maintaining its political tradition, which prioritises the interests of British elites, large corporations and businesses. The political ethos within the Conservative Party extends support to the ideology of white supremacists under the guise of national interests and conservative British cultural values, thereby perpetuating a system of political patronage. This alignment with white supremacist ideals not only undermines the principles of equality and inclusivity but also exacerbates societal divisions and tensions in twenty-first-century Britain (Allchorn, 2024).

These two parties in British politics bear striking similarities in their policies, ideological commitments and interactions with the populace. Both the Conservative Party and the Labour Party share commonalities in their approaches to governance, often aligning on key issues such as economic strategy, social welfare and foreign policy. Their ideological foundations, while distinct in certain aspects, frequently converge on matters of corporate interests branded as national importance.

The electoral rituals of democracy, orchestrated by these two parties, fail to provide a genuine alternative for the common people. The forthcoming general election on July 4 merely perpetuates a cycle wherein an unpopular ruling party and its leadership are replaced by an equally unpopular opposition party and its leadership. This recurring pattern underscores the disillusionment felt by many citizens who perceive little substantive difference between the policies and priorities of the incumbent government and the opposition. Despite the democratic façade of electoral choice, the fundamental interests of ordinary people often remain marginalised amidst the political theatre enacted by these parties in Britain (Kenny, 2024).

The mere act of alternating power between two unpopular entities does little to address the systemic issues and challenges facing society. Instead, it reinforces a sense of political inertia and cynicism, eroding trust in the democratic process itself. In such a climate, the need for genuine alternatives and transformative leadership becomes increasingly evident. Citizens deserve more than a superficial exchange of power; they deserve meaningful representation and policies that genuinely reflect their interests and aspirations. Until such alternatives emerge, the electoral rituals orchestrated by the dominant parties will continue to ring hollow for many disenfranchised voters. However, the result of the forthcoming general election is crucial as it will determine the direction of the Unted Kingdom's political landscape amidst ongoing economic, political challenges and social issues. Many are calling for a shift towards policies that more directly benefit the broader population, rather than maintaining the status quo that favours the elites.

Will the British electoral irony offer any alternatives?

The British electoral irony, characterised by the cyclic exchange of power between unpopular parties, may indeed present opportunities for alternative voices to emerge. While the dominant parties may seem entrenched in their positions of influence, historical precedents demonstrate that shifts in political landscapes can occur, often catalysed by grassroots movements, new political parties or charismatic leaders. In recent years, people have witnessed the rise of smaller progressive parties, green politics and independent candidates challenging the status quo, offering alternative visions and policies that resonate with disenchanted voters. These movements, although initially marginalised, can gradually gain momentum, reshaping the political discourse and forcing established parties to adapt or risk irrelevance.

Moreover, societal changes and evolving public attitudes can create fertile ground for new ideas and progressive ideologies to take root in the expansion of working-class politics. Issues such as climate change, social inequality and technological innovation have the potential to galvanise diverse coalitions and mobilise support for unconventional political platforms. Ultimately, the British electoral system, despite its limitations and paradoxes, remains dynamic and responsive to changing realities. While entrenched interests may resist change, the inherent unpredictability of politics means that genuine alternatives can emerge from unexpected quarters, offering hope for a more inclusive and representative democracy despite its current irony.

Elections Sans Electoral Alternatives and Democratic Stagnation in Europe

Free and fair elections are considered to be the festivals of democracy, where the electorates have the opportunity to choose their leaders from a pool of alternative candidates listed on the ballot. This democratic process allows citizens to express their preferences and have a direct impact on the governance of their country or community. Through elections, individuals are empowered to voice their opinions on policies and leadership, ensuring that those in power are representative of the people's will. The diversity of candidates provides a range of options, reflecting various ideologies and policy proposals, which enrich the democratic experience and encourage healthy political competition. This fundamental aspect of democracy not only legitimises the authority of elected officials but also fosters civic engagement and political accountability.

In the ongoing elections in France, the electorates face a choice between the far-right National Rally (RN) party, led by Marion Anne Perrine Le Pen and the liberally centrist right-wing Ensemble alliance, headed by Emmanuel Jean-Michel Frédéric Macron. The left-wing New Popular Front (NFP) coalition is trailing behind these right-wing contenders. The results of the first round of the country's parliamentary elections indicate that the RN party has won a substantial majority, positioning it to form the next government in France. This significant right-wing political shift challenges the radical legacies of the French Revolution. The flag-waving nationalism of the RN has overshadowed the revolutionary promises of *Liberté, Égalité, Fraternité*, potentially altering the historical and ideological landscape of French politics (Steger, 2008).

The general election in the United Kingdom did not offer any new alternatives in terms of radical electoral choices, with the main contenders being the Labour Party, led by Sir Keir Rodney Starmer, and the Conservative Party, under the leadership of the previous prime minister, Rishi Sunak. Both parties uphold the interests of the establishment and follow similar policy trajectories, both domestically and in terms of foreign policies. Interestingly, the Labour Party leader, Mr Starmer, appears more conservative in his approach than Mr Sunak, who, in turn, evokes comparisons to Tony Blair, albeit without Blair's charm as a political marketer (Kenny, 2024).

Similarly, the presidential election between the Democrats, under the leadership of the current president, Mr. Joseph Robinette Biden Jr., and the Republicans, led by the ex-president, Mr Donald John Trump, offers nothing radical to the American people. Both these political traditions consistently pursue, nourish and implement their neo-imperialist ambitions, both domestically and internationally. These two political parties are supported by the American establishment, which betrays the very foundations of the American Revolution, a revolution that was built on the ideals of equal citizenship rights, liberty, equality and self-government (Warren, 2021).

From alcohol and cars to drugs, many goods are conveniently delivered to people's homes, yet hungry and homeless individuals still stand in line at soup kitchens or food banks. This stark contrast highlights the capitalist reality of so-called advanced democracies in America and Europe. Elections in France, the United Kingdom and the United States, three advanced capitalist democracies, offer nothing radical that can change the everyday sufferings of the working masses.

The limited electoral choices available to the people in the ongoing elections underscore the absolute grip of the establishment on democratic practices, including periodic elections. This stranglehold curtails genuine democratic engagement and reduces the elections to a mere formality, rather than a true expression of the people's will. Moreover, these elections have proven inadequate in curbing the pervasive issues of neocolonial and imperialist wars that threaten democracy in the world. Despite the democratic facade, the underlying power structures continue to perpetuate policies that undermine democratic values and destabilise global peace and justice while exploiting the working masses in Europe and America.

Market forces are celebrating the forward march of right-wing culture and politics in advanced capitalist democracies, particularly in France, the United Kingdom and the United States. This celebration reflects the alignment of economic interests with the political shifts towards conservatism and nationalism in these nations. The rise of right-wing ideologies is often accompanied by policies that favour deregulation, lower taxes and reduced government intervention in the economy, which align with the goals of powerful market entities. Consequently, the entrenchment of right-wing politics in these countries signifies not only a cultural shift but also a transformation in economic policies that benefit market-driven interests. As a result, the synergy between market forces and right-wing politics is reshaping the political landscape in these advanced capitalist democracies (Nilges, 2019).

Elections have increasingly become a monopolised practice of the powerful, failing to adequately foster the deepening of democracy. The corporatisation of the current electoral landscape often sidelines diverse voices and perpetuates inequalities in representation. As a result, the fundamental principles of democracy, such as inclusivity and fair representation, are undermined. In this context, it becomes increasingly clear that the preservation of democracy and the resurgence of its core values – equality, liberty, justice and fraternity – can only be achieved through a robust working-class mass movement. This movement is essential not only to counteract the erosion of democratic norms but also to reclaim the foundational principles of working-class democracy. These principles are rooted in the idea that every citizen should have equal rights and opportunities, ensuring that justice is accessible to all and fostering a sense of solidarity and community.

By championing these inalienable foundations of citizenship, a working-class mass movement can serve as a potent force in safeguarding democracy against threats posed by authoritarianism, inequality and the unchecked influence of powerful interests. Thus, by mobilising around these ideals, the working class can play a pivotal role in revitalising democracy and advancing a society where all individuals can thrive and participate fully in civic life and control public resources for their well-being. Elections can be a tool for political mobilisation, driving the democratic transformation of society, the state and the government towards peace and prosperity for all citizens, regardless of their backgrounds.

Is It a Labour Victory or the Consolidation of Conservative Oligarchy in United Kingdom?

The crushing defeat of the Conservative Party and their local version called the Scottish National Party in the UK general election today is a cause for celebration. The Labour Party has returned to power after 14 years of Tory rule. It is a clear electoral victory for the Labour Party under the leadership of Sir Keir Rodney Starmer, who is now the new prime minister of the United Kingdom. The Labour Party's victory marks a pivotal moment in British politics, reflecting widespread dissatisfaction with the Conservative Party's handling of key issues over the past decade. The new government faces the formidable task of uniting a divided nation and delivering on the promises that fuelled their electoral success. However, despite this significant political shift, a wave of disillusionment continues to ripple through the public. In his victory speech, the new prime minister pledged to 'restore trust in politics' and vowed to rebuild and govern Britain with a vision 'unburdened by doctrine'. Such a political position promotes ideology-free politics, which is the foundation of opportunistic politics (Colley & Head, 2013).

How can anyone trust a word from Keir Starmer, who has a habit of taking opportunistic political positions and changing his views on policies and his commitment to manifestoes? He changes more often in politics than the British weather. His politics of being 'unburdened by doctrine' means establishing an ideologically free zone of politics and governance, which aligns with conservative values of capitalism and the interests of British and international elites. Even the Conservative Party leadership and supporters claim that the Labour policy offering is not drastically different from the policy agendas of the Conservative Party. There is no fundamental difference between Mr Starmer and Mr Sunak in terms of their approach to welfare policies. Both are committed to the requirements of capital more than to the everyday needs of people. How can Mr Starmer promise to rebuild Britain while standing on the foundations and values of Conservative politics and policies?

The scepticism surrounding Sir Keir Starmer's leadership stems from his perceived lack of a consistent ideological stance. Critics argue that his flexible approach to policymaking raises questions about his authenticity and reliability as a leader. Many question his commitment to working people and their needs. This concern is further amplified by the notion that his governance style might cater more to the interests of the corporate elite rather than addressing the pressing needs of the general populace. Moreover, the fact that the Labour's policy platform mirrors that of the Conservatives suggests a troubling continuity rather than the transformative change many voters desire. If the new Labour government under Starmer's leadership fails to distinguish itself significantly from the previous Conservative administration, it could lead to further disillusionment among the electorate.

However, Mr Starmer's public positions on the privatisation of public services, economic austerity, social welfare and even on foreign policy issues like Gaza, Ukraine, war, nuclear weapons and NATO are not markedly different from those of Mr Sunak. Both leaders follow similar policy trajectories in British politics, reflecting a convergence in their approaches on key issues shaped by the Conservative political culture. While Mr Starmer and Mr Sunak come from different political parties – Labour and Conservative, respectively – their stances on privatisation show a shared inclination towards involving private sector efficiencies in public services. On the issue of economic austerity, both have advocated for fiscal prudence, albeit with nuanced differences in their approaches to government spending and debt management.

In terms of social welfare, Mr Starmer's proposals do not deviate significantly from Mr Sunak's policies, suggesting a consensus on the need to balance welfare provisions with economic sustainability. Foreign policy positions of both leaders also align in many respects, particularly in their support for NATO and their firm stance on international security challenges. This alignment indicates a broader trend in British politics where major parties exhibit similarities on fundamental policy issues, reflecting a right-wing shift in their political positions. Therefore, the landslide victory of the Labour party is not a victory for progressive politics or social democracy. It is the consolidation of the victory of extreme right-wing politics.

The dominance of the Labour and Conservative parties has transformed British politics into a political oligarchy where a very small number of unmeritorious economic elites shape public policy to uphold their interests with the support of the British state and government. This concentration of power within a limited political framework has led to significant consequences for the broader democratic process. The political influence wielded by these elites often results in policies that favour their economic and social interests, rather than reflecting the diverse needs and aspirations of the working people (Mount, 2012).

This collaboration between the ruling elites and opposition politics undermines the principles of democratic practice in Westminster, where decisions are frequently driven by the priorities of a privileged few. The intertwining of political power and economic clout means that these elites can effectively circumvent mechanisms designed to ensure accountability and transparency.

Their deep connections within both the Labour and Conservative parties enable them to exert disproportionate influence over legislative and regulatory frameworks, often to the detriment of wider societal welfare. In essence, the current oligarchic political landscape in Britain is detrimental to the deepening of democracy and public welfare. This has far-reaching implications for social equity, public trust in government and the overall health of the democratic system.

The rise of far-right political parties like Reform UK, led by Mr Nigel Paul Farage, in this election reveals disturbing trends of conservative consolidation in British politics. Such a political trend indicates a significant shift towards more extreme conservative ideologies, reflecting growing discontent and polarisation among the electorate. The increasing support for such parties suggests a backlash against traditional political establishments and a demand for more radical solutions to economic, social and cultural issues (Looney, 2017).

The presence of far-right parties like Reform UK in the political arena also raises concerns about the potential erosion of democratic norms and values. Their often inflammatory rhetoric and divisive policies can exacerbate social tensions and undermine efforts to foster inclusivity and cohesion within society. It signals a troubling trend towards conservative consolidation, with potential implications for the country's democratic integrity and social harmony. The electoral success of these parties encourages mainstream political entities to adopt more hardline stances to retain their voter base, further shifting the overall political discourse to the right. This conservative consolidation poses a challenge to the principles of pluralism and tolerance that are foundational to a healthy democracy in Britain (ibid).

For Starmer to truly rebuild Britain, he must go beyond the rhetoric of being 'unburdened by doctrine' and present a clear, progressive vision that prioritises social welfare, economic equality and robust public services focusing on health, education, employment and transportation. Only by doing so can he hope to bridge the gap between his promises and the expectations of a public weary of political platitudes. This requires a commitment to bold, tangible policies that address the root causes of societal issues and a willingness to challenge the status quo entrenched by years of conservative governance. Given Mr Starmer's political record, he is unlikely to break through the iron curtain of the conservative British establishment.

The overwhelming victory of Mr Jeremy Corbyn, other independent candidates and the Green Party shows that there is still electoral space for the revival of alternative and progressive politics in Britain. Mass mobilisation of all working people can ensure the defeat of conservative values and halt the forward march of right-wing politics in Britain, establishing a society based on peace and prosperity for all in this small island nation.

Tragedy of Hoi Polloi and Farce of Western Democratic Values

The reality of Western democracy is structured in such a way that it effectively excludes the majority of people from meaningful participation in decision-making processes. While citizens do vote and participate in elections, this engagement often serves as a veneer of inclusivity and equal opportunity that masks the underlying dominance of elites within the political system. Despite the semblance of democratic participation, the political structure is heavily influenced and controlled by a small group of elites who have the power to shape policies and allocate resources in ways that primarily serve their own interests. This elite dominance undermines the core democratic principle of equal representation and results in a political landscape where the voices of ordinary citizens are marginalised by the so-called democratic governments and states in Europe and America (Fabbrini, 2010).

The concentration of power among elites leads to a political process that is less responsive to the needs and desires of the broader population. Instead, it tends to prioritise the agendas of those with significant economic and social influence. This dynamic perpetuates inequality and fosters a sense of disenfranchisement among the general populace, who may feel that their votes and voices do not translate into actual influence over the governance of their countries.

The principles of democratic governance – transparency, accountability, the rule of law and inclusiveness – are increasingly eroding within Western political systems. Despite the theoretical framework supporting broader political participation and fairer representation, the fundamental nature of capitalist states in Europe and America remains unchanged. This persistent decline highlights a critical issue: the mechanisms designed to ensure a vibrant democracy are failing to counterbalance the entrenched power structures within these societies. Even as citizens engage in elections and other forms of political participation, their ability to influence substantive policy decisions is severely limited. This discrepancy underscores a troubling trend where democratic ideals are subverted by the economic interests of few capitalists.

In Western democracies, the alignment of government policies with the interests of capitalist corporations rather than those of the general populace is evident. This alignment manifests in legislation and regulatory frameworks that often prioritise corporate profitability and market stability over social welfare and equitable resource distribution. The interests of ordinary citizens are sidelined and their needs and aspirations are inadequately represented. The foundational principles of democracy are destroyed, as a result of which citizens are no longer the shareholders of Western democracy (Kitschelt et al., 1999).

The so-called Western democratic countries, which often engage in imperialist wars, promote conflicts and impose sanctions under the pretext of exporting democracy to countries in Asia, Africa and Latin America, are experiencing a significant decline in their own democratic values and practices. This situation highlights a profound irony and exposes the inherent contradictions within their political systems. The tragedy of these undemocratic foundations lies in their persistent assault on the very democratic values they claim to uphold. While advocating for democracy abroad, these nations frequently undermine democratic principles at home. This duality not only erodes the credibility of Western democracies but also reveals the farcical nature of their commitment to genuine democratic ideals. As these countries continue to prioritise geopolitical interests over the promotion of authentic democracy, the gap between their rhetoric and reality widens. This ongoing hypocrisy challenges the legitimacy of their democratic institutions and calls into question their role as global champions of democracy. So, it is imperative to critically examine and address these contradictions to foster a more genuine and consistent approach to democratic governance both domestically and internationally (Reid-Henry, 2020).

The so-called Western governments seemingly have the financial resources to engage in wars, military interventions and conflicts in various countries across Asia, Africa, Latin America and Eastern Europe. However, these same governments often fall short when it comes to investing in the critical infrastructures of health, education and employment within their own nations. This disparity reveals a troubling prioritisation of resources. Significant amounts of money are allocated to defence budgets and military operations, ostensibly to promote the interests of global corporations in the name of global stability or protect national interests. Yet, when it comes to addressing pressing domestic issues, such as expanding healthcare services, improving educational systems and creating meaningful employment opportunities, these governments often claim budgetary constraints (Reid-Henry, 2020).

The consequences of this democratic deficit and misallocation of resources are profound. Underfunded health systems struggle to provide adequate care, leading to disparities in health outcomes and accessibility. Educational institutions face resource shortages, impacting the quality of education and future prospects for students. Meanwhile, the lack of investment in creating sustainable and meaningful employment opportunities contributes to economic inequality and social instability (van Niekerk, 2020).

The growth of hunger, homelessness, food insecurity, unemployment and poverty represents a democratic disgrace for the so-called developed capitalist countries, where democracy is sacrificed to uphold the interests of corporate capitalism. In these nations, the gap between the wealthy elite and the average citizen continues to widen, highlighting the failure of democratic systems to address the fundamental needs of their populations. Despite the immense wealth and resources available in these countries, a significant portion of the population struggles with basic necessities. This stark contrast reveals the extent to which democratic ideals have been compromised in favour of maintaining and expanding corporate power and profits (Bakan, 2012).

The prevalence of hunger and food insecurity is particularly alarming in affluent societies. Many individuals and families face difficulty accessing nutritious food, leading to widespread health problems and diminished quality of life. Similarly, homelessness and inadequate housing conditions reflect the inability of the system to provide for its citizens, despite the presence of vast economic resources. Unemployment and underemployment further exacerbate these issues of individual dignity, as individuals are unable to secure stable, well-paying jobs that allow them to support themselves and their families. The resulting poverty traps many in a cycle of deprivation, with limited opportunities for upward mobility (Silver, 2023).

These social and economic issues in western countries are symptoms of a broader political problem: the prioritisation of corporate capitalism over the well-being of the populace. Policies and practices that favour large corporations and the wealthy elite often come at the expense of the broader citizenry, undermining the principles of fairness, equity and representation that are supposed to underpin democratic governance.

Such a situation not only calls for a re-evaluation of national priorities but also highlights the urgent need for mass struggle to deepen radical democracy and reclaim citizenship rights in western Europe and America. This mass mobilisation can serve as a powerful force to challenge and change the existing power dynamics. By advocating for a more equitable distribution of resources and greater public participation in decision-making processes, citizens can work towards a political system that truly represents their interests. The push for radical democracy involves creating mechanisms for more direct citizen involvement, ensuring that policies and practices reflect the will of the majority rather than the interests of a privileged few. It requires transparency, accountability and a commitment to social justice. Only through sustained collective action can citizens reclaim their rights and create a more just and equitable society.

These challenges also require a fundamental re-evaluation of the relationship between democracy and capitalism. It is essential to implement policies that ensure economic justice, such as fair wages, affordable housing, accessible healthcare and robust social safety nets. It is vital to curb corporate influence in politics and promote greater transparency and accountability within the government. The restoration of the integrity of democracy in these developed capitalist countries involves reclaiming it from the clutches of corporate interests and redirecting its focus towards serving the needs and rights of all citizens. By doing so, it is possible to build a society that is more just, equitable and reflective of true democratic values.

Politics of Confusion and Capitalism

The world is witnessing growing confusion in politics, economy, culture, society and life on a scale never seen before. There is confusion in different aspects of life perpetuated by the ruling elites, who use 'confusion' as a strategy to spread dominant narratives without any form of scrutiny. The global, national, regional and local landscapes are mired in unprecedented levels of 'confusion', determining various facets of everyday lives. It looks as if confusion has become an omnipresent force, infiltrating every aspect of our existence. From politics to the economy, culture to society and even personal lives, people find themselves navigating a web of confusion. These confusions produce uncertainties and crises, which are tools of control and domestication. This state of bewilderment is not a happenstance occurrence but rather a calculated tactic employed by those in power (De Mul, 2014).

The Brexit referendum in the United Kingdom, the involvement of the ex-deputy prime minister of Russia, Vladislav Surkov, who funded both human rights activists and anti-immigrant groups and the undemocratic consensus for an electoral alliance between the ruling BJD and the opposition BJP in Odisha show that there is no contradiction among ruling elites when it comes to power. There is only political confusion for the masses. The ruling elites, vested with authority and influence, have mastered the art of utilising confusion as a strategic tool to propagate their agendas and ideologies without any form of scientific mass verification. The ruling class crafts and disseminates dominant narratives, exploiting the fog of confusion to shield their actions from scrutiny and dissent. By obfuscating the truth and clouding the collective understanding, the ruling class maintains control and perpetuates capitalist hegemony (Stoddart, 2007).

At the global, national, regional and local levels, this phenomenon of mass confusion manifests in myriad forms, shaping the contours of our everyday lives as per the requirements of the ruling elites of capitalism. In the political arena, conflicting narratives and disinformation campaigns sow seeds of doubt and discord, undermining democratic processes and eroding public trust. Economic policies shrouded in complexity leave the masses bewildered, while benefiting the few at the top who profit at the cost of mass misery. The collective foundations of cultural norms and religious values of peace and solidarity are manipulated and distorted, blurring the lines between truth and fiction. Mass confusion helps to hide the ugly realities of capitalism with its fantasies. The spread of mass confusion also helps in the normalisation and naturalisation of ruling class falsehood in society. The normalisation of falsehood through confusion generates apathy towards understanding the predicaments of capitalism (Bell, 1972).

In society, the proliferation of fake news, disinformation, misinformation and polarisation fuels division and unrest, fracturing communities and exacerbating social, cultural and religious tensions. Social, cultural and religious conflicts help the security state to rise, which protects capitalism as a system of governance. Even on a personal level, individuals grapple with uncertainties and ambiguities, unsure of whom or what to believe in a world mired in confusion spread by fake news. The mainstream media also acts as the mouthpiece of ruling elites, where unaccountable governance defines governing and non-governing elites in every layer of society and state and where capitalism becomes the dominant force without any form of opposition (Hirst, 2017).

In order to establish dominance in the battle for narrative supremacy, the capitalist classes shape public discourses by spreading confusion with the help of sophisticated propaganda techniques to manipulate the masses in favour of right-wing reactionary forces. Such a project of mass confusion works as a strategy of ruling and non-ruling elites who are centrally responsible for the erosion of trust in public life, which is concomitant with the requirements of capitalism. Trust-free social, political and cultural zones are helpful for the elites to exploit the masses and push their agenda to govern without accountability. Accountable and trustworthy democratic and constitutional institutions are an anathema to capitalism. Therefore, weakening public institutions and public trust by spreading mass confusion is good for capitalism to sustain itself as a system. The spreading of mass confusion weakens citizenship rights by promoting a culture of disengagement and resignation among the masses (Vujnovic & Kruckeberg, 2023).

The spread of mass confusion isn't just a random occurrence but seems to be deliberately propagated by those in power, often termed the ruling elites. These elites utilise confusion as a potent strategy to disseminate dominant narratives without facing significant scrutiny or challenge to capitalism and its dominant order. There is a fundamental difference between organic confusion, which is a product of curiosity in seeking knowledge or discovering ignorance and the confusion manufactured by information warfare and mass media. The latter is a product of ruling and non-ruling elites seeking to uphold the interests of capitalism by destroying the critical thinking abilities of the working masses (Lelo & Fígaro, 2021; Farkas & Schou, 2018).

The struggle for clarity, critical thinking, reflection on everyday realities, transparency and accountability requires mass consciousness based on science and secularism, which can provide a glimmer of hope amidst this fog of mass confusion. As awareness grows and people awaken to the mechanisms of manipulation at play, they can see through the haze and question the narratives imposed upon the masses. Through critical thinking, dialogue and collective action, there is potential to pierce through the veil of confusion and reclaim agency over working-class lives and the future of the planet. This entails challenging dominant narratives, fostering media and digital literacy and holding those in power accountable for their actions. Mass struggle against confusion is the only way to aspire and forge a path towards clarity, understanding and genuine progress towards peaceful and prosperous coexistence sans capitalism. Truth and knowledge triumph in all pages of history.

Electoral Democracy and Hereditary Politics of Inheritance

Democracy is not only a product of the struggles of the working classes, but its survival against all odds also depends on the unwavering commitment of the working people. Historically, the working class has played a pivotal role in the establishment, promotion and preservation of democratic processes and institutions. Their collective actions, from organising labour movements to participating in political processes, have been fundamental in shaping democratic societies, states and governments. The ongoing resilience and active participation of the working class are crucial for maintaining and enhancing democratic cultures and values (Lind, 2020).

In times of political turmoil and economic challenges, it is often the working people who stand at the forefront, advocating for rights, justice and equality. Their dedication ensures that democracy remains a dynamic and inclusive system, capable of addressing the needs and aspirations of all its citizens, irrespective of their backgrounds. Therefore, acknowledging and supporting the contributions of the working class is essential for the continued health and growth of democratic governance (ibid).

However, the propertied classes, industrialists and business owners, ruling and non-ruling elites continue to employ various strategies to undermine the working-class origins of democracy by promoting and practising hereditary politics, as if political power is a property that must be inherited and controlled by a family. This approach not only contradicts the fundamental principles of democracy but also reinforces a system of entrenched privilege and inequality. By perpetuating the notion that political authority should remain within certain families, these elites aim to consolidate their power and maintain the status quo. This practice often results in a concentration of power that excludes the broader population, particularly women, the working class, the poor, marginalised communities, castes and people of colour, from meaningful participation in the political processes (Usmani, 2018).

Hereditary politics undermines the democratic ideal of equal opportunity and representation, fostering an environment where political positions are passed down through generations without regard to experience in public life, merit or public service. The rich and powerful do not consider elections as tools for deepening democracy in society. They often use elections as a means to capture state power, control government and pursue their own interests. By leveraging their substantial resources, they influence electoral outcomes through extensive campaign financing, media control and lobbying efforts. This enables them to shape policies and legislation in ways that favour their economic and political agendas. This manipulation of the democratic process undermines the principle of fair representation, as it skews the political landscape in favour of those with wealth and influence. Ordinary citizens find their voices drowned out by the sheer volume of money and power wielded by elite groups. As a result, policies that should serve the broader public interest are frequently designed to benefit a privileged few (Bachrach, 2017).

Such a strategy erodes public trust in democratic institutions and processes. When political power is perceived as a family heirloom rather than a public mandate, citizens become disillusioned with the democratic system and its ability to address their needs and concerns. This disillusionment leads to apathy, reduced civic engagement and even social and political unrest. The influence of the rich and powerful extends beyond elections. They often maintain their grip on power by funding think tanks, political action committees and other organisations that promote their interests. This creates a cycle where the same elite groups continue to dominate the political arena, perpetuating inequality and limiting social, political and economic mobility (Rahman, 2013).

Hereditary politics and the inheritance of state power are fundamentally opposed to the democratic transformation of society, which seeks to ensure individual liberty, social and economic equality and political justice. This system of inherited political power undermines the core democratic principles of participation, representation and equal opportunity by concentrating authority within specific families or groups. Moreover, hereditary politics hampers political justice by limiting the diversity of perspectives and ideas within the government. When political power is confined to a few reactionary families or groups, the range of voices and viewpoints that influence policymaking is significantly reduced. This exclusion of diverse opinions weakens the democratic process and can lead to governance that is out of touch with the realities and aspirations of the citizenry (Basu, 2016).

Electoral and constitutional democracies are not properties to be inherited based on family lineages. These forms of government are founded on the principles of egalitarian participation and representation, equal opportunity and the collective will of the people. They are designed to ensure that political power is derived from the consent of the governed, not from inherited privilege. Hereditary politics erodes the integrity of democratic institutions by creating an uneven playing field where a select few enjoy disproportionate advantages. This practice often leads to governance that prioritises the interests of a narrow elite over the broader population. It stifles innovation and progress by limiting political leadership to a small, privileged group, regardless of their experiences, skills, or public support (Fernandez, 1995).

Moreover, the perception that political power can be inherited diminishes public trust in democratic processes. Citizens become disillusioned with a system that appears rigged in favour of entrenched elites, leading to apathy and disengagement. This weakens the very foundation of democracy, which relies on active and informed participation from all segments of society.

In a true democracy, political positions should be accessible to all citizens based on their abilities, ideas and dedication to public service, rather than on their family lineage. Democratic political leaders are chosen through free and fair elections, reflecting the choices of the electorate. This process is meant to provide every eligible citizen with an equal opportunity to participate in the political arena, either as a voter or candidate. When political power is concentrated within specific families and passed down through generations, it undermines these democratic ideals.

Hereditary politics contradicts the foundations of democratic ideals, fostering an environment where power is passed down through generations, often irrespective of competence or public approval. Such a system perpetuates social and economic inequalities by entrenching a ruling class that is insulated from the experiences and struggles of ordinary people. This leads to policies and decisions that favour the interests of the elite, rather than addressing the needs of the broader population. As a result, the gap between the wealthy and the poor widens and social, economic and political mobility is stifled, derailing the democratic empowerment of people.

It is necessary to dismantle the structures that support hereditary politics to foster a truly democratic society that upholds individual liberty, social and economic equality and political justice. It is also essential to encourage and facilitate wider political participation. Implementing strict anti-nepotism laws and promoting transparency and accountability in government are crucial steps to ensure democratic outcomes. By ensuring that political power is earned and not inherited, people can create a more equitable and just society that reflects the democratic values that working people aspire to uphold as equal citizens and shareholders of democracy, state and government. People's democracy is the only form of sustainable democracy that working people need to reclaim to save their citizenship rights.

Elections and Democratic Consciousness

In electoral democracies, periodic elections conducted according to constitutional provisions serve as essential tools for deepening democratic consciousness and ensuring people's governance. These elections aim to humanise power and establish a state and government that prioritises the well-being of both people and the planet. However, there is a concerning trend in recent years where authoritarian, undemocratic and reactionary forces use electoral means to capture state power. These forces often pursue interests that conflict with those of the working population, undermining the principles of democracy in various countries (Halikiopoulou, 2018).

These alarming anti-democratic developments highlight a significant issue: elections alone are necessary but insufficient in cultivating a secular, scientific and democratic consciousness among the populace. Despite the regular occurrence of elections, many societies struggle to instil these fundamental values in their citizens. The failure to foster a more informed and democratically engaged citizenry allows anti-democratic elements to exploit the electoral system, posing a threat to the core ideals of democratic governance (Friedrich, 2014).

People across the globe continue to cast their votes based on narrow silos of religion, race, regional affiliation, caste and other immediate, assigned, majoritarian, dominant and reactionary identities. This tendency to vote along these lines often leads to a fragmented and polarised electorate, which undermines the broader goals of democratic governance. Voting driven by such narrowly assigned affiliations prevents individuals from considering the larger societal implications of their electoral choices. It contributes to the perpetuation of social divisions and hinders the development of policies that address the needs of the broader population. When voters prioritise their immediate identity group over the common good, it becomes challenging to build inclusive and equitable societies (Mondon & Winter, 2020).

Political parties, interest groups, propagandists and lobbyists often exploit fragmented and polarised electorates to mobilise the masses in pursuit of their own agendas. These entities manipulate divisions based on nationality, religion, race, caste and regional affiliations to garner support and advance their specific goals. This strategy is highly effective in rallying segments of the population during elections to capture state power at the cost of deepening societal divides. By appealing to narrow dominant identity-based interests, these groups can distract from real issues that affect the collective well-being of the entire population. (Gianoncelli, 2021).

The tactics of populist mobilisation based on dominant and narrow identities often lead to the prioritisation of divisive policies that reinforce existing inequalities and hinder the development of inclusive and equitable societies. The use of dominant identity politics can also undermine democratic processes by shifting the focus away from policy discussions and towards emotional and majoritarian identity-driven rhetoric. This can result in voters making decisions based on fear, prejudice, or loyalty to their identity group rather than on a rational assessment of policies and their potential impact on society as a whole (Betz, 2003).

The rise of fraudulent propaganda, disinformation campaigns, anti-minority and anti-migrant hate speeches and targeted advertisements by political leaders and media outlets threaten the very foundation of electoral democracy by manipulating elections. This manipulation undermines the integrity of the democratic process, eroding public trust in the fairness and transparency of elections. Disinformation campaigns spread false or misleading information, which can confuse voters and skew their perceptions of candidates and issues (McKay & Tenove, 2021).

Anti-working class, anti-women, anti-minority and anti-migrant rhetoric foster division and prejudice, marginalising vulnerable communities and inciting social unrest. Targeted advertisements, often fuelled by data analytics and social media algorithms, can micro-target specific voter groups with tailored messages that reinforce biases and polarise opinions. These tactics not only distort the electoral landscape but also create an environment where informed decision-making is compromised. As a result, elections have failed as a tool to foster democratic consciousness among people and deepen the democratic practice of governance (Harnecker, 2007).

Political participation grounded in progressive, democratic, secular and scientific consciousness is crucial for determining the quality of an electoral democracy. When citizens engage in the electoral process with these values in mind, it enhances the functioning and integrity of democratic systems. However, the weakening of such participation due to reactionary dominant or minority forms of mobilisation poses a significant threat to democracy as a practice. When political engagement is driven by narrow identity-based appeals or manipulated by powerful political groups and parties, it undermines the foundational principles of democratic governance. This type of mobilisation can lead to a less informed and more polarised electorate, where decisions are made based on immediate affiliations rather than on a rational evaluation of policies and their broader societal impact (Croly, 2017).

Dominant and reactionary electoral mobilisation often involves leveraging societal divisions – such as those based on nationality, religion, race, caste and region – to rally support. While this can be effective in the short term, it risks entrenching existing inequalities and perpetuating divisive politics. Over time, such practices can erode public trust in democratic institutions and processes, making it harder to achieve inclusive and equitable governance.

To safeguard people's democracy, it is essential to promote and sustain political participation that is informed by progressive, democratic, secular and scientific principles. This involves not only encouraging citizens to vote but also fostering a political culture that values critical thinking, inclusivity and evidence-based decision-making. Accountability, transparency and rule of law can help in restoring faith in electoral democracy and upholding its core constitutional principles in defence of people and the planet. Civic education also plays a key role in this, equipping individuals with the knowledge, skills and democratic consciousness needed to participate meaningfully in the democratic processes to strengthen democracy in practice (Levine, 1999).

Political Landscape in India in Search of an Alternative

Ideologically speaking, the landscape of Indian politics is dominated by the Hindutva ideology propagated by the Bharatiya Janata Party (BJP), which effectively occupies the entire spectrum of right-wing politics. The BJP's strategy revolves around mobilising Indians on the grounds of Hindu religion and nationalist sentiments, portraying itself as the guardian of Hindu identity and cultural heritage. In contrast, the Indian National Congress (INC) has historically positioned itself as ideologically centrist, with a penchant for socialist policies tempered by a commitment to secularism. Rooted in the principles of Mahatma Gandhi and Jawaharlal Nehru, the Congress Party has long championed the cause of a pluralistic and inclusive India, built upon the pillars of constitutionalism and liberal democracy (Nayak, 2021b).

However, the Congress Party's recent string of electoral defeats has prompted a re-evaluation of its ideological stance. Faced with the formidable electoral machinery of the BJP, the Congress finds itself compelled to adapt its strategy in order to regain political relevance. This has led to a noticeable shift towards embracing elements of Hindutva ideology, albeit in a more moderate and nuanced manner. This departure from its traditional ideological moorings has raised concerns among some within the party ranks, who fear that it may dilute the Congress's distinct identity and compromise its long-standing commitment to secularism and pluralism. Critics argue that this tactical manoeuvring risks alienating the party's core supporters and eroding its moral authority (ibid).

Furthermore, the Congress's flirtation with soft Hindutva for electoral gains may prove to be a double-edged sword. While it may attract some voters who are swayed by the BJP's overtly Hindu nationalist agenda, it runs the risk of alienating progressive and secular-minded voters who view such overtures with scepticism. In essence, the Congress Party finds itself at a crossroads, torn between the imperative of electoral pragmatism and the preservation of its ideological integrity. Whether it can strike a delicate balance between these competing demands and carve out a distinct political identity in the increasingly polarised landscape of Indian politics remains to be seen. One thing is certain: in the volatile arena of Indian electoral politics, mere imitation rarely succeeds in winning over the discerning electorate (Siddiqui, 2017).

The mass organisations affiliated with left, socialist and communist parties are experiencing a decline, mirroring the shrinking of their electoral support base. This downward trend can be attributed, in part, to their perceived disconnection from working-class politics. Historically, these parties have been champions of the proletariat, advocating for their rights and interests. However, in recent years, there has been a strategic disengagement from these grassroots movements, leading to a loss of relevance among the very communities they once represented. Compounding this issue is the ideological fragmentation and electoral disunity prevalent among left-wing parties. Internal conflicts and lack of cohesive strategy have rendered them ineffective in countering the ascendancy of right-wing politics. This strategic disarray has created an opening for right-wing forces to capitalise on the vacuum left by the left, effectively occupying the ideological space traditionally held by leftist movements (ibid).

Meanwhile, the landscape of Indian politics is also shaped by the presence of strong regional parties such as the Samajwadi Party (SP), Bahujan Samaj Party (BSP), Biju Janata Dal (BJD), Dravida Munnetra Kazhagam (DMK), Rashtriya Lok Dal (RLD) and Trinamool Congress (TMC), among others. While these parties wield significant influence in their respective regions, their impact on the national political stage is often hindered by a lack of ideological consistency and clear direction. In particular, the absence of a coherent national political agenda among these regional parties has allowed the BJP to forge alliances with them for electoral gain. While some, like the Rashtriya Janata Dal (RJD), maintain a degree of ideological opposition to the BJP's Hindutva politics, others have formed electoral pacts with the ruling party, inadvertently bolstering the growth of Hindutva ideology in Indian politics (Pinatih, 2024).

This phenomenon underscores the complex dynamics at play within the Indian political landscape, where shifting alliances and ideological pragmatism often take precedence over steadfast principles. As the political landscape continues to evolve, the challenge for left-wing parties and regional forces alike lies in formulating a cohesive strategy that not only resonates with the electorate but also safeguards the pluralistic and secular fabric of the nation.

Within this context, the formidable electoral dominance of Hindutva politics spearheaded by the BJP, under the leadership of Mr Narendra Modi, appears insurmountable. Despite the availability of political space and the advantage of incumbency, opposition parties have struggled to forge a cohesive front uniting secular, democratic and progressive forces against the BJP juggernaut. One of the key factors contributing to the BJP's sustained electoral success is the extensive grassroots mobilisation efforts undertaken by the Rashtriya Swayamsevak Sangh (RSS) and its 36 affiliated organisations. Through their extensive reach, they have penetrated even the remotest villages, effectively consolidating the Hindutva vote bank. This consolidation poses a significant long-term threat, as it has the potential to reshape the very fabric of Indian society, eroding its syncretic, liberal and secular ethos (Shani, 2021).

Despite the clear dangers posed by the rise of Hindutva politics, there has been a notable absence of concerted efforts to develop an ideological counter-narrative capable of challenging its hegemony. The failure to articulate a compelling alternative vision not only hampers the immediate electoral prospects of opposition parties but also undermines the long-term sustainability of India's pluralistic and secular democracy. In order to effectively counter the growing influence of Hindutva ideology, it is imperative for opposition parties and civil society actors to come together and articulate a robust ideological framework grounded in the principles of pluralism, secularism and social justice. Such a narrative must resonate with the aspirations of diverse segments of Indian society, offering a compelling vision for a future that celebrates diversity and inclusivity (Mayal, 2021).

Moreover, efforts to combat Hindutva politics must extend beyond electoral alliances and encompass grassroots mobilisation, public education campaigns and advocacy for progressive policies that promote social cohesion and economic justice. By promoting a culture of pluralism and tolerance and by championing the values of democracy and human rights, India can resist the encroachment of divisive ideologies and safeguard its democratic traditions for generations to come.

The Aam Aadmi Party (AAP), under the leadership of Mr Arvind Kejriwal and the Suraj Abhiyan, led by Mr Prashant Kishor, have indeed emerged as significant players on the national political stage, signaling aspirations beyond regional politics. However, a critical challenge they face is the absence of a distinct and coherent ideological narrative that sets them apart from the established political parties in India. The over-reliance on a model of political mobilisation borrowed from NGOs, while effective in certain contexts, is not sustainable as a long-term strategy for mass mobilisation in the realm of politics. This approach, characterised by issue-based campaigns and grassroots activism, lacks the depth and breadth required to attract widespread support and sustain meaningful political engagement beyond specific campaigns or movements (Sharma, 2014).

Moreover, without a well-defined ideological framework underpinning their political agendas, initiatives like the AAP and Suraj Abhiyan risk being perceived as transient and politically inexperienced, unable to offer a compelling alternative to the entrenched party politics dominating the Indian landscape. Indeed, while issue-based politics can serve as a valuable tool for drawing attention to pressing social, economic and cultural issues, it must be complemented by a robust ideological narrative that provides a coherent vision for long-term transformation. Such an ideological framework serves as the guiding force behind policy formulation and political action, anchoring movements in principles of justice, equality and democracy (Singh, 2014).

In essence, the challenge for emerging political entities like the AAP and Suraj Abhiyan lies in developing a distinctive ideological identity that resonates with the aspirations of the Indian electorate. This requires not only articulating a clear set of values and principles but also translating them into concrete policies and actions that address the multifaceted challenges facing the country. By grounding their political agendas in a coherent ideological narrative, these emerging forces can position themselves as credible alternatives to the status quo, offering a vision for a more inclusive, equitable and progressive India. This, in turn, holds the potential to galvanise mass support and pave the way for meaningful social, economic and cultural transformation in the years to come.

Many voters indeed feel disillusioned with the existing political parties, perceiving a lack of genuine commitment to addressing the long-term social, economic and political challenges facing the country. This sentiment reflects a growing desire among the electorate for an alternative form of politics – one that prioritises the interests of the people and the planet over narrow partisan agendas. While various parties may pay lip service to the idea of transformation and progress, the reality often falls short of the lofty rhetoric. Genuine efforts towards sustainable development, social justice, environmental protection and inclusive growth are frequently overshadowed by short-term electoral considerations, intra-party squabbles and the pursuit of power for its own sake.

In this context, there is a palpable yearning among Indian voters for a political movement or party that embodies a vision of progressive, peaceful and prosperous change. Such a movement would be grounded in principles of social equity, environmental sustainability, participatory democracy and respect for human rights. This alternative politics would prioritise the well-being of all citizens, especially marginalised and vulnerable communities, while also recognising the interconnectedness of global challenges such as climate change, economic inequality and political instability. It would seek to foster dialogue, collaboration and consensus-building among diverse stakeholders, transcending traditional divides of caste, religion, region and ethnicity. Moreover, this movement would be characterised by a commitment to transparency, account-ability and ethical governance, rejecting the entrenched culture of corruption and cronyism that has plagued Indian politics for far too long.

While the emergence of such a transformative political force may still be on the horizon, the widespread disillusionment with the status quo indicates a fertile ground for change. The challenge lies in channelling this discontent into constructive action, mobilising citizens around a shared vision of a better future and building the institutions and movements necessary to bring about lasting social, economic and political transformation in India in a path of peace and prosperity. The working masses of India deserve politics of dignity.

Who is going to offer them dignified lives and citizenship rights based on equality and liberty?

Modi-led Hindutva Politics: A Threat to Indian Citizenship

Mr Narendra Damodardas Modi, serving as the 14th prime minister of India, has successfully completed two terms in office and is in office for a third term after the 18th Lok Sabha elections victory. Widely recognised as a prominent figure in Hindutva politics, Modi is often viewed as the face of a political ideology marked by division and animosity. Throughout his tenure, Modi has been disseminating misleading information to sway public opinion in his favour. One of the most contentious aspects of his leadership has been his portrayal of Indian Muslims as outsiders or 'intruders'. This rhetoric not only under-scores his divisive approach but also exacerbates religious tensions, leading to increased polarisation and communal strife in the country. Such divisive tactics not only undermine the unity of India but also pose a threat to its secular fabric and citizenship rights (Nayak, 2021b).

Modi's policies and governance have often been evident in marginalising minorities, lower castes and the working classes. This marginalisation can be traced back to the core principles of the BJP, which is deeply influenced by the RSS, an organisation espousing a racist Eurocentric ideology. The RSS's emphasis on cultural nationalism and its hierarchical view of society have shaped the BJP's approach, leading to policies that often neglect the rights and welfare of marginalised communities. Modi's past remarks about Indian Muslims, first likening them to 'puppies' and now branding them as 'intruders' offer a telling insight into the nature of Hindutva politics rather than merely reflecting on Modi's personal beliefs. These comments indicate a troubling tendency to overlook and undermine the secular and inclusive principles that are at the heart of India's Constitution (ibid).

Indian Muslims have been an integral part of the country's fabric, actively participating in its democratic processes and contributing significantly to its growth and progress. They have made invaluable contributions across various fields such as social work, science, education, history, culture, religion, language and literature. Their role in India's anti-colonial struggles and nation-building efforts has been substantial, often involving sacrifices that have helped shape the nation's identity, ethos and destiny. Hindutva political forces collaborated with British colonialism in their aim to create a Hindu Rashtra. In contrast, anti-colonial Muslim leaders not only participated and sacrificed their lives but also helped shape India's secular and scientific ethos as a modern constitutional democracy (Roy, 2005).

By branding Indian Muslims as 'intruders', Mr Modi not only undermines the sanctity of the Indian Constitution but also negates the rich tapestry of contributions that Muslims have made to India's diverse heritage. Such rhetoric not only threatens to erode the concept of Indian citizenship but also perpetuates a divisive narrative that undermines national unity. Moreover, Modi's statements are deeply offensive to all Indians who uphold the principles of equality, secularism and the rights enshrined in the Constitution. Modi and his Hindutva forces send a message that contradicts the inclusive vision of India as a pluralistic society where every citizen, regardless of their religious or cultural background, has an equal stake and contribution to make in the deepening of Indian democracy. Muslims are as much shareholders of Indian democracy as any other citizens of India (Behl, 2022).

In essence, Mr Modi's remarks reflect a broader Hindutva challenge to India's foundational values and principles. The Hindutva ideology is a foreign import that has intruded into the fabric of Indian politics, society and culture. While claiming to represent authentic Indian values, its ethnonationalistic tendencies and focus on religious and ethnic identity have more in common with European ideologies than with India's rich and diverse history, society and culture. Rather than drawing from India's pluralistic traditions and composite culture, Hindutva's roots can be traced back to European concepts of ethnonationalism, religious nationalism and racialised democracy. This imported ideology of Hindutva politics has sought to redefine Indian pluralistic identity in narrow, exclusionary terms, often at the expense of religious and cultural minorities (De Souza & Hussain, 2023).

Historically, there are parallels between Hindutva and the ideologies that emerged in Europe during the early twentieth century. One of the most striking comparisons can be drawn with Nazi Germany, where ethnonational-ism and religious intolerance were central tenets of the regime. The ideology of Adolf Hitler, with its emphasis on racial purity, scapegoating of minorities and use of fear and hatred to mobilise the masses, seems to provide a blueprint for Hindutva political practices in India. In both cases, fear and hatred are employed as powerful tools to manipulate public opinion and garner electoral support. The Hindutva ideology can be seen as a true intruder in Indian poli-tics, society and culture, drawing inspiration from European ethnonationalism rather than India's own rich traditions. Its reliance on fear, hatred and divisive tactics undermines the principles of secularism, pluralism and unity that are integral to India's democratic ethos (Ahmad, 1993).

By stoking communal tensions and promoting a divisive agenda, Hindutva politicians seek to consolidate their power base and rally support among cer-tain segments of the population. This approach not only undermines India's secular and democratic principles but also threatens to unravel the country's social fabric by fostering mistrust and animosity among its diverse communi-ties. It's crucial to recognise that such divisive ideologies are antithetical to the pluralistic ethos that has been a hallmark of Indian civilisation for centuries. India's strength lies in its diversity, and any attempt to impose a monolithic vision of identity runs counter to the country's democratic values and inclusive heritage (Desai, 2016).

The tactics employed by Hindutva politics, including its anti-Muslim prop-aganda and diversionary strategies, serve multiple purposes for its proponents. First, these tactics serve to distract from the ideological shortcomings and lack of substantive policy achievements within the Hindutva framework. By focusing public attention on divisive issues and fostering communal tensions, Hindutva leaders like Mr Modi can deflect scrutiny from their governance failures and policy inadequacies. Secondly, by creating a climate of fear and suspicion, Hindutva politics seeks to consolidate its voter base by appealing to religious and ethnic identities. This strategy aims to rally support among certain segments of the population by portraying minorities, particularly Muslims, as the 'other' or as threats to national identity and security (ibid).

However, in the long run, such divisive politics by Hindutva forces have detrimental effects on both India and its people. Firstly, it undermines the social fabric of the country by fostering mistrust and animosity among its diverse communities. India's strength has always been its pluralistic ethos, which celebrates its rich cultural, linguistic and religious diversity. Hindutva's divisive agenda threatens to erode this diversity by promoting a narrow and exclusionary vision of Indian identity. Secondly, the focus on divisive issues and religious polarisation detracts from addressing the real challenges facing the country, such as economic development, social inequality and progressive governance reforms. By prioritising dominant identity politics over issues that affect the daily lives of ordinary citizens, Hindutva politics hampers India's progress and development. Lastly, the international perception of India as a secular and democratic nation is also at risk due to Hindutva's divisive agenda (Leidig, 2020).

Therefore, Hindutva politics may offer short-term electoral gains by exploiting religious and ethnic divisions; its long-term consequences are detrimental to India's unity, progress and international standing. By prioritising divisive tactics over inclusive governance, Hindutva weakens the fabric of Indian society and undermines the democratic values that are integral to India's identity. Mr Modi's bid for a third term is a continuation of his divisive Hindutva politics, characterised by misinformation, religious polarisation and marginalisation of vulnerable groups. His leadership style and policies reflect the broader ideological framework of the BJP, influenced by the RSS's racist Eurocentric worldview, which prioritises certain segments of society at the expense of others (ibid).

The 18th Lok Sabha elections in India present an opportunity to mend the fractured republic led by the Hindutva figurehead, Modi. The crisis facing Indian democracy under Hindutva politics highlights the urgent need for political transformation to uphold the principles of secularism and inclusivity that are fundamental to India's democratic values. Instead of employing divisive tactics that marginalise communities based on religion or ethnicity, it's crucial to nurture unity. It is time to defeat Modi, BJP and RSS to steer India away from a destructive path politically, socially, culturally, religiously and economically. Progress and prosperity in India depend on secular solidarity.

Defeating a Dictator: Fighting Hindutva Dictatorship in Indian Elections

The general election in India, conducted from 19 April 2024 to 1 June 2024, which elected the 543 members of the 18th Lok Sabha and the new Government of India, carries immense significance for the preservation of India's identity as a liberal, secular and constitutional democracy. The prevailing fascist ideology of the RSS, coupled with the authoritarian rule of the BJP and the dictatorship of Mr Narendra Modi, poses a grave threat to every democratic achievement of the Indian working people. Their agenda appears to be focused on serving the interests of crony capitalists entrenched in Hindutva politics. These unscrupulous crony capitalists are driven by a desire to monopolise all natural resources and state revenues, prioritising the expansion of their business empires at the expense of India and its citizens (Nayak, 2017).

Indian democracy and its values are experiencing a decline under the Hindutva approach to public governance, characterised by the arbitrary arrest and imprisonment without trial of opposition leaders, academics, researchers, journalists, writers, political figures, writers and social activists. This suppression is indicative of a broader erosion of democratic values. Constitutional institutions and laws are being undermined to suppress any form of opposition to Hindutva fascism and to stifle the struggles for the survival of Indian democracy. The defeat of the Modi-led BJP government is imperative to rejuvenate India as a pluralistic society founded on constitutional democracy. Reinstating respect for democratic principles and ensuring the protection of fundamental rights are essential steps towards preserving the integrity of Indian democracy (Nayak, 2021b).

The Hindutva politics espoused by the BJP under the leadership of Mr Modi not only poses a threat to Indian democracy but also presents a harmful prospect for the Indian people if elected once again. Indians are witnessing the regression of Hindutva politics under the authoritarian rule of Mr Modi, which draws its philosophical and political roots from Europe.

Contrary to its purported intentions, Hindutva politics does not serve the interests of Hindus or Indians at large. Instead, it represents a perilous path, akin to a suicidal trap, fuelled by deceptive propaganda. Those advocating Hindutva ideology are not true nationalists; rather, they are adept practitioners of deceptive politics, employing diversionary tactics to further their agenda and promote corporate capitalism in India. It is imperative to recognise the dangers inherent in Modi and his Hindutva politics of hatred and falsehoods. The time has come to thwart their efforts and reject their divisive rhetoric in favour of upholding the principles of unity, inclusivity and truth in Indian democracy.

Approximately 970 million (97 crore) Indians, out of a total population of 1.44 billion (144 crore), are eligible to participate in the general elections. These numbers represent more than mere entries in the spreadsheets of political parties and the Election Commission of India; they signify Indian citizens with a keen political consciousness. The united electoral consciousness and collective struggle of these 970 million Indians possess the potential to consign Hindutva's electoral prospects to the annals of Indian political history. By defeating Modi, the BJP and the RSS, they can pave the way for authoring a new chapter in Indian political discourse, one that seeks to rejuvenate Indian constitutional democracy on the bedrock of scientific principles and secular values. This collective effort holds the promise of steering India towards a future founded on peace, solidarity, science, secularism, inclusivity, rationality and pluralism.

Hindutva fascism, epitomised by its politics of hatred under Mr Modi's leadership, has only yielded a grim harvest of deaths and destitution. The propaganda orchestrated by Modi and his authoritarian regime serves as a smokescreen, concealing the multitude of failures plaguing the BJP-led government. The imperative to defeat Modi, the BJP and the RSS emerges as the primary and indispensable alternative for safeguarding India's democratic fabric. Should Modi, the BJP and the RSS emerge victorious in the upcoming elections, the unchecked cocktail of arrogance and ignorance of Hindutva ideology will engulf us all, laying waste to the beauty and diversity inherent in India. Therefore, it is incumbent upon every conscientious citizen to unite in opposition to this looming threat and strive to uphold the cherished values of democracy, inclusivity and pluralism in the general election (Nayak, 2017).

History has borne witness to the downfall of every dictator and their oppressive schemes. It has also celebrated the triumph of the people. Indian history, too, stands as a testament to the power of the populace. Indian citizens possess the collective strength to overcome challenges, including the divisive policies of leaders like Modi, the political dominance of the BJP and the reactionary ideological influence of the RSS. By uniting and mobilising their efforts in general elections, the people of India can safeguard their nation from the brink of destruction, ensuring a brighter future for generations to come.

Rising Debt, Deepening Destitution and Widening Inequalities in India Under Modi

No amount of propaganda can hide that Mr Narendra Modi is riding on the rising tides of debt and destitution. The Modi-led Hindutva government of India is pushing the country into an economic landscape that breeds billionaires while increasing the central government debt to 58 per cent of GDP in the financial year 2024. Additionally, the general government debt has surged to 82 per cent of GDP. There is also a dramatic decline in real wages, incomes and savings. The rise of household debt, unemployment, inflation, rural distress and increased inequality highlight the failures of the Modi government. Modi and Hindutva define deceptive politics for the masses.

Despite promises of economic growth and development, the actual economic indicators paint a grim picture. The wealth gap is widening, with a few individuals amassing significant wealth while a large portion of the population struggles with financial instability. Real wages have stagnated or declined, eroding the purchasing power of ordinary citizens. Savings rates are falling, leading to greater household debt as families struggle to make ends meet. Unemployment remains a critical issue, with many young people unable to find jobs that match their skills and qualifications (Nayak, 2021b).

The rising inflation is eroding the value of money, making basic necessities more expensive and inaccessible for many. Rural distress is another pressing concern, as farmers face challenges such as low crop prices, inadequate infrastructure and insufficient government support. The combined effect of these issues is increased inequality, where the benefits of economic growth are not shared equitably across the population. Modi government's economic policies have led to significant financial challenges for many Indians, contributing to a more divided and unequal society (Desai, 2011).

Modi and his Hindutva politics do not address the economic distress of the working masses. The Modi government is an utter failure on all fronts. Hindutva politics and its master manipulators, like Modi, excel at diverting public attention from the everyday material issues people face to reactionary propaganda based on falsehoods. The economic struggles of ordinary citizens, including rising unemployment, inflation and household debt, are overshadowed by divisive rhetoric and identity politics. Instead of focussing on creating sustainable economic policies that would benefit the majority, the government's strategy often involves stirring up communal tensions and promoting a nationalist agenda (Desai, 2011).

Such an approach by the Modi-led Hindutva government serves to distract from the failures in addressing crucial economic challenges. For instance, while the wealth gap widens and many people face financial instability, the government's emphasis is frequently on cultural and religious issues rather than substantive economic reforms. Moreover, this diversionary tactic undermines democratic discourse and prevents the development of policies that could genuinely improve the standard of living for all citizens. By shifting the focus to reactionary propaganda, the government avoids accountability for economic mismanagement and social inequalities. The Modi-led Hindutva politics prioritises ideological agendas over the economic well-being of the population, using manipulation and distraction to sidestep pressing economic, social and political issues.

The World Inequality Database (2024), published by the World Inequality Lab, reveals that income inequality in India is the highest in the world. The Modi government is very generous to the rich while enforcing austerity and minimal government support for the masses. 'The Income and Wealth Inequality in India from 1922 to 2023: The Rise of Billionaire Raj' (2024), also published by the World Inequality Lab, further reveals that Modi's government has accelerated the concentration of wealth in the hands of a tiny class of crony capitalists. Meanwhile, the working masses suffer from hunger, homelessness, illiteracy and illness.

The data indicates that the economic policies of the Modi government disproportionately benefit the wealthy elite, exacerbating existing inequalities. While billionaires see their fortunes grow, the majority of the population faces severe economic hardship. Austerity measures have led to cuts in social services and public welfare programmes, leaving the underprivileged with little support. The report highlights the deepening divide between the rich and the poor. As the government continues to favour business magnates and influential capitalists who fund election campaigns of Hindutva politics, essential services such as education, healthcare and housing remain underfunded and inaccessible to many. This has resulted in widespread illiteracy, deteriorating health conditions and increased homelessness among the working class. Without significant changes, the economic disparity in India will continue to grow, further entrenching the divide between the affluent and the impoverished. The World Inequality Lab's reports provide a stark illustration of how current government policies have led to extreme income inequality in India, prioritising the interests of the wealthy at the expense of the broader population's well-being.

Hindutva politics is designed and pursued for the benefit of crony capitalists. Hindutva only mobilises the masses for its electoral gain by destroying the social, cultural, religious and secular fabric of India as a republic. Modi's rule represents lost decades for development for Indians. The political strategy behind Hindutva serves to entrench the power of a select few, fostering an environment where crony capitalism can thrive. By prioritising the interests of the wealthy elite, the government ensures substantial support and financial backing from these influential individuals and groups. This relationship between the government and crony capitalists results in policies that further deepen economic inequalities and undermine democratic principles (Desai, 2011; Nayak, 2017).

In pursuit of electoral victories, Hindutva politics exploits societal divisions and fosters a climate of intolerance and communalism. This divisive approach distracts from pressing economic and social issues, redirecting public discourse towards polarising topics. As a result, the social, cultural, religious and secular integrity of India suffers, weakening the nation's unity and democratic foundations.

Modi's tenure has been marked by significant neglect of developmental goals that could benefit the broader population. Investments in education, healthcare, infrastructure and social welfare have taken a backseat to the interests of the wealthy and powerful. The Modi-led Hindutva government represents lost decades for the development and progress of the average Indian citizen, who is bearing the brunt of Hindutva policies, which augment debts and destitution. Modi and Hindutva politics are committed to crony capitalism and its growth. The only alternative is to defeat Modi, defeat Hindutva and save India and Indians.

Tragedies of Hathras Stampede to Kallakurichi Liquor

More than one hundred and twenty-one people died in a stampede at a religious gathering in the Pulrai village of Hathras district, located in the northern Indian state of Uttar Pradesh. This tragic incident highlights the deeper economic, social, cultural and spiritual crises that India faces today. The prevalence of massive religious gatherings and the rise of self-styled godmen and godwomen point to these underlying issues. In contemporary India, many people turn to figures like Bhole Baba (Narayan Sakar Vishwa Hari), also known as Suraj Pal Singh, to address their everyday problems.

This reliance on self-styled spiritual leaders is partly due to the retreat of the welfare state and the weakening of secular and scientific education systems, which are essential for fostering a more informed and scientifically conscious society. The incident in Pulrai village is a stark reminder of the urgent need to address these multifaceted crises. Ignorance is the breeding ground for all forms of religious dogma, and godmen are the living examples of such dogmatic practices. The perpetuation of ignorance serves the interests of both the godmen and the political class, creating a cycle where people remain trapped in a state of dependency and manipulation (Chandra, 2011). To break free from this cycle, it is essential to promote education, critical thinking and scientific reasoning. By empowering individuals with knowledge and encouraging rational thought, society can reduce the influence of dogmatic practices and create a more enlightened and equitable environment. Strengthening public welfare programmes and enhancing the quality of education could help mitigate the dependence on such spiritual figures and prevent such tragedies in the future.

These self-styled spiritual leaders exploit the lack of education and critical thinking among the masses, perpetuating superstitions and unscientific beliefs. By manipulating the faith and desperation of vulnerable individuals, they gain power and influence, often with the support of political leaders seeking to mobilise voters and maintain control (Radhakrishnan, 2004). The political leaders and political parties often promote these self-styled godmen and godwomen for their electoral mobilisation efforts. The political patronage extended to these figures bolsters their religious enterprises among the unsuspecting masses, who suffer under a caste-ridden society where spiritual freedom is constrained and economic exploitation is rampant. In such a society, religion is a good business where these self-styled godmen and godwomen seek rent and offer fake spiritual freedom that gives hope to many working people and marginalised people to survive the everyday onslaught of a caste-based capitalist and feudal society.

This alliance between politicians and self-styled spiritual leaders perpetuates a cycle of dependency and manipulation. By leveraging the influence of godmen and godwomen, political leaders can galvanise support during elections, ensuring their continued dominance. Meanwhile, the masses remain entrapped in a system that limits their spiritual autonomy and subjects them to ongoing economic hardships. People fall back on quacks in the absence of modern medicines and doctors. People fall back on religion and various religious denominations to outsource and survive the onslaught of their spiritual and material sufferings perpetuated by political and economic conditions shaped by ruling elites in the country (McKean, 1996).

Similarly, more than sixty-five people have died after consuming spurious liquor in Karunapuram village, located in the Kallakurichi district of Tamil Nadu in southern India. Additionally, over one hundred and eighteen people are currently undergoing treatment in various hospitals. The rent-seeking state promotes the liquor business as a means to raise revenue, which is then used to beautify cities and create conditions favourable for private investment in the name of economic development. This prioritisation of revenue generation over public health and safety leads to dire consequences, as evidenced by the tragic incident in Karunapuram village. This incident highlights the urgent need for stricter regulations and enforcement to prevent the distribution of illicit liquor. Furthermore, it underscores the importance of re-evaluating state policies that prioritise economic gain at the expense of the well-being of its citizens. A more balanced approach that considers both revenue generation and public health is essential for preventing such tragedies in the future.

Who are these people who died in Hathras and Kallakurichi? What is the common thread among these two tragic incidents? These are working people who build our parks, homes, hospitals and schools but live a life of everyday sufferings. Many of these working people turn to liquor as a means to escape and forget their everyday pain. Similarly, these individuals often rely on religion to endure the hardships of their daily material existence. The dual dependency on alcohol and religion among the working class reflects deeper societal and economic issues. Economic instability, social inequalities and a lack of comprehensive support systems contribute to the prevalence of these coping mechanisms. People seek solace and temporary relief from their struggles through alcohol, while religion provides them with hope and a sense of purpose amidst their everyday challenges.

The rent-seeking state, government, reactionary political class and exploitative religious institutions are the real evils perpetuated by the hegemonic system, which is responsible for the tragic loss of lives in Hathras and Kallakurichi. In Hathras, the reliance on self-styled godmen and the inadequacies of the welfare state contribute to social and spiritual crises. In Kallakurichi, the unchecked liquor business prioritised over public health reflects the state's focus on revenue generation at the expense of its citizens' well-being. Both instances reveal the darker facets of the capitalist state, where profit and power often take precedence over human lives and dignity. Capitalism's influence on political and religious institutions exacerbates these issues. Political leaders use religious figures for electoral gains, fostering dependency and manipulation among the masses. Meanwhile, the state's focus on revenue through harmful means, such as the liquor trade, leads to dire consequences for the vulnerable.

Both alcohol and religion undermine reason and weaken the critical thinking abilities of human beings. When people turn to alcohol as a means of escape, they may find temporary relief from their problems, but this often comes at the cost of impaired judgment and reduced cognitive function. Prolonged reliance on alcohol can lead to addiction, further eroding an individual's capacity for rational thought and decision-making. Similarly, all forms of religious belief, particularly those propagated by self-styled godmen, can discourage questioning and critical analysis. These dogmatic practices often exploit the lack of education and the desperation of individuals, fostering a reliance on superstition and unverified claims. By promoting unquestioning faith over inquiry and scepticism, such religious practices can stifle intellectual growth and diminish the ability to think critically. Such a society is fertile ground for ruling and non-ruling elites to continue their hegemony over the masses. Such hegemonic conditions are concomitant with the requirements of capitalism.

Therefore, struggles against religion and capitalism are also struggles for mass consciousness grounded in science and secularism. These avoidable tragedies highlight the urgent need for the expansion of scientific and secular education to foster critical political, social and scientific awareness. By doing so, individuals can be empowered to question exploitative systems, challenge dogmatic beliefs and make informed decisions that contribute to a more equitable society. It equips people with the tools to analyse their circumstances, understand the broader socio-economic forces at play and advocate for systemic changes that benefit the common good. This requires a collective commitment to advancing education, promoting rational discourse and ensuring that knowledge is accessible to all.

These issues require a concerted effort to dismantle the structures that enable such exploitation. This includes promoting genuine spiritual freedom, ensuring equitable economic opportunities and fostering a political environment that prioritises the well-being of all citizens over short-term electoral gains. Improving economic opportunities, ensuring access to mental health services, and creating robust social support networks can help reduce the dependency on such coping mechanisms. By addressing the root causes of their pain and hardship, society can help individuals find healthier and more sustainable ways to navigate their daily lives.

Manufacturing Myths of Hindutva Economic Development

The messiah of Hindutva politics, Mr Narendra Modi, assumed office as the Prime Minister of India on 26 May 2014. He pledged to transform the Indian economy and deliver a developed nation with prosperous citizens. However, despite Mr Modi's continued tenure as the Prime Minister, his ambitious electoral promises seem increasingly elusive. When Mr Modi took office, there was widespread optimism among the corporate class and upper middle class about the future of India. He even managed to manipulate the working masses with his relentless propaganda to get their votes. He claimed he would boost economic growth, improve infrastructure and promote innovation and entrepreneurship. He guaranteed he would create millions of jobs, enhance the quality of life for all citizens and position India as a global economic powerhouse (Kaul, 2017).

However, more than one decade into his administration, the reality reveals that the Hindutva myth of economic growth and development. The glaring failure of the Modi-led BJP government is visible in every sector of the Indian economy, which does not work for the masses. While Hindutva politics has kept its promises to large corporates, it has failed to deliver for the common people. Under Mr Modi's leadership, initial promises were made to uplift the entire nation, bringing prosperity and growth to all. Yet, as time passed, it became evident that the benefits of his policies were largely skewed in favour of large corporations and wealthy individuals. The agricultural sector, which supports a significant portion of India's population, has struggled and many farmers continue to face economic hardship despite promises of better support and fair prices for their produce. Farmer suicides are an everyday reality that reveals the agrarian crisis in the country.

Similarly, the manufacturing and small business sectors have not seen the anticipated growth. The implementation of policies such as the Goods and Services Tax (GST) and demonetisation created additional challenges for small and medium-sized enterprises, leading to disruptions and financial strain. The Indian manufacturing sector is declining on a massive scale, causing significant job losses and contributing to the growth of unemployment. The NSSO surveys reveal that there has been a 12 per cent decline in manufacturing enterprises in the informal sector from 2015–16 to 2021–22. Additionally, there has been a nearly 22.50 per cent decline in employment during the same period. This decline in the manufacturing sector is alarming, given its critical role in providing employment to a large segment of the Indian workforce, especially in the informal sector. The contraction of manufacturing enterprises not only affects those directly employed in these businesses but also has a ripple effect on ancillary industries and services.

The reduction in employment opportunities in manufacturing is a significant concern for the Indian economy. With fewer jobs available, many workers are forced to seek employment in other sectors, often with lower wages and less job security. This shift exacerbates the issue of underemployment and leads to a decline in the overall standard of living for many families. Several factors contribute to this decline, including inadequate infrastructure and lack of investment and government support. Moreover, the COVID-19 pandemic has further strained the manufacturing sector, leading to disruptions in supply chains and reduced consumer demand. The Modi-led BJP government did nothing to address the concerns of the people.

Social sectors, including healthcare and education, have also seen insufficient progress. Public healthcare facilities remain underfunded and overburdened, and the quality of education in rural and economically disadvantaged areas has not improved significantly. The gap between the rich and the poor continues to widen, with wealth and resources increasingly concentrated in the hands of a few. This economic disparity has led to growing discontent among the population, who feel neglected and marginalised by a government that prioritises corporate interests over their welfare (Siddiqui, 2017).

Modi-led BJP government has largely failed to address the needs and aspirations of the broader population. The myth of widespread economic growth and development propagated by the Hindutva narrative stands exposed, highlighting the need for more inclusive and equitable policies that truly benefit all segments of society. The promise of a 'developed India' by Mr Modi is still a work in progress, as the Hindutva model of alternative economic development is a myth. The achievement of such a goal looks elusive, like salvation after death (Kaul, 2017).

The new narratives and election propaganda of Hindutva politics obscure old elusive promises by making new ones. In the ever-evolving landscape of Hindutva politics, new narratives and election propaganda often serve to obscure the unfulfilled promises of the past. Mr Modi frequently adopts fresh slogans and pledges to garner support, diverting attention from the commitments he failed to deliver in previous terms. Transparency and accountability are alien words in Hindutva political praxis of governance. Modi's guarantee means poverty, underdevelopment, unemployment, homelessness, food insecurity and Hindutva of unreason. The Hindutva politics of arrogance and ignorance is pushing India in a direction of backwardness where poor people live in a rich country.

Morbid Symptoms of Hindutva Politics

The recent decline in the BJP's seat numbers in the Indian parliament, along with their electoral losses in the latest bypolls, indicates a diminishing marginal utility of Hindutva politics. The defeats in significant temple towns such as Badrinath and Ayodhya suggest that Hindutva is losing its political currency. The strategy of majoritarian mobilisation and the consolidation of Hindu votes in the name of religion and nationalism are no longer yielding political dividends. This shift can be attributed to the deteriorating living standards and material conditions of the working people, which are overshadowing religious and nationalistic appeals in everyday life.

The widespread disenchantment with Mr Modi and the BJP government is evident, but the morbid symptoms of Hindutva politics in elections do not mean that the Indian ruling and non-ruling elites have abandoned their consensus on the dominant narratives of Hindutva politics. This dissatisfaction is evident in various public opinion polls, social media discussions and grassroots movements that highlight the growing discontent with the Hindutva model of politics, policies and governance.

Despite this, the persistent and powerful presence of Hindutva politics in different regions indicates that the Indian ruling and non-ruling elites have not entirely rejected the dominant narratives associated with Hindutva ideology. Hindutva, which advocates for the primacy of Hindu culture and identity in India, continues to shape political discourse and influence voter behaviours significantly, but it upholds the interests of crony capitalists. The ruling elites, comprising political leaders, influential business magnates and media moguls, often find themselves aligned with or at least sympathetic to the Hindutva agenda. This alignment is driven by various factors, including the assured and insured political and economic benefits of supporting a narrative that resonates with a substantial segment of the electorate.

Similarly, the non-ruling elites, which include intellectuals, academics, lawyers, doctors, civil society members and certain segments of the opposition, also grapple with the pervasiveness of Hindutva narratives. While some vocally oppose it, others might adopt a more cautious approach, acknowledging its impact on the sociopolitical landscape and sometimes strategically engaging with it to advance their own agendas. While the visible discontent with Mr Modi's leadership and the BJP government signifies a critical juncture in Indian politics, it does not necessarily translate into a complete departure from the entrenched narratives of Hindutva politics among the elites and even among working masses. The influence of these narratives remains robust, shaping the contours of political strategy and public discourse in contemporary India.

The morbid symptoms of Hindutva reflect the weakening of Hindutva politics, but this alone is not a sufficient condition for the complete defeat of the reactionary Hindutva ideology. While there are clear indications of its diminishing influence, a more comprehensive approach is needed to address and counteract the ideological and cultural underpinnings that sustain it.

The current morbid political conditions in Indian election results highlight a significant rift between the ruling ideology of Hindutva and the working masses. This disconnect underscores the growing dissatisfaction among the people with the policies and rhetoric associated with Hindutva, which pretends to prioritise a Hindu-centric national identity often at the expense of economic and social inclusivity of the Indian masses. This rift is not just a symptom of discontent but also a potential catalyst for meaningful political change. The palpable disillusionment with Hindutva politics among the working class and other marginalised communities offers a unique political opportunity. It is a moment ripe for the emergence of alternative political movements that can advocate for and implement a radical transformation of Indian society.

Such a transformation would involve addressing the underlying socio-economic inequalities and injustices that have been exacerbated by the current political climate. It would necessitate a shift towards inclusive policies that prioritise the needs and aspirations of the working masses, irrespective of their religious or cultural backgrounds. In order to seize this opportunity, progressive political forces need to articulate a clear and compelling vision for India's future. This vision should be grounded in principles of social justice, economic equity and democratic participation. It should challenge the divisive narratives of Hindutva by promoting unity and solidarity among diverse social groups.

Historically, morbid conditions in politics often give rise to crisis, giving way to fascist and authoritarian regimes (Sassoon, 2021). If democratic, left, socialist, liberal and progressive forces do not combat Hindutva with a viable political, economic and cultural alternative, the current morbid symptoms in politics can transform into an imminent crisis. This crisis has the potential to empower Hindutva forces once again, leading to the consolidation of Hindutva fascism in India. Therefore, it is crucial for these diverse groups to unite and present a cohesive and compelling vision that addresses the needs and aspirations of the working masses, countering the reactionary ideology with progressive and inclusive policies.

Moreover, this alternative politics must be grassroots-driven, empowering local communities to actively participate in the democratic process. By fostering a culture of civic engagement and political activism, it is possible to build a broad-based movement capable of challenging the status quo and bringing about lasting social change. The current political climate, marked by a rift between Hindutva and the working masses, presents a critical juncture. It is an opportunity to envision and strive for a radically transformed Indian society, one that is more just, equitable and inclusive.

Hindutva Onslaught on Higher Education

Higher education is an anathema to Hindutva politics in India, similar to any other right-wing reactionary politics worldwide. Their aversion to scientific and secular education is a deliberate political strategy aimed at undermining scientific and secular consciousness. These right-wing reactionaries fear education because it challenges the very foundations of their reactionary and right-wing ideologies. In societies where right-wing politics prevail, the suppression of educational advancement is often used as a means to maintain control. By limiting access to comprehensive education, these groups can perpetuate ignorance and foster an environment where their ideologies remain unchallenged. Scientific education, in particular, encourages critical thinking and evidence-based reasoning, both of which are seen as threats to dogmatic beliefs.

Secular education, on the other hand, promotes an inclusive worldview that transcends religious and cultural boundaries, fostering a sense of common humanity. This inclusive approach is antithetical to the divisive tactics employed by right-wing groups, which often rely on creating an 'us versus them' mentality to garner support. The aversion to higher education exhibited by Hindutva and similar right-wing movements globally is not merely a byproduct of their ideologies but a calculated effort to stifle intellectual growth and maintain socio-political dominance. Emphasising the importance of education in fostering a scientifically literate and secular society is crucial in countering these regressive forces.

The Hindutva government, led by the BJP under the leadership of Prime Minister Narendra Modi, has shown little focus on higher education. Finance Minister Nirmala Sitharaman presented the Indian Union Budget for 2024, which clearly indicates a significant reduction in funding for higher education. The budget allocation for higher education has been cut from Rs. 57,244 crores in 2023–24 to Rs. 47,619 crores in 2024–25. Moreover, there is a substantial reduction in funding for the University Grants Commission (UGC) of India. The funding for the UGC has been slashed by 60.99 per cent by the Hindutva government. This drastic cut highlights the government's stance on higher education, potentially undermining the quality and accessibility of higher education in the country. In principle, the financial decisions made by the current government reflect a broader strategy that adversely affects the development and progression of higher education institutions in India. This will have long-term implications for the nation's scientific, technological and socio-economic advancement.

The funding cuts are a strategic decision by the Modi government to facilitate Hindutva politics and crony capitalism in higher education by privatising it. The reduction in funding will diminish the quality and efficiency of higher education institutions. As these institutions become defunct due to financial constraints, the Modi government plans to sell them to the crony capitalist allies of Hindutva politics. Therefore, this funding cut serves as a prelude to the mass privatisation of higher education in India. This strategy aligns with the broader agenda of promoting privatisation and weakening public institutions, which could lead to increased inequality in access to quality education. The privatisation of higher education results in exorbitant fees, making it inaccessible to a large segment of the population, thereby undermining the fundamental principle of education as a public good. These funding cuts represent a calculated move to shift the control of education from public to private hands, aligning with the interests of a few at the expense of the many. This shift will have long-lasting detrimental effects on the educational landscape of India, impacting its socio-economic fabric profoundly (Lall & Anand, 2022).

By implementing funding cuts in the Union Budget 2024, Hindutva forces undermine higher education and its ability to produce new knowledge based on science and secularism. These cuts not only weaken the infrastructure and resources of educational institutions but also stifle intellectual growth and critical thinking. Scientific research and secular education are crucial for fostering innovation, progress and a well-informed citizenry. By reducing funding, the Hindutva agenda effectively hampers the development of these essential areas, promoting an environment where dogma can thrive over reason and evidence. The strategic defunding of higher education by the Modi government is a deliberate attempt to curb the generation of new, scientifically grounded knowledge and to diminish the role of secularism in India. This move threatens to compromise the future of higher education in India, making it less capable of contributing to global scientific and cultural advancements.

Hindutva politics is opposed to human progress and educational growth in India. The funding reduction in the Budget 2024 is just yet another example. This deliberate underfunding not only hampers the quality of education but also threatens the very foundation of a progressive and inclusive society in India.

Hindutva Gift to Corporates

On July 23, Indian Finance Minister Nirmala Sitharaman presented the Union Budget (2024–25), which highlights the priorities of Hindutva politics of economic growth sans human development. The Modi-led BJP government, along with its finance minister, continues to pursue failed and rejected neoliberal economic policies, including the reduction of corporate taxes, in an attempt to spur economic growth. However, historical evidence suggests that corporate tax cuts have not effectively stimulated economic growth. Despite this, neoliberal capitalists and their corporate allies persist in advocating for these tax reductions, arguing that they lead to increased profits and economic expansion. In reality, these policies often result in greater income inequality and benefit large corporations at the expense of working people.

The Congressional Research Service (CRS) studies have revealed that taxes have no significant effect on economic growth in the United States. They also found that higher tax rates contributed to economic growth in the United States after the Second World War. Most reliable studies on the relationship between tax cuts and economic growth show that there is no significant relationship between the two. Corporate tax cuts have been found to have an insignificant to zero effect on economic growth. Even the biased empirical studies of institutions like the World Bank and the Tax Foundation indicate that a 10 per cent point reduction in corporate tax rates contributes only 0.2 per cent points to annual GDP growth. This insignificant and imprecise contribution of tax cuts to GDP continues to be the opium of Hindutva politics, which competes in the global race to cut taxes to uphold corporate interests.

Despite all international experiences and evidence, Hindutva politics continue to support corporate interests while the people suffer from unemployment, hunger, homelessness and poverty. The lowering of corporate taxes encourages corporations to save for their own investments, which circulates corporate capital for profit accumulation. Therefore, the corporate tax cut is not a social good but a saving gift to corporations.

The Indian Budget 2024 is a Hindutva gift to corporates, while it designs systems that put students, farmers and entrepreneurs into debt traps created by banks, furthering the interests of an unproductive, rent-seeking economy. Students need scholarships, fellowships and good academic infrastructure to study and gain skills that contribute to India's economic and social development. However, the budget's provision of loans to students is likely to create a debt trap for them, with banks emerging as the net beneficiaries.

Similarly, the credit line extended to Micro, Small and Medium Enterprises (MSMEs) will likely only create debt traps for entrepreneurs. This approach fails to create conditions for innovative development and does not provide the necessary support for MSME leaders to thrive. Instead of fostering genuine growth and innovation, these measures merely increase the financial burden on small business owners, leaving them struggling under the weight of debt rather than contributing meaningfully to the economy.

The corporate tax reduction is not the final gift of Hindutva politics to corporate capitalism. Hindutva leadership has also promised tax reform, which is an obsession of every radical bourgeois represented by Mr Modi and his finance minister Nirmala Sitharaman. The reduction of corporate taxes is bourgeois socialism of the Hindutva variety which robs the pockets of working people for corporate saving in the name of economic growth. Critics argue that a more balanced approach, including investments in social infrastructure and equitable taxation, would better serve the country's economic interests and lead to sustainable growth.

The tax policies can be a tool for redistribution. Such a proposal is not even radical redistribution, but by ensuring that corporations and wealthy individuals pay their fair share, the government can generate revenue to fund social programmes, infrastructure, education and healthcare. Such redistributive tax policies can help reduce income inequality and provide more opportunities for marginalised and disadvantaged groups. Instead of relying on debt-inducing schemes, a focus on equitable taxation and investment in public services could lead to more sustainable and inclusive economic growth.

The praxis of Hindutva politics continues to neglect the broader goals of mass welfare and the long-term transformation of Indian society towards economic and social equality. Rather than addressing the pressing needs of the working people and striving for a more equitable distribution of wealth and opportunities, Hindutva politics is increasingly focused on supporting and promoting the interests of large corporations (Chacko, 2019). Tax cut is just an example. This approach prioritises the establishment and maintenance of corporate dominance within the country, often at the expense of the common citizen's needs and rights. By doing so, it helps in widening the gap between the rich and the poor, undermining the principles of democracy and social justice. The emphasis on corporate hegemony suggests a shift away from policies that can promote inclusive growth and social harmony, raising concerns about the future direction of India's socio-economic development under the directionless leadership of Hindutva politics and economy.

Meditation as a Political Act

After spreading the venom of deceptive Hindutva politics during his election campaign meetings, the master propagandist, Prime Minister Narendra Modi, plans to meditate for forty-eight hours at the Vivekananda Rock Memorial in Tamil Nadu as the general election campaign comes to an end in India. His choice of the Vivekananda Rock Memorial for meditation, a site of historical and spiritual significance, is seen by many as a strategic move, aiming to fraudulently convey an image of reflection and spiritual grounding amid the political turmoil. As the nation awaits the election results, Modi's retreat for meditation raises questions about the intersection of Hindutva politics and Modi's personal image management in the post-electoral landscape of Indian politics. However, there is no spiritual sojourn in Hindutva politics of hate. Mr Modi can televise his meditation, but it can never erase the inherent Hindutva toxicity in his political praxis.

Meditation, rooted in the practice of mindfulness, assists individuals in concentrating on the present moment and navigating the complexities of daily life. It is a discipline embraced by various religious, non-religious and spiritual traditions, each of which values meditation for its potential to provide self-help and spiritual comfort within an inherently alienating capitalist society. In times of suffering, meditation offers a pathway to inner peace and resilience, allowing practitioners to find solace and strength. Whether through structured sessions or informal practice, meditation serves as a versatile tool for enhancing mental clarity, emotional stability and overall well-being. Its universal appeal lies in its ability to foster a deeper connection with oneself and the surrounding world, making it a vital component of so-called holistic health and spiritual practice.

It is also claimed that meditation enhances cognitive processes, enabling individuals to think more clearly, contemplate deeply, devise effective strategies and ponder complex issues. By fostering a calm and focused mind, meditation allows for greater introspection and creativity. This mental clarity can lead to more insightful problem-solving and innovative ideas. As a result, many people find that regular meditation practice not only improves their emotional well-being but also boosts their intellectual and creative capacities. Despite the public display of meditation, it remains challenging to discern what Prime Minister Modi truly thinks, contemplates, devises and ponders in his everyday life. Such acts of public meditation can be seen as symbolic or strategic, but they do not necessarily provide insight into his private thoughts or intentions beyond Hindutva electoral engineering and personal image makeover. While meditation is a personal practice that can offer numerous mental and emotional benefits, the public nature of Modi's meditation might obscure rather than reveal the deeper aspects of his inner life that offer any public good for Indian society and politics.

The public display of meditation by Prime Minister Modi can be seen primarily as an act of propaganda, aimed at influencing public perception rather than revealing genuine introspection. Such meditative displays are strategically orchestrated to bolster his image as a thoughtful and spiritual leader. While meditation is typically a personal and introspective practice, when performed publicly by a political figure, it often serves more as a tool for managing public opinion than for personal enlightenment. Thus, the true nature and impact of Modi's reflections during these moments appear to be geared more towards propaganda than sincere contemplation or problem-solving.

The practice of meditation as a public and political act has gained traction beyond the borders of India and the influence of Prime Minister Modi. In the United Kingdom, over 120 MPs and 180 peers have participated in meditation courses, reflecting a wider acceptance and integration of mindfulness practices within the political sphere. This trend underscores a broader recognition of the benefits of meditation, leading to proposals for the establishment of a dedicated meditation room within the British Parliament, akin to the facility already available in the Australian Parliament in Canberra. The corporate world is also embracing meditation, with many companies introducing meditation training programmes for their employees. These programmes aim to enhance mental well-being, reduce stress and improve overall productivity. By incorporating meditation into the workplace, corporations acknowledge its potential to create a more focused, resilient and innovative workforce. This growing trend illustrates the increasing value placed on mindfulness and meditation across various sectors of society. Whether in politics, business or personal life, meditation is being recognised as a powerful tool for fostering mental clarity, emotional stability and overall well-being (Cook, 2016).

The marketisation, medicalisation and popularisation of meditation represent significant trends within contemporary therapeutic cultures, driven largely by the pressures and alienation associated with worldwide capitalist societies (Karelse, 2019; Nehring et al., 2020). As individuals seek ways to cope with the stress, disconnection and fast-paced nature of modern life, meditation has emerged as a widely accessible tool for mental and emotional relief. Marketisation refers to the commercialisation of meditation practices, where an increasing number of products, apps and services are designed and sold to meet the demand for mindfulness and stress reduction. From guided meditation apps to retreats and workshops, the industry surrounding meditation is expanding rapidly, catering to a diverse audience seeking solace and improved mental health in the crisis created by capitalism. Medicalisation involves the integration of meditation into mainstream healthcare as a recognised therapeutic intervention (ibid). However, meditation cannot conceal the shortcomings of toxic Hindutva politics and the failures of Mr Modi's leadership, nor can it resolve the flaws of capitalism.

There are unverified claims that meditation can reduce symptoms of anxiety, depression and other mental health issues, leading to its adoption by medical professionals as part of a holistic approach to treatment. Hospitals, clinics and wellness programmes now frequently include meditation as a complementary therapy, validating its effectiveness through scientific studies. Popularisation, on the other hand, reflects the widespread acceptance and practice of meditation across various sectors of society. Once considered a niche or alternative practice, meditation is now embraced by people from all walks of life, including political figures, corporate employees and the public. This mainstream acceptance is evidenced by initiatives such as meditation rooms in parliaments, workplace mindfulness programmes and the incorporation of meditation into educational curriculums. The growing trend of meditation within therapeutic cultures is a response to the feelings of alienation and disconnection that often accompany capitalist lifestyles. By promoting mindfulness and self-awareness, meditation offers a way to counteract the negative effects of a high-pressure, materialistic society, fostering a sense of inner peace and connectedness.

For working people, meditation has evolved into a practice of moral obligation, essential for navigating the daily challenges and ordeals presented by a market-led state, government and society. In an environment where capitalist exploitation is normalised and justified by promises of prosperity, individuals often find themselves under immense pressure and stress. The relentless pursuit of economic growth and personal success can lead to feelings of alienation, burnout and mental fatigue. Meditation offers a counterbalance to these pressures, providing a means for individuals to maintain their mental health and emotional resilience. By fostering mindfulness and inner peace, meditation helps workers cope with the demands and injustices of a capitalist system that often prioritises profit over people. It serves as a tool for self-care and survival, enabling individuals to reclaim a sense of control and well-being amidst the turbulence of modern life. The widespread adoption of meditation among working people signifies a collective response to systemic exploitation. It reflects a growing awareness of the need for personal and communal strategies to mitigate the adverse effects of capitalism. As a practice rooted in mindfulness, meditation empowers individuals to cultivate inner strength, focus and clarity, helping them endure and resist the dehumanising aspects of their socio-economic environment. Through meditation, working people find a way to navigate the complexities of a market-driven world while striving to preserve their collective dignity and sense of self.

Centrist Politics: An Insidious and Opportunist Ideology

Many political parties and their leaders adopt a so-called middle political path, commonly known as centrist politics, by maintaining an equal distance from both left-wing and right-wing ideologies or aligning with any ideological orientation based on selfish requirements. This approach allows them to appeal to a broader spectrum of voters by adopting shallow policies and avoiding the extremes of the political spectrum. Centrist politics often claims to focus on pragmatic solutions and liberal compromise, aiming to balance progressive and conservative values in order to address the needs and concerns of the general population effectively. Centrist politics is the shock absorber of reactionary right-wing politics (Elhefnawy, 2021).

Such a centrist worldview and its political project are neither political naivety nor an effective method for deepening democracy and citizenship rights. Centrist politics is often an insidious and opportunistic ideology that masquerades as pragmatic and free from ideological bias. By positioning themselves in the middle ground, centrist politicians may claim to offer so-called balanced, credible and reasonable solutions. However, this stance is a mask, and in reality centrists lack genuine commitment to substantive political change and always prioritise maintaining the status quo over addressing deeper societal, economic and political issues (Colley & Head, 2013).

Centrist political path is neither neutral nor an ideology-free zone. It is an opportunistic project of both ruling and non-ruling elites. By positioning themselves as centrists, these elites appeal to a broad range of voters, avoiding polarising ideological positions. This strategy allows them to maintain their influence and control, presenting their approach as balanced and pragmatic while potentially prioritising their interests over those of the common people (Stern, 2023).

Centrist political tendencies generally oppose radical transformations in political, social, economic and cultural spheres aimed at achieving an egalitarian society. They advocate for a so-called balanced approach that seeks gradual improvements and reforms within the existing system rather than sweeping changes. Centrists believe that stability and incremental progress are more sustainable and less disruptive than drastic shifts, aiming to find an opportunistic ground between opposing viewpoints in the name of fostering social cohesion and political stability.

Centrist political movements, parties and their leadership often seize any opportunity to undermine radical politics, policies and people-oriented movements advocating for social change. They typically prioritise so-called stability and incremental reform over drastic shifts, viewing radical approaches as potentially disruptive and impractical. This centrist political opposition manifests in various ways, including political maneuvering, public discourse and legislative actions aimed at discrediting or stalling progressive initiatives. Centrists strive to maintain a balanced status quo, believing that gradual change within the current system is more effective and sustainable. In reality, this is not the case, and it is a process where the unjust status quo is maintained in the name of reforms.

Centrist politics, which typically presents itself as a balanced or moderate alternative, frequently forms alliances with right-wing forces in its pursuit of power. This alignment is achieved by pandering to reactionary religious and moral factions within society, which often hold conservative views on social and cultural issues. By doing so, centrists hope to broaden their appeal and secure electoral success. However, this approach is indicative of an underlying ideological emptiness. Instead of adhering to a coherent set of principles or values, centrist politics is driven primarily by the goal of maintaining and advancing the interests of capital. This focus on economic gain often comes at a significant cost, including the well-being of the working people and the health of the planet. Environmental degradation and social inequality are frequently overlooked or worsened as a result.

The adoption of a liberal veneer is a tactical move designed to attract support from a broader base. By presenting themselves as progressive or forward-thinking, centrist politicians aim to win over those who might otherwise be wary of their true allegiances and policy priorities. This deceptive strategy allows them to rally people to their cause, even as their actions ultimately serve the interests of the wealthy and powerful.

Centrist politics is neither dependable nor a viable alternative to pursue for a progressive, prosperous and peaceful future. Unmasking centrist politics is crucial to shaping the nature and future of radical politics focused on social, political, cultural and economic transformation for an egalitarian and fair future based on reason, science and secularism.

Conclusion

From the colonial and capitalist core to postcolonial countries, capitalism tends to promote political oligarchy. In both the so-called developed democracies, such as those in Britain, France and the United States and in developing countries like India, Sri Lanka, Pakistan, as well as various African and Asian nations, democracy is increasingly under threat. This peril arises due to the pervasive control of market forces over political processes. The undemocratic capitalist onslaught produces a democratic crisis across the world.

In the historical context, colonial powers established economic systems that favoured their interests, leading to the concentration of wealth and power in the hands of a few. This legacy has persisted in postcolonial societies, where the economic structures remain largely intact, facilitating the rise of political oligarchies. These oligarchies, often composed of a small number of wealthy individuals and corporations, exert significant influence over political decisions and policies, undermining democratic principles. In developed democracies, the influence of capitalism manifests through extensive lobbying, campaign financing and corporate influence over media and public opinion. The market-led democracy amplifies the voices of the wealthy over the average voter. Similarly, in Britain and France, corporate interests often have privileged access to policymakers, leading to legislation that favours business over the public good.

In developing countries, the situation is compounded by weaker institutions and regulatory frameworks, making it easier for market forces to dominate political processes. In India, for instance, large conglomerates have significant sway over political parties and policies, which can lead to corruption and a focus on business-friendly policies at the expense of social welfare. In countries like Sri Lanka and Pakistan, economic dependencies on powerful nations and multinational corporations further erode democratic governance, as political leaders often prioritise economic agreements over the will of their citizens.

The influence of capitalism on democracy is also evident in the erosion of social safety nets and the widening gap between rich and poor. As economic policies increasingly favour the wealthy, social inequalities grow, leading to public disillusionment with democratic institutions. This disillusionment can result in lower voter turnout, the rise of religious, right-wing and populist movements, and increased political instability.

The working people are suffering from exploitative economic conditions, rising debt, dictatorship, deepening inequalities, uneven development, religious conflicts, misinformation campaigns and the consolidation of political oligarchy. These issues are defining features of capitalist politics, often disguised as centrist policies.

CHAPTER 4

LOCALISATION OF RELIGIOUS AND CAPITALIST POLITICS IN INDIA

Introduction

Capitalism as an economic system tends to align itself with reactionary and religious political movements to enhance its growth and solidify its presence at the local level. This engagement is often pursued to the detriment of progressive cultural, political and economic advancements. When capitalism localises, it forms strategic alliances with conservative regional and religious groups. These alliances are designed to achieve control over state mechanisms and resources, both natural and human, by leveraging governmental power and influence. The motive behind this alliance is to secure a stable environment that favours regional capitalist expansion and local accumulation. By partnering with reactionary forces, capitalism ensures a political climate that is resistant to progressive changes that might threaten its interests. This collaboration allows for a concentrated effort to maintain and enhance capital accumulation on a regional and local scale (Kumral, 2023).

Moreover, the localisation strategy of capitalism involves tailoring its approach to the specific socio-political context of each region. By doing so, it can effectively navigate and manipulate local political dynamics to its advantage. This often includes promoting policies that benefit capitalist enterprises, suppressing progressive movements that advocate for equitable distribution of resources and maintaining a socio-political order that supports continuous capital accumulation.

The interactions between capitalism and reactionary politics pursued by the BJP and BJD are not merely byproducts of economic and political activities but a deliberate and strategic manoeuvre to ensure the perpetuation and dominance of capitalist systems in various regions of India and Odisha. This interaction highlights the complex interplay between economic forces and political structures, illustrating how capitalism adapts and evolves by aligning itself with local power dynamics to sustain its growth and influence. Capitalism promotes religious politics, gods and goddesses to weaken people and their citizenship rights. It is a strategy of mass domestication to ensure compliant politics, culture and people.

Alliance with the BJP: Political Suicide Mission or Electoral Arithmetic?

There are numerous sources of political leadership in Indian politics, spanning from familial political legacies to issues rooted in economics, society and culture. Political leadership emerges from various quarters, including familial lineages, socio-economic concerns, religious affiliations, ethnic identities, cultural movements, linguistic divisions and ideological mobilisations. Additionally, the evolution of market-driven democracies has ushered in leaders from corporate and bureaucratic backgrounds. Odisha politics is no different when looking at the nature and origin of political leadership in the state. Mr Naveen Patnaik is a product of power, prosperity and privilege due to the lineage of his father, Mr Biju Patnaik. He neither understands Odisha nor the everyday struggles of working people in the state. He has managed Odisha's political landscape for more than two decades with shrewd political managerialism.

In the backdrop of Odisha, the passing of Biju Patnaik and the autocracy of the Congress Party sparked a profound political crisis. This void paved the way for the emergence of the Biju Janata Dal (BJD), a regional political entity spearheaded by Mr Naveen Patnaik. Initially perceived as a somewhat hesitant leader, Mr Patnaik gradually rose to prominence, enticed by the promises of influence, gratification and privilege. However, such pragmatic and opportunistic leadership often faces its downfall, weaving a narrative of political demise through self-inflicted wounds. These leaders navigate a political terrain lacking ideological foundations, propelled solely by the pursuit of power, devoid of principled governance. Mr Naveen Patnaik, in aligning with Hindutva forces in the state, seems to be scripting his own political demise. By aligning with the BJP, Patnaik seeks to pre-empt any potential threat to his political dominance and ensure the continuity of his governance agenda, albeit within a new alliance framework.

In the opportunist political landscape of Indian politics, political alliances often define the course of governance and the fate of political leaders. The recent move by Mr Naveen Patnaik, the seasoned leader and chief minister of

Odisha, to align with the BJP has sparked intense speculation and debate. Is this decision a political suicide mission, risking the support base carefully nurtured over decades or a shrewd calculation to secure electoral gains?

Mr Naveen Patnaik, the projected enigmatic figure at the helm of Odisha's political affairs for over two decades, has carved a niche for himself in Indian politics. His regional party, the BJD, has enjoyed unparalleled dominance in Odisha, largely owing to Patnaik's astute leadership, welfare schemes and ability to maintain a delicate balance between various socio-political factors. The BJD's success has often been attributed to its non-alignment with national parties, allowing it to focus on Odisha's unique needs and aspirations.

However, in a surprising turn of events, Patnaik's BJD recently decided to join hands with the BJP. This move has left many political analysts baffled, questioning the rationale behind Patnaik's departure from his long-standing policy of equidistance from national parties. One perspective suggests that this decision could spell political suicide for Patnaik and the BJD, alienating their core support base, which has been nurtured on the platform of regional autonomy and identity. Patnaik's decision to align with a party often viewed as centralising and majoritarian could erode the trust of Odisha's diverse populace, comprising various ethnic, linguistic and socio-economic groups.

On the other hand, a closer examination of the political landscape reveals the intricate arithmetic behind Patnaik's move. With the BJP's growing influence across India and its ambitious expansion plans in eastern states, including Odisha, Patnaik's alliance with the NDA could be seen as a pragmatic step to safeguard Odisha's interests within the central government. By forging ties with the ruling coalition at the center, Patnaik aims to secure developmental projects, funds and policy support for Odisha, leveraging his position as a crucial ally in the BJP fold.

The burgeoning alliance between the BJD and the BJP heralds a significant shift in the state's political dynamics, paving the way for a closely watched electoral spectacle. This strategic alignment is poised to alter the contours of democratic politics in Odisha, with both Mr Narendra Modi and Mr Naveen Patnaik emerging as key beneficiaries. While power itself may not be the cohesive force in politics, the shared pursuit of political opportunism often unites leaders under the guise of serving the people's welfare.

Mr Naveen Patnaik's reintegration into the political alliance under the stewardship of Mr Narendra Modi signals yet another manifestation of the prevailing principle-free landscape in Indian politics. In this milieu, the relentless pursuit of state power through majoritarian politics stands as the singular objective. The alliance between the BJD and BJP casts Odisha into an inadvertent whirlwind of political and democratic turmoil, wherein the ruling party forges ties with its principal adversary to erode the foundations of democracy within the state.

This partnership is devoid of any semblance of ideological underpinning or principled governance. Its sole ambition is the consolidation of state power to serve the interests of corporate entities, thereby sacrificing the welfare of the populace at large. Moreover, the tacit objective of this alliance is to pave the way for the ascension of Hindutva forces, which poses a grave threat to the societal fabric of Odisha in the long run.

Mr Naveen Patnaik's return to the BJP can be viewed solely through the prism of political suicide for the sake of electoral arithmetic. Only time will tell whether this alliance proves to be a masterstroke or a miscalculation in Patnaik's political journey. The current political equilibrium in Odisha teeters on the brink of both democratic peril and potential political transformation.

While the prevailing political stability hints at a semblance of order, beneath the surface lies a brewing democratic crisis, intertwined with a burgeoning opportunity for change. It is imperative for the people of Odisha to seize upon this momentous juncture to usher in an era of alternative – one that prioritises the welfare of the masses above all else. In harnessing this opportunity, the citizens of Odisha hold the key to steering the state away from the precipice of political stagnation and towards a future characterised by inclusivity, accountability and genuine democratic representation. By actively engaging in the political process and demanding meaningful change, they can propel Odisha towards a trajectory defined by peace, progress and prosperity for all its inhabitants.

Failed Electoral Philanthropy in Odisha

All attempts by senior leadership to form an electoral alliance between the BJD and BJP in Odisha have failed due to popular opposition to such an alliance in forthcoming elections. Both parties have declared their candidates for the general and state elections. Mr Naveen Patnaik has also announced his candidates for the BJD. At this stage, it seems like the narrative of the ruling party under the leadership of Mr Patnaik resembles that of a surrendered general who wishes to become a philanthropist in electoral politics to hide his failures for more than two decades.

The notion of philanthropy in politics may seem conceivable, yet within the realm of electoral politics, there exists no straightforward or adept method of disarming and overcoming political opposition. Despite this, the political opposition, led by the BJP in the state, has operated akin to a second-hand ruling party, lacking the vigour expected of a true opposition force in democracy. As chief minister, Mr Patnaik currently faces minimal political opposition within the state, yet he has still failed to deliver the oft-quoted development for the masses.

In his initial decade as chief minister, Mr Patnaik espoused the non-existent dreams of his father, Mr Biju Patnaik, to the people of Odisha. Now, after two decades at the helm, he presents his own dreams of 'New Odisha, Naveen Odisha'. These dreams resemble the fictitious and supercilious American dreams or the aspirations of salvation in Hindu spiritual teachings – illusive and intangible. Their realisation remains elusive, as even the dreamer himself seems uncertain about their true essence.

Mr Patnaik has not only squandered the political goodwill of the working masses in the state, but he has also failed to mobilise the internal resources of the state for the welfare of the people. He has failed to generate wealth and employment for the masses and failed to deliver health and education for the masses. Additionally, he has failed to develop the state on a prosperous and peaceful path, as he indirectly hands over the state and government to the Hindutva forces led by the BJP. He has redeployed his tainted MLAs and weak leaders as candidates who are likely to lose the election to the viciously organised Hindutva forces. It is evident from the way he manages to maintain a resigned state of leadership with the withdrawn mindset of a defeated commander in politics.

By fielding tainted MLAs and feeble leaders as candidates – many of whom are poised to lose against the well-organised Hindutva electoral machinery – Mr Patnaik appears to be acquiescing to the impending dominance of these forces. His approach reflects a leader resigned to his fate, adopting the demeanour of a defeated commander in the political arena, rather than actively steering the state towards a more robust and resilient progressive political future.

In the forthcoming elections, the BJP sells Modi's dream, and the BJD sells Naveen Patnaik's dreams to the masses. What are these dreams? What do these dreams mean for the working masses? No one knows these elusive dreams. The truth is that the essence of these elusive dreams remains shrouded in mystery. People must be careful of such political quacks who sell dreams during elections to control the everyday lives of the masses after their victory. People must defeat these dream sellers and choose candidates who talk about secular, scientific, successful and alternative policy visions for the masses. It's imperative for the public to exercise caution amidst the electoral cacophony, wary of those who peddle dreams during elections only to support the capitalist class post-victory. Instead, voters should reject these purveyors of dreams and opt for candidates who espouse historically grounded successful policy visions that truly benefit the masses. By doing so, they can ensure a future governed by tangible progress rather than fleeting promises.

The current candidate profiles of all mainstream political parties in Odisha resemble an ideology-free zone in politics, devoid of principles, policies and visions for people. The present and future of the state and its people are poised to be in the hands of individuals lacking vision. The prevailing camaraderie between the ruling party and the opposition party has transformed democracy in the state into a corporate joint venture aimed at capturing and sharing power to serve the ruling and non-ruling elites. This collusion sidelines democratic scrutiny, allowing the state's resources to be monopolised by the corporate class unchecked. Politics for profit is the only motto of a market democracy led by the BJD and BJP in the state. Both parties are working overtime in handing over the mining and marine resources of the state to the corporate class without any form of democratic scrutiny.

As the forthcoming elections approach, they bring to light the deep-rooted political crisis plaguing the state. With no champions to represent the interests of the working masses, the future governance of Odisha hangs in the balance underscoring the urgent need for a paradigm shift towards policies that prioritise the welfare of the people over elite interests. The election without democratic principles and vision for the people reveal the deeply ingrained political crisis in the state where no one is there to represent the interests of the working masses.

In this critical juncture, it is imperative for the people in Odisha to unite and reject both the BJP and BJD, seeking instead a political alternative rooted in substantive policies aimed at the development and welfare of the masses. Only through this concerted effort can the populace alter their democratic destiny, breaking free from the grip of various iterations of the ruling class and castes that serve the interests of crony capitalists. These vested interests have long plundered the state's forest, water, agricultural, mineral and marine resources, leaving the people mired in poverty and deprivation. It is only by dismantling this entrenched system and electing a government that genuinely prioritises the needs of the working masses that a new political dawn can emerge in Odisha. Therefore, the power lies in the hands of the people to forge a new path forward, one that fosters genuine progress and prosperity for all, rather than perpetuating the cycle of mass exploitation and neglect. History is the only witness to political victories of the masses over all empires and their powerful agencies. The Odia people defeated Ashoka and they can defeat the political friendship between Modi and Naveen too.

Emerging Class Collaboration in Odisha Politics

Amidst the flurry of frantic speculations, clandestine discussions and fleeting moments of camaraderie, the anticipation of an electoral alliance between the ruling BJD and the opposition BJP fizzled out. The BJP decided to go alone in the forthcoming elections. The aspirations of Mr Naveen Patnaik to position himself as a junior partner to the BJP were dashed as the BJP chose to distance itself from any such arrangement, ultimately abandoning his overtures. Despite the failed attempts to forge a formal political alliance due to issues regarding seat sharing, the brotherhood between the BJP and BJD appears to only strengthen. What seems to emerge is a facade of a friendly electoral contest between the ruling BJD and the opposition BJP. However, in reality, these two parties have orchestrated a mockery of democracy within the state, eroding the trust of the people in the democratic electoral processes as the bonhomie between the two continues.

The apparent friendly electoral match between the BJD and BJP in the forthcoming elections in Odisha may indeed be indicative of a deeper phenomenon: class collaboration in state politics. While on the surface, the two parties may engage in electoral competition, their underlying alignment on key issues and policies suggests a shared interest in serving certain privileged classes or elites. This collaboration, whether explicit or implicit, can have significant implications for governance and policymaking, potentially sidelining the needs and concerns of marginalised masses in the state.

In the annals of political history, there exists no ruling party nor leader quite like Mr Naveen Patnaik, who has demonstrated a unique penchant for surrendering and squandering away the vast reservoir of mass support he once commanded in Odisha for over two decades. His relentless endeavours to forge political alliances with Hindutva forces have not only weakened the BJD but have also tarnished his political image within the state. Indeed, tracing back to the inception of his political career, Mr Naveen Patnaik has maintained close ties with the BJP, whether through direct collaboration or indirect support of various political projects and governance policies. As asserted by the Congress party, there exists a symbiotic relationship between the BJD and the BJP, suggesting an inseparable bond that transcends mere political alliances.

Mr Naveen Patnaik appears to have retreated from the political fray and disengaged from the intricate processes of governance, as though he is under immense pressure from the BJP. His demeanour suggests a sense of resignation, as if he is encircled by the looming spectre of vindictive Hindutva politics, instilling a palpable fear within him. Rarely does a political leader with such a formidable mass base and a strong political party apparatus exhibit the propensity for surrender seen in Mr Patnaik.

The political capitulation of the BJD under the stewardship of Mr Patnaik towards the BJP and its leadership exemplifies a form of class collaboration in Odisha politics. This dynamic blurs the lines between the BJD and BJP, particularly in their approach to politics, policies and governance issues. Their shared outlook extends to matters of economic development, where the welfare of the masses often takes a back seat to the relentless pursuit of political power through any means necessary, regardless of political and ethical considerations. Today, Odisha politics seems to have devolved into an ideology-free zone, where discernible differences between political parties and their leadership are scant or altogether absent.

The ideological underpinnings of mainstream political parties and their leadership often stem from a foundation rooted in higher caste and class affiliations. This dynamic fosters an environment conducive to the politics of class collaboration, allowing those from higher castes to govern the masses with relative ease, devoid of significant political resistance in the state. Whether the BJD and BJP maintain a formal political alliance or not, the distinction becomes increasingly negligible, as both parties, when in power, tend to advance each other's interests within and outside the state.

The strong class collaboration between the BJD and BJP suggests a cooperative relationship wherein both parties, despite ideological or superficial differences, work together to serve the interests of privileged classes or elites, often at the expense of the broader populace in the state. This collaboration can manifest in various forms, including policy alignment, mutual support in elections or shared governance objectives that prioritise the interests of certain socioeconomic groups over others.

Patnaik's dreams are fraudulent dreams like American dreams. While the American Dream is characterised by ideals of individual achievement, success, upward mobility and societal progress, labelling Patnaik's dreams as fraudulent implies a lack of authenticity or substance. After two decades of experience, it suggests that the promises or aspirations put forward by Patnaik are perceived as deceitful or unattainable, failing to materialise into tangible benefits for the people of Odisha. Such a comparison underscores a sentiment of scepticism or disillusionment regarding Patnaik's leadership and the fulfilment of his vision for the state.

In this context, the people of Odisha deserve an alternative politics that transcends the class collaboration seen between the BJP and BJD. This alternative should be grounded in principles of social justice, economic and political empowerment, electoral transparency, secularism, cultural inclusivity and participatory governance models. By prioritising policies and initiatives aimed at uplifting marginalised communities, addressing socioeconomic disparities and empowering individuals from all backgrounds, Odisha can pave the way for a more inclusive and equitable society. It's through such concerted efforts that the state can truly realise its democratic potential and ensure that all its citizens have the opportunity to thrive, participate fully in the democratic process and access equal resources available in the state.

An alternative politics in Odisha can only harness all available natural resources in the state for the collective welfare of its people. By effectively managing and leveraging these resources, the state can generate sustainable economic growth, create employment opportunities and improve the overall standard of living for its citizens. This approach requires a commitment to responsible and equitable resource allocation, ensuring that the benefits derived from these resources are distributed fairly and contribute to the advancement of health, education and well-being of all segments of society. Additionally, prioritising environmental sustainability and conservation efforts is essential to safeguarding the long-term viability of Odisha's natural assets for future generations.

The urgency for alternative politics in Odisha is palpable, especially in light of the disillusionment caused by fraudulent promises and stagnant governance under the Patnaik administration. The time is ripe for transformative change that prioritises the genuine welfare of the state's people. Embracing an alternative political vision rooted in transparency, accountability and the empowerment of all citizens is imperative to address the pressing issues facing Odisha. This moment calls for bold leadership and collective action to chart a new course that fulfils the aspirations of the populace and builds a more equitable, progressive, peaceful, prosperous, secular and scientific future for the state.

Divisive Dividends of Hindutva Politics in Odisha

Over two decades ago, Professor Pralay Kanungo outlined the ways in which Hindutva politics and its organisational strategies adapt to the diverse cultural, social, religious and political conditions in Odisha. His analysis demonstrated how Hindutva politics led by the RSS and affiliated organisations could effectively navigate and integrate into the unique cultural landscape of Odisha, ensuring their ideology resonated with local sentiments. By meticulously examining these adaptive strategies, Professor Kanungo's work provides critical insights into the historical roots to understand the contemporary success of Hindutva politics in the state.

In his seminal article *Hindutva's Entry into a 'Hindu Province': Early Years of RSS in Orissa*, Professor Kanungo (2003) provides a comprehensive analysis of the initial phases of Hindutva politics led by the RSS in Odisha. This work serves as a crucial lens to understand the current electoral successes of Hindutva politics in the state. By examining the historical context and strategic manoeuvres detailed in Kanungo's research, one gains valuable insights into the enduring appeal and resilience of Hindutva ideology in contemporary Odisha, based on majoritarian identity mobilisation.

The Hindutva politics led by the BJP raised issues of Odia pride and dignity (Odia Asmita) to outmanoeuvre and defeat the BJD in the recently concluded state and parliamentary elections. The BJP highlighted the Tamil origin of Mr V. K. Pandian, the former personal secretary to Mr Naveen Patnaik, who was newly inducted into the BJD to manage political affairs assigned to him by Mr Patnaik. This strategy aimed to question Mr Pandian's commitment to Odia culture and identity, thereby appealing to regional sentiments and swaying voter opinion against the BJD.

However, the BJP itself has several prominent leaders in Odisha who are not originally from the state. Despite their non-Odia origins, these leaders have frequently been elected to parliament, often with the tacit or explicit support of the BJD. This situation reveals a complex political landscape where regional identity and political alliances intersect, demonstrating that the issue of local versus non-local leadership can be selectively emphasised based on strategic needs. The BJP's tactic of questioning Mr Pandian's Tamil origin while having non-Odia leaders in its own ranks highlights the nuanced and sometimes contradictory nature of Hindutva political rhetoric and political strategy in the state. It also reveals the hypocrisy of Hindutva politics, which claims to champion one nation, national unity and national pride. Despite all divisive Hindutva political attempts, Odisha continues to be a relatively inclusive and peaceful society that embraces all its inhabitants as citizens, irrespective of their backgrounds. The practice of Mahima Dharma and the celebration of Satya-Pir spiritual, religious and cultural traditions continue to represent Odisha's rich and pluriversal society and stand in opposition to Hindutva hegemony. The BJP in state power threatens the very foundation of Odia society.

Historically, Hindutva forces have regarded Odisha as a Hindu province and have leveraged the identity-seeking Odia Hindu upper caste-middle classes to advance their political agenda. By doing so, they have managed to exert significant influence over the lives of diverse working people and marginalised communities in the state. This approach has allowed them to mobilise support and consolidate power, often at the expense of addressing the unique needs and challenges faced by these diverse and under-represented groups. The emphasis on a homogenised Odia Hindu identity has sometimes overshadowed the rich cultural, religious and social diversity within Odisha, impacting the socio-political dynamics and perpetuating existing hierarchies.

The question of Odia identity (Odia Asmita) largely stems from the perspectives and interests of the Odia Hindu upper castes and middle classes, who wield significant influence over every apparatus of the state and its resources. This dominant group has historically shaped and defined what constitutes Odia identity, often to the exclusion or marginalisation of other socio-cultural groups within the state. Their control over political, economic and cultural institutions has reinforced their privileged position and continues to perpetuate inequalities and limit the representation and participation of marginalised communities in decision-making processes. These dynamics underscore the complexities of identity politics in Odisha, where the narrative of Odia Asmita is not universally shared or experienced. It reflects broader issues of power dynamics and social hierarchies within the state, highlighting the ongoing challenges in achieving inclusive and equitable development that addresses the diverse needs and aspirations of all inhabitants of Odisha as citizens and shareholders of democratic politics.

The Hindutva forces have successfully established their first majority government in a so-called Hindu province, threatening the very foundation of Odia society. Hindutva politics relies on dominant identity politics for successful political mobilisation. The recently concluded election results indicate a diminishing marginal utility of identity-based politics across India. However, Odisha presents fertile ground for the divisive dividends of Hindutva politics in the state, especially as it incorporates lower castes and tribal communities within its political fold for electoral gains. Such electoral, political and cultural assimilation helps to weaken the emancipatory struggles of marginalised communities and their citizenship rights.

It is within this context that the BJP has chosen Mr Mohan Charan Majhi as the new Chief Minister of Odisha. He comes from a marginalised tribal community that struggles every day with different forms of underdevelopment, marginalisation and the ongoing havoc caused by mining in their lives. Mr

Majhi's ascension to Chief Minister is a beacon of hope for his community and working people in the state.

Will Mr Majhi break away from the dominant caste-class-led Hindutva politics of development that serves only a few and marginalises the masses in the state? Will he adopt a different approach from Hindutva politics to ensure inclusive and egalitarian development, where lower castes, lower classes, tribal communities and working people will be equal stakeholders in the state's mineral and other resources? These questions are more crucial for the majority of working people in the state than Odia Asmita. Time will reveal the answers to these questions as the Hindutva government led by the BJP, under the leadership of Mr Majhi, unfolds.

Surrender to Hindutva: Ignominious Fall of the Naveen Era in Odisha Politics

Here richly, with ridiculous display,
The Politician's corpse was laid away.
While all of his acquaintance sneered and slanged
I wept: for I had longed to see him hanged.
Another on the Same

— **Hilaire Belloc**

The twentieth-century conservative French and English poet Hilaire Belloc did not write this poem, 'Epitaph on the Politician Himself', to pen the political obituary for the long-serving outgoing chief minister of Odisha, Mr Naveen Patnaik. However, each word of the poem aptly resonates with the political and electoral transformation in Odisha. Ordinary people push the all-powerful to the dustbin of history and make them irrelevant in public life while exercising their democratic dissent in the form of voting during elections.

No one is studying Odisha politics immediately after the recent electoral defeat of Mr Naveen Patnaik led (BJD), which has governed the state for more than two decades. The 4th of June election result has already written the political epitaph of much of the BJD leadership including its founder Mr Patnaik. It is an ignominious end to the long-standing political dominance of BJD and its future in the state. It has effectively become irrelevant in national politics with no seats in the Lok Sabha.

This electoral defeat and the dissatisfaction of the Odia people and their discontent was directed not just at the party but personally at Mr Patnaik, who had been a central figure in Odisha politics for decades. He was defeated in the Kantabanji assembly seat and his vote share declined in Hinjili, where he won with a smaller margin of votes than in the previous state election. Mr Patnaik has squandered the political goodwill of the working masses in the state. His political demise is a product of his own making. Mr Patnaik's political demise and precarious political future can be attributed to several factors.

Mr Patnaik's resigned state of leadership with the withdrawn mindset, overdependence on ignorant and arrogant bureaucrats, technocratic political interventions, over-engagement with religion, imposition of unpopular leadership on the party and the state, disengagement with working masses, failure to deliver development, employment, livelihoods and empowered citizenship to people and so forth have alienated many within his party and among Odia voters as well. Additionally, there were growing concerns over corruption, lack of development in key areas of health, education, agriculture and a failure to address the needs and aspirations of the younger generation. These issues cumulatively eroded the trust and support that the BJD once enjoyed. Furthermore, opposition parties like BJP capitalised on these weaknesses, mounting a more effective campaign that resonated with the public's desire for change.

The defeat of the BJD, therefore, is not merely a reflection of Mr Patnaik's political missteps but also a testament to the evolving political sentiments in Odisha, where people have rejected the imposed leadership of an unelected bureaucrat. Voters in the state are increasingly demanding accountability and progressive governance – qualities that Hindutva politics is unlikely to provide. This shift in voter sentiment highlights a broader trend in which citizens are prioritising effective leadership and tangible improvements in their quality of life over the ideological agendas pursued by Hindutva politics.

Mr Patnaik has played a significant role in the rejuvenation of Hindutva politics in the state. His alliance government with the BJP marked the initial step in Hindutva politics' quest to capture state power in Odisha. The BJP, acting as a secondary partner to Mr Patnaik's BJD, failed to deliver meaningful results for the people of the state while serving in the opposition. Moreover, under Mr Patnaik's leadership, the BJD has consistently supported BJP policies and bills in the Indian parliament, blurring the lines between the two parties in terms of governance. As a result, there has been very little distinction between the BJD and the BJP in their approach to governing Odisha in terms of economic policies for development. Both pander to primitive crony capitalists who plunder the natural resources in the state.

In the coming months, it will be crucial to monitor how the BJD attempts to regroup and rebuild itself as a political entity and whether Mr Patnaik will play any role in this process. Equally important will be the actions and policies of the new government led by the BJP, as they will set the course for Odisha's future development and political stability as per the Hindutva requirements.

Interreligious and intercultural harmony is the hallmark of Odisha. It is the duty of all to protect it from the Hindutva onslaught. There is no place for the Hindutva culture of religious violence in the state. The people of Odisha must remain vigilant about the divisive policies and politics of Hindutva forces, ensuring that the state and its government work for the peace and prosperity of all its residents without any form of discrimination.

As Odisha moves forward, political parties will need to adapt to these changing expectations. They must focus on addressing the real issues facing the populace, such as economic development, education, employment, healthcare and infrastructure, rather than relying on divisive or outdated rhetoric of Hindutva politics. The recent electoral outcomes suggest that only those who can genuinely respond to the needs and aspirations of the people will find lasting success.

The fall of BJD and the rise of Hindutva politics led by BJP also offer alternative experiments in Odisha, where all progressive, left, democratic, liberal and secular forces can consolidate to create a political movement for the progressive, peaceful and prosperous future of the Odia people and their planet.

New Chief Minister and Old Habits of Hindutva Culture in Odisha

Mr Mohan Charan Majhi took the oath as the new chief minister of Odisha following the electoral defeat of the BJD led by Mr Naveen Patnaik, who served as chief minister for twenty-four years. The new chief minister is the son of a security guard and a four-time MLA who hails from the remote village of Raikala in the Keonjhar district. He belongs to the Santali tribe and comes from a working-class family. Such achievements and political mobilities are possible only in a democratic society. Mr Majhi's leadership even in the form of symbolic representation in a democracy deserves celebration.

Mr Majhi is the third chief minister of Odisha from the tribal community, which constitutes 22.84 per cent of the state's total population, 9.20 per cent of the nation's Scheduled Tribes and about 0.79 per cent of the nation's entire population as per the 2011 census. The first two tribal chief ministers did nothing visible for the social, economic and political empowerment of tribal communities in the state. However, this democratic representation of indigenous leadership highlights the progress of Odisha's political landscape, ensuring that even individuals from remote and under-represented communities can ascend to significant positions of power and responsibility. Therefore, the election of Mr Majhi as the new chief minister of Odisha is a cause for celebration – a celebration of electoral democracy.

Even before taking the oath, when Mr Majhi was declared by the BJP as the chief ministerial candidate, social media and WhatsApp groups were filled with memes and messages reflecting the snobbery of the Brahminical social order composed of caste and class hierarchies empowered by the Hindutva politics that Mr Majhi represents. Caste and class snobbery find favour within the framework of a Brahminical social order, receiving political patronage from Hindutva politics. This political ideology often perpetuates and reinforces existing caste-based social, economic and political hierarchies, privileging certain social groups while marginalising others. Hindutva's endorsement of such hierarchies not only sustains caste-based discrimination but also reinforces social stratification, thereby entrenching inequalities within society. The BJP has selected Mr Majhi as their chief minister. However, Hindutva politics, which promotes a Brahminical social order, undermines him due to his origin, accent, attire and tribal background.

Despite being elected to such a prominent position, Mr Majhi faces significant challenges. His tribal heritage and unique cultural attributes set him apart from the Brahminical norms promoted by Hindutva ideology. This ideological clash can lead to tensions and challenges in his leadership, as these aspects of his identity may not align with the dominant social order within the party and its broader political framework. By highlighting these issues, it becomes clear that while the BJP's choice of Mr Majhi reflects a certain inclusivity, it also exposes underlying conflicts within the party's ideological stance, potentially affecting his effectiveness and acceptance as Chief Minister. It is incumbent upon Mr Majhi's leadership to overcome these contradictions by promoting reforms in Odia society through constitutional, secular, scientific and progressive values and ideals, which stand in contrast to the Hindutva culture in politics. His ability to navigate these complexities will be crucial in fostering a more inclusive and equitable society in Odisha.

Hindutva politics often relies on symbolic representation and scapegoating of tribal communities and working-class people within the framework of electoral democracy. This political ideology tends to utilise symbolic gestures and narratives, sometimes at the expense of marginalised groups such as tribal communities and the working classes. It strategically employs these tactics to garner support and maintain power within the electoral system while upholding the interests of the crony capitalists, propertied caste and class.

Mr Majhi's political journey has been deeply influenced by Hindutva ideology, a worldview he has been steeped in since the early days of his leadership. His ideological perspectives bear the imprint of the RSS and its Brahminical caste hierarchy. This ideological grounding informs his approach to governance and decision-making, reflecting a commitment to the principles and values espoused by the exclusionary Hindutva movement.

The BJP and BJD have maintained fraternal relations since the inception of their alliance, a bond that endures to this day. However, despite being the principal opposition party in Odisha, the BJP has struggled to effectively advocate for the interests of the state and its people during the twenty-four-year tenure of BJD rule. Instead, they often exchange support with rare instances of face-saving criticisms. This political camaraderie persists, evident in the recent oath-taking ceremony of Mr Majhi, leaving the people of Odisha questioning the depth of opposition politics and the nature of democracy in the state.

As time progresses, the people of Odisha will observe Mr Majhi's leadership and performance closely. They will see whether he adheres to the egalitarian outlook rooted in tribal values or succumbs to the old Brahminical social order promoted by the exclusionary Hindutva ideology. This period will be critical in determining Mr Majhi's legacy and the direction of his leadership. If he remains true to his tribal heritage and its values of equality and inclusivity, he may inspire significant social progress and gain widespread support. Conversely, if he conforms to the Brahminical norms, it may lead to further marginalisation of tribal communities and reinforce existing social hierarchies. The people of Odisha will be keenly watching to see which path he chooses and the impact it will have on the state's social and political landscape.

Time will ultimately determine whether Mr Majhi follows in the footsteps of historical power dynamics, where prominent figures like Indira Gandhi, Benazir Bhutto and Hillary Diane Rodham Clinton, despite being women in positions of power, may not have always represented the interests of women effectively. Similarly, numerous male leaders from the working class have not always championed the interests of their fellow working people in politics. Throughout history, there are numerous examples of leaders who have fallen short of truly advocating for the causes they ostensibly represent. Time will reveal where Mr Majhi's legacy falls within this continuum of representation and deepening of democracy in Odisha. Viva la democracy in Odisha and beyond.

Odisha's Democracy in Search of Identity

Democratic identity encompasses more than just political processes and governance structures; it is about the empowerment and development of citizens. At its core, democratic identity reflects the intricate interplay between the state, government, political parties and citizens, influenced by diverse ideologies aimed at fostering democratic progress and ensuring the well-being of the populace. This postcolonial state-government-citizenship identity is not merely a static construct but a dynamic relationship that evolves through the active participation of citizens in shaping their societies. It thrives on the principles of inclusivity, accountability and respect for human rights, fostering an environment where all voices are heard, and all individuals are afforded equal opportunities for political engagement and socio-economic advancement. The democratic identity also extends beyond the boundaries of formal institutions; it permeates the social fabric, cultural norms and collective consciousness of a society. It encompasses a shared commitment to the values of freedom, justice and equality, serving as a unifying force that transcends individual differences and fosters a sense of common purpose and belonging. In essence, democratic identity is not just a matter of political allegiance or legal frameworks; it's a reflection of the collective aspirations and ambitions of a people united in their pursuit of a more just, equitable and prosperous society based on science and secularism. It is through nurturing and upholding this identity that nations can truly realise the promise of democracy and fulfil the aspirations of their citizens.

In such a context, the prospect of an alliance between the ruling BJD and the opposition BJP in the upcoming state and general elections raises significant concerns for democracy in the state. Such a collaboration, while potentially advantageous for the parties involved in terms of electoral gains, threatens to undermine the very foundation of democratic principles and processes. At the heart of democracy lies the concept of political pluralism, where diverse voices and viewpoints are encouraged to compete openly and fairly within a framework of rules and institutions within a constitutional framework. The formation of an alliance between the ruling BJD and opposition party BJP risks eroding this essential aspect of democracy by limiting political competition and diminishing the accountability of those in power. Such an alliance could further consolidate political power in the hands of a few, potentially leading to a monopolisation of governance and a weakening of checks and balances. This concentration of power not only undermines the principle of separation of powers but also deprives citizens of meaningful alternatives and avenues for dissent and opposition.

The alliance between the ruling BJD and opposition party BJP raises questions about the integrity of the political process and erodes public trust in the democratic system. It creates perceptions of backroom deals and compromises that prioritise partisan interests over the welfare of the electorate, thereby delegitimising the electoral process and disenfranchising the populace. It is imperative for stakeholders in Odisha's democracy to reaffirm their commitment to the principles of transparency, accountability and political competition. Instead of resorting to alliances that may undermine these principles, political parties should focus on engaging with citizens, addressing their concerns and offering viable solutions to the challenges facing the state. Ultimately, the strength and vibrancy of Odisha's democracy will depend on the ability of its citizens and leaders to uphold the core values of democratic governance and resist efforts to subvert them for short-term political gain. Only by safeguarding the integrity of the democratic process can Odisha truly fulfil its potential as a beacon of democracy and progress.

The trend of political leaders in Odisha frequently switching parties reflects a concerning erosion of ideological integrity and a prioritisation of electoral calculations over democratic principles. In this scenario, democracy appears to have devolved into an ideology-free zone, where the pursuit of power trumps adherence to core values and beliefs. The cynical view of citizens as mere numbers in a vote box, rather than as active participants in the democratic process, is a troubling reflection of this trend.

When electoral victory becomes detached from principles and values, democracy itself is diminished and the trust between citizens and political leaders is eroded. In a healthy democracy, citizens are empowered to make informed political decisions based on the principles and policies espoused by political parties. However, when leaders prioritise party politics over the interests of the electorate, they undermine the very foundation of democratic governance. The constant shifting of political allegiances not only breeds cynicism among voters but also weakens the accountability mechanisms that are essential for a functioning democracy.

Without a clear commitment to principles and values, political leaders may prioritise short-term gains over long-term development, leading to a cycle of instability and disillusionment among the populace. To address this challenge, there is a need for an alternative politics with a renewed focus on restoring trust and accountability within Odisha's political landscape. Political leaders must demonstrate a genuine commitment to democratic principles, transparency and ethical conduct. Additionally, citizens must actively engage in holding their representatives accountable and demand integrity and consistency in political leadership. Ultimately, a robust democracy depends on the active participation and vigilance of its citizens, as well as the principled leadership of elected officials. By upholding democratic values and rejecting opportunistic politics, Odisha can reclaim its identity as a beacon of democratic governance and ensure that the voices of its citizens are heard and respected.

The trajectory of Odisha's democracy reflects a dynamic interplay of historical legacies of feudalism, contemporary realities of a market-led society and shifting power dynamics between higher caste and class leadership shaped by rising Hindutva politics. From the early years of statehood to the present day, political parties have played a crucial role in shaping governance and policy frameworks. The dominance of regional parties like the BJD has redefined the contours of Odisha's political landscape, propagating the so-called indigenous leadership and grassroots empowerment. It is neither indigenous nor grassroots politics. It is purely feudal politics based on family legacies and opposition parties are no different from ruling parties.

Odisha's democracy, in its search for identity, epitomises resilience, adaptability and a commitment to inclusive development. As the state grapples with contemporary challenges and navigates the complexities of governance, it remains anchored in its rich cultural heritage and ethos of participatory democracy. By embracing innovation, fostering social cohesion and prioritising sustainable development, Odisha is poised to carve a distinct identity within Indian democracy, embodying the spirit of resilience and evolution. However, the time is crucial if democracy in the state wishes to survive and remain vibrant. When will the people of Odisha rise and reclaim their democracy from the few?

Prosperous Gods and Goddesses in the World of Pauperised People

Homelessness is on the rise in both urban and rural areas of Odisha, exacerbating the struggles of its inhabitants. Currently, 11.07 per cent of the population in the state lives in poverty, reflecting widespread economic hardship. Hunger and malnutrition continue to be pressing concerns, with many families unable to access sufficient food, safe drinking water and nutrients. The high levels of unemployment and the resulting distress migration highlight the dire economic situation, as people leave their homes in search of better opportunities. The government policies have directly and indirectly supported private educational and health infrastructures, while public health and educational infrastructures are in decline in the state.

Despite the severity of these problems, neither the previous nor the current government has made them a priority. This lack of attention has hindered progress and left many citizens without the welfare support they need. Effective policies and initiatives are urgently required to address homelessness, poverty, hunger, malnutrition, unemployment and migration. Only through welfare efforts can the state improve the living conditions and prospects of its people, but the government is busy with gods and goddesses in the name of heritage protection.

The new Chief Minister of Odisha, Mr Mohan Majhi, follows in the footsteps of Mr Naveen Patnaik. Like his predecessor, Mr Majhi continues to emphasise the welfare of gods, goddesses and their abodes, demonstrating considerable generosity in this regard. Both leaders have prioritised the reconstruction and maintenance of religious sites, allocating substantial portions of the budget to ensure the divine opulence and sacred welfare of deities within the state. Meanwhile, the schools and hospitals are in decimated conditions. The working people continue to dream of prosperity while grappling with everyday poverty.

This juxtaposition of divine prosperity with human pauperisation starkly defines the developmental trajectory in the state. Both BJP, BJD and their leaders prioritise the reconstruction of homes for gods and goddesses, while the people of Odisha suffer from hunger, hopelessness and homelessness. The focus on religious infrastructure stands in sharp contrast to the neglected needs of the populace. While funds are abundant for temple renovations and deity worship, essential public services such as public healthcare, mass education and social welfare remain underfunded and inadequate. This disparity highlights a critical issue in governance: the prioritisation of spiritual and religious concerns over the immediate, tangible needs of the citizens.

Under the leadership of both Mr Patnaik and Mr Majhi, the state continues to witness efforts to enhance religious sites. However, this has often come at the expense of addressing pressing social issues such as poverty, hunger and homelessness. The people of Odisha continue to face daily hardships, dreaming of prosperity amidst their struggles. The leadership of both the BJD and BJP argue that the investment in religious sites promotes cultural heritage and tourism, potentially leading to economic benefits. However, this perspective overlooks the pressing realities faced by the state's residents. The lack of employment opportunities, insufficient support for farmers and inadequate housing conditions are issues that demand urgent attention and resources.

Despite the significant investment in temples and other religious sites, many citizens of Odisha still struggle with basic necessities due to misplaced priorities. The contrast between divine prosperity and human impoverishment underscores a glaring issue: the urgent needs of the population are often over-shadowed by spiritual and religious concerns.

Odisha is a mineral-rich state with huge potential for alternative, green, clean and sustainable industrialisation. It has huge potential for agricultural, forest and marine resource development. The mobilisation of these resources is central to the development of the state and its people. But the visionless leadership in an ideological free zone of politics in Odisha is pauperising its people, while allocating abundant budgetary resources for the abodes of gods and goddesses. The constitutional principle of a secular state and government is undermined by both BJD and BJP governments. The new BJP government and its Hindutva politics are fuelling communal conflicts and destroying harmony in Odia society.

It is clear that the government in Odisha does not want to create conditions for economically prosperous and politically conscious citizens who can question the government and its legitimacy. The government ensures compliant citizens by promoting religion in public life, as religious citizens seldom question the legitimacy of state and government activities.

It is imperative that the government re-evaluates its priorities and focusses on a balanced approach that addresses both cultural preservation of religious sites and human welfare, which can pave the way for a more equitable, secular, progressive and prosperous Odisha. By addressing the basic needs of the people – such as healthcare, education and housing – the government can pave the way for a better quality of life for all its residents. This balanced approach will ensure that while the state's rich cultural heritage is maintained, its citizens do not continue to suffer from neglect and deprivation. People can protect their culture, religion and heritage only when they have economic stability in their lives and livelihoods.

It is the working people who construct roads, schools, colleges, hospitals, temples, churches, mosques and even space stations. The working masses have also removed kings and established democracies to assert their supremacy. History bears witness to the transformative power of people over empires and emperors. There would be no religions or gods without people. Therefore, the state and government should start working for the people. Gods and goddesses can take care of themselves. Viva la People!

Conclusion

Religion, religious politics and regional chauvinisms are capitalist strategies designed to create conditions and institutions that facilitate and ensure local accumulation processes. These strategies aim to operate without interference from progressive political transformations that seek to deepen democracy and empower citizens. The informal and formal political alliances between the BJP and the BJD aid in the localisation of capitalism, as well as the entrench- ment of capitalist social and political relations, in Odisha and India. Both parties promote religious politics under the guise of preserving culture and religion, all while the working class continues to suffer from various forms of marginalisation.

Religion, as utilised by these political entities, serves to distract and divide the people, redirecting attention away from pressing socio-economic issues. The infusion of religious sentiments into politics not only bolsters the power structures of these parties but also perpetuates a cycle of exploitation and ine- quality. By championing regional chauvinisms, these parties further fragment society, fostering divisions based on regional identity and pride. This fragmen- tation weakens collective efforts towards progressive change and sustains the status quo of capitalist dominance.

The BJP and BJD's collaboration exemplifies a broader trend of political manoeuvrings where alliances are forged to maintain control over economic resources and political power. In Odisha, this partnership has led to policies and practices that favour capitalist interests, often at the expense of social wel- fare and equitable development. The invocation of cultural preservation serves as a smokescreen for policies that undermine workers' rights and deepen socio- economic disparities. The strategic use of religion and regionalism by the BJP and BJD reveals a calculated effort to sustain regional and national capitalist hegemony. This approach not only stifles progressive political movements but also ensures that the mechanisms of marginalisation and exploitation remain firmly in place, to the detriment of the working masses.

CHAPTER 5

CONTRADICTIONS, CONFLICTS, COLLABORATIONS AND CONTOURS OF CAPITALISM

Introduction

Contradictions, conflicts and collaborations are three integral features of capitalism in all its forms (Shaikh, 2016). Capitalism adopts these three strategies either together or separately, depending on local, regional, national and global conditions. Consistency is not a characteristic of capitalism. Contradictions arise within capitalism when the pursuit of profit leads to opposing outcomes, such as wealth for some and poverty for others. These contradictions can manifest in various ways, including economic inequalities, market failures and environmental degradation. They highlight the inherent tensions within a system that prioritises profit maximisation, often at the expense of broader social and environmental concerns. Conflicts are another inherent feature of capitalism, stemming from competition between businesses, workers and governments. These conflicts can lead to labour strikes, trade wars and political disputes, as different stakeholders vie for a larger share of resources and power. The competitive nature of capitalism often results in a constant struggle for dominance, both within and between nations. Collaborations, on the other hand, occur when businesses, governments and other entities work together to achieve common goals. These collaborations can take many forms, such as public-private partnerships, international trade agreements and corporate alliances (Hancké et al., 2007).

The adaptability of capitalism allows it to respond to varying conditions across different levels of society. At the local level, small businesses may collaborate to support community development. Regionally, industries might compete or collaborate based on shared resources or market opportunities. Nationally, governments and corporations might engage in conflicts over regulations and policies while also forming alliances to enhance economic stability. Globally, multinational corporations and international organisations navigate a complex web of contradictions, conflicts and collaborations to drive global economic dynamics. Finally, the inconsistency of capitalism is one of its defining traits. Its ability to fluctuate between contradictions, conflicts and collaborations makes it a dynamic and resilient system, capable of adapting to changing circumstances and evolving over time.

The capitalist systems and their Eurocentric proponents persist in applying double standards to serve their capitalist interests. These forces consistently undermine alternative narratives and successful practices of development and governance in Asia, Africa and Latin America. For instance, their economic policies, such as subsidies and banking regulations, and their geopolitical stances on issues like Ukraine and Palestine highlight the Eurocentric bias embedded within the fictitious democratic ideals. These inconsistencies shape a narrative that prioritises Western capitalist perspectives over local, regional, national and global concerns.

Two Tales of Subsidies

The secretary of the US Department of the Treasury, Janet L. Yellen, visited the People's Republic of China (PRC) from 3rd April to 9th April 2024 for bilateral meetings aimed at strengthening healthy economic relationships and engaging in other diplomatic discussions. During her visit, Yellen expressed concerns about Chinese state subsidies, stating in a press conference that they 'pose significant risks to workers and businesses not only in the United States but also globally'. While on a subsidies boat cruise along the Pearl River in the southern Chinese city of Guangzhou, Yellen further criticised China for its industrial overcapacity and unfair trade practices. These comments underscored the ongoing economic tensions between the two countries and highlighted the importance of addressing these issues through dialogue and cooperation.

US Treasury Secretary Janet L. Yellen goes further to say that 'China is too large to export its way to rapid growth'. European leaders have been echoing Yellen's views for a while now. So, she is not acting in isolation with her criticisms aimed at Chinese economic growth and human development. Her Sinophobic views are part of a broader political and economic campaign to undermine the Chinese model of alternative postcolonial developments. This perspective is influenced by long-standing colonial legacies and Eurocentric knowledge traditions that have shaped the worldviews of American and European policymakers. These traditions often guide the strategies of their governing bodies, which prioritise protecting their hegemonic interests even if it comes at the expense of people and the planet. The criticisms and concerns expressed by Yellen reflect a historical context where Western powers have sought to maintain their dominance in global economic and political affairs. Such colonial, imperialist and hegemonic mindset often draws its justifications from Eurocentric knowledge traditions. These traditions have historically positioned themselves as the sole arbiters of scientific truth and morality, aiming to assert dominance globally. This perspective sometimes employs what can be perceived as half-baked philosophies and science, tailored to serve market forces to expand the pyramid of capitalist profits.

Historically, the United States has benefited from state-led protectionist industrial and trade policies that played a significant role in its post-war economic growth. However, American policymakers and politicians have often urged countries like China and other postcolonial nations not to adopt similar strategies. Likewise, European nations have frequently employed discriminatory protectionist policies to safeguard their economic interests. While practising protectionism themselves, both American and European leaders advocate for what they describe as 'free trade' to postcolonial countries. This so-called free trade is often neither free nor fair, as it tends to favour the economic interests of the developed Western nations at the expense of developing countries. This double standard in trade policies highlights the complexities and contradictions inherent in global economic relations. It underscores the need for a more transparent, equitable and mutually beneficial approach to international trade. Developing countries should be given the space to pursue policies that best suit their economic development needs, rather than being pressured into adopting one-size-fits-all capitalist solutions that are not in the best interest of people living around the globe.

The colonial and imperialist plundering of people and their resources laid the foundation for European and American industrial overcapacity and capitalist development, leading to deindustrialisation and underdevelopment in Asia, Africa and Latin America. Similarly, corporatisation and hegemonic trade practices by Americans and Europeans, and their wars continue to destroy livelihoods around the world. This historical plunder and its continuity have had lasting effects, contributing to deindustrialisation, unemployment and poverty in regions like Asia, Africa and Latin America. As a result, many of these regions have struggled to develop their own industries and economies on an equal footing. The corporatisation and hegemonic trade practices in the name of so-called free trade championed by Americans and Europeans, and their neo-colonial policies continue to pose challenges for people around the globe. These practices often prioritise profit over people and the planet, leading to the displacement of local industries and the destruction of livelihoods.

Similarly, Americans and Europeans provide different forms of subsidies and tax relief to their farmers, industrialists, bankers, corporates and even to fertiliser and defence manufacturers to be competitive in the global market. The European agricultural subsidies are destroying agriculture in Africa. The American federal government spends a massive amount on subsidies for farm businesses and agriculture. Corporate agriculture receives the lion's share of subsidies in the United States. Despite unequal subsidy distribution, the policies of subsidies have a positive impact on production, price and on environment in the United States under the Environmental Quality Incentives Program (EQIP), Conservation Stewardship Program (CSP) and Conservation Reserve Program (CRP).

European and American policymakers often leverage institutions like the World Bank, IMF and WTO to label subsidies as non-merit goods and oppose them, particularly when dealing with postcolonial countries in Asia, Africa and Latin America. This approach promotes unfair trade practices that benefit Western economies at the expense of developing nations. While European and American farmers and corporations receive subsidies to remain competitive in the global market, these same benefits are frequently denied to farmers in postcolonial countries. This selective application of subsidy policies serves to protect and expand American and European food and agricultural markets, industrial and manufacturing sectors, while hindering the growth and competitiveness of agricultural and industrial sectors in developing countries. Such practices perpetuate economic disparities and contribute to the dependency of postcolonial countries on Western markets and technologies. They also undermine efforts to achieve food security and sustainable agricultural development in these regions.

China's approach challenges the double standard often employed by Western nations regarding state subsidies. China provides subsidies to promote the production of essential goods and services, aiming to support economic growth and human development while remaining competitive in the global market, much like American and European practices. However, this stance taken by China is often viewed as untenable by American and European policymakers. The capitalist insecurities stemming from China's rapid economic development and its challenge to Western economic dominance contribute to the emergence of Sinophobia or a fear and hostility towards China. The

Western narrative often portrays China's economic policies as a threat rather than a legitimate strategy for development. This portrayal overlooks the historical and ongoing subsidies provided by Western nations to their own industries and highlights the selective application of free-market principles. The reality is that state subsidies have been and continue to be an integral part of economic development strategies for many countries, including Western nations. China's use of subsidies to support key industries and promote economic growth should be understood within this broader context.

There are two contradictory tales on subsidies, trade, industrialisation and development that define the hypocrisy of the capitalist Western nations and their governing elites. The postcolonial countries must unite and reject such a narrative, working together towards an egalitarian international economic order that benefits both people and the planet.

Myths and Realities of Eurocentric Fables on Chinese International Debt Trap Diplomacy

Debt-driven capitalism persists through the implementation of liberalisation, privatisation, globalisation and structural adjustment policies enforced by creditors on borrowing nations. These policy mechanisms establish an international debt trap, wherein credit-fuelled economic expansion ultimately leads to an escalating cycle of debt (Dejuán, 2013). A debt trap manifests as an economic predicament where a borrower finds themselves ensnared in a perpetual cycle of debt, rendering it nearly impossible to repay (King & Parrish, 2007). Within this framework of indebtedness, countries often resort to further borrowing to service their existing debt obligations. Consequently, this creates an unsustainable level of debt dependency that reverberates across all facets of human development and welfare, impacting societies at various levels.

The global undemocratic institutions, such as the World Bank and International Monetary Fund (IMF), serve as the driving force behind debt-driven policies under the guise of economic reforms and modernisation (Payer, 1975). Through debt-driven policies and processes, there has been a significant transfer of money, capital and resources from the poorest countries to the wealthiest nations worldwide. Debt operates as the supply chain and logistical backbone of the capitalist system. The impoverishment of the poor and their respective countries due to debt is often portrayed as the emergence of economies and modernisation efforts. However, the payment and repayment of debt operate within a moral framework (Graeber, 2011) that sustains the institutions and processes of international debt, facilitating the expansion of capitalism and its control over both natural resources and human capital. Deaths and destitution emerge as twin outcomes of a debt-driven capitalist economic system.

The International Debt Statistics (IDS) primarily comprises the World Bank's Debtor Reporting System (DRS), which meticulously documents the debt of 123 low- and middle-income countries. According to its 2022 report, the combined external debt stock of these nations surged to $8.7 trillion by the end of 2020. This includes a ten percent increase in publicly guaranteed external debt and a three percent rise in long-term private non-guaranteed debt. Despite worsening debt indicators across all geographic regions, the World Bank and the IMF managed to secure $117 billion from multilateral creditors to further expand the international debt regime. Such a debt-driven economic system is inherently unsustainable in the long run. It carries an inherent risk of perpetuating a cycle of permanent debt crisis, which is integral to capitalism as an economic system.

The former colonial powers have historically employed debt as a strategic tool to assert control over the economic policies and natural resources of postcolonial nations, often through stabilisation and structural adjustment programmes (John, Messina, & Odumegwu, 2023; Stallings, 1992; Young, 1986). These debt policies were portrayed as instruments of economic development, yet they frequently undermined locally sustainable alternative development trajectories (Nayak, 2023).

In contrast, Chinese development finance and aid, along with associated debt, have been labelled as 'debt trap diplomacy' by critics from former colonial countries and their supporters. Chellaney (2017) argues that Chinese debt trap serves as a tool of diplomacy for China. Other writers like; Panda (2019), Rana and Xianbai, (2020) have argued that debt trap diplomacy is a neo-colonial strategy of Chinese statecraft. However, such narratives of Chinese debt trap diplomacy have been challenged by several studies (Himmer & Rod, 2022; Singh, 2020), indicating myth of Chinese debt trap diplomacy. The debunking of Chinese debt trap diplomacy (Jones & Hameiri, 2020) is important to expose anti-Chinese propaganda. However, the Eurocentric and American narratives continue to undermine Chinese alternative modes of development, debt and diplomacy.

Eurocentric Fables on Debt Trap Sans History

The international debt trap emerges because of historical colonial and neo-colonial exploitation, imperialist hegemony and the imposition of neoliberal economic policies by developed countries on the developing world. This phenomenon affects regions across the globe, including Asia, Africa, Latin America and even parts of the capitalist West, all under the sway of the Westphalian capitalist system that wields significant influence over global economics and politics (Backiel, 2015; Gardner, 2017; Kwet, 2022; Uwakwe & Onebunne, 2022).

Nevertheless, reactionary and capitalist ideologues, along with their mouthpiece mass media, writers, journalists, consultants, think tanks and leaders, are engaged in a relentless campaign to discredit, delegitimise and downplay Chinese accomplishments. This concerted anti-Chinese propaganda aims to undermine the alternative development model pursued by China and numerous other nations in Asia, Africa and Latin America (Kochegurov, 2022).

The economic and political involvement of China in regions such as Asia, Africa and Latin America presents a formidable challenge to the prevailing development model based on debt dependence. This Chinese engagement calls into question the very foundation of the Western-designed debt trap, which has long been used to exploit natural resources in the developing world. Debt, in this context, serves as both a political and economic tool wielded by Western powers to exert control over the politics and economic systems of developing nations, thereby perpetuating capitalist hegemony. Consequently, China's emergence as a global player poses a threat to this established world order. However, narratives portraying Chinese authoritarianism and the so-called 'Chinese debt trap' campaigns are often driven by ideology and myths rather than grounded in reality (Brautigam & Rithmire, 2021). These campaigns rely on falsehoods as a means to uphold Western hegemony over both people and the planet (Kochegurov, 2022).

The narratives surrounding the so-called 'Chinese Debt Trap' are indeed largely unfounded and serve as propaganda aimed at undermining Beijing and its relationships with developing nations (Brautigam & Rithmire, 2021; Singh, 2020). In reality, China's approach to lending encompasses three distinct types of loans: interest-free loans, long-term infrastructure loans with minimal interest rates and commercial loans. Moreover, China demonstrates flexibility by allowing for the restructuring of loan terms based on the changing economic conditions of borrowing countries. It's crucial to note that China has never resorted to seizing assets from countries that have borrowed from it. While acquisitions, investments and integrations are common strategies employed by Western entities in international trade, China distinguishes itself through its lending patterns and policies towards developing nations. Rather than adopting a coercive approach, China's engagements prioritise mutual benefit and sustainable development (Nayak, 2023).

China stands out as one of the largest official creditors globally, boasting a significant presence on the international stage. However, unlike traditional Western creditors, China refrains from imposing conditions such as structural adjustments, alterations to labour laws, or demands for economic liberalisation and privatisation when extending loans. Despite this, the Western propaganda machine consistently depicts China's integration and acquisitions as evidence of dominance and the infamous 'debt trap'. In reality, China's economic engagement with developing countries presents a formidable challenge to Western hegemony. Consequently, Beijing often finds itself demonised as an authoritarian force with ambitions of global colonisation and domination. Yet, there is no truth to these allegations; they are merely products of Western ideologues viewing the world through their own distorted lens. The colonial past serves as a mirror, reflecting the true nature of the colonisers who now attempt to play the victim card to obscure their own historical atrocities. However, China's approach to international relations offers a departure from this legacy, emphasising mutual cooperation and development rather than coercion and exploitation (Nayak, 2023).

The economic and political challenges confronting nations across Asia, Africa and Latin America today are deeply rooted in their colonial past and perpetuated by a neo-colonial present dominated by the United States and Western Europe. In this context, China's provision of loans for infrastructure development emerges as a crucial counterbalance, offering developing countries the opportunity to break free from their historical dependency on the West and mobilise their own natural resources for sustainable growth and development. By extending loans for infrastructure projects, China empowers developing nations to enhance their economic infrastructure, strengthen their industrial base and improve their connectivity both domestically and internationally. This facilitates economic diversification and reduces reliance on Western aid and influence. Moreover, China's approach to lending typically avoids the stringent conditions often imposed by Western creditors, providing greater flexibility and autonomy for recipient countries to chart their own development paths. Ultimately, China's engagement in infrastructure development represents a significant shift in the global economic landscape, offering developing countries an alternative route to economic empowerment and self-reliance amid the ongoing challenges posed by colonial legacies and neo-colonial dynamics (Nayak, 2023).

The level of Chinese debt in African, Asian and Latin American countries is relatively minimal compared to their total debt-to-GDP ratios (Brautigam & Rithmire, 2021). Therefore, it's imperative to dispel the unfounded narratives and propaganda surrounding the notion of Chinese debt trap diplomacy. The expansion of Chinese economic and political engagement with developing nations plays a crucial role in reducing their dependency on Western capital. This shift in economic ties understandably makes Western powers uneasy, leading them to propagate falsehoods against China. However, such efforts serve as a diversionary tactic by Western leaders to conceal their own political and economic shortcomings. Blaming China solely for global issues does not absolve the failures inherent within capitalism and so-called Western democracy. True progress towards democracy requires a world economy free from the shackles of debt. This can be achieved through fostering politics centred on unity, peace, solidarity and shared prosperity. The Chinese model, based on principles of peace, cooperation, development and socialism, presents an alternative framework for the world to consider. By embracing these principles, nations can collectively move towards a more equitable and sustainable future (Nayak, 2023).

Indeed, a debt-driven Western dominance rooted in capitalism offers neither an economic nor political alternative, as evidenced by its failures throughout history. The world needs a new paradigm, one that transcends the confines of a unipolar, bipolar or even multipolar world order led by traditional global powers such as the United States, China, France, Britain, Germany, Russia and India. Instead, the focus of world politics needs to centre on people, peace and the planet, grounded in the egalitarian values of liberty, justice, fraternity and citizenship rights. This call for a people and planet-centric world order reflects the urgent need for a sustainable tomorrow. Such a paradigm shift would prioritise the well-being of humanity and the environment over narrow geopolitical interests, fostering a more equitable and harmonious global community without any form of debt traps.

Tale of Two Stories in International Debt

The IDS (2022) published by the World Bank has unveiled a stark reality: the external debt of 123 low- and middle-income countries surged by an average of 5.6 per cent to reach a staggering $8.7 trillion in 2020. This revelation underscores the devastating impact of the pandemic on the economies of developing nations. It lays bare the profound challenges these countries face in navigating a path towards sustainable development. At the forefront of this economic struggle, the G20 creditors have introduced a policy framework known as the Debt Service Suspension Initiative (DSSI), seemingly casting themselves as benevolent benefactors to the impoverished inhabitants of the developing world. However, beneath this facade of goodwill lies a more insidious truth: the international debt trap, a mechanism that ensnares both individuals and nations within an economic system where borrowing becomes normalised to service an ever-expanding burden of debt (Jubilee Debt Campaign, 2015).

The repercussions of this debt trap are profound, extending far beyond mere financial strain. It erodes incomes, diminishes well-being and jeopardises livelihoods, driving many individuals, particularly the impoverished, to despair and tragically, to suicide. Moreover, it perpetuates a cycle of dependency wherein poor and developing countries forfeit their economic independence and political sovereignty, ceding decision-making power over their people, resources and territories to external creditors (Jubilee Debt Campaign, 2015). This dynamic underscores a systematic strategy employed by developed countries to exploit their developing counterparts. Debt emerges not merely as a financial instrument but as a potent tool of control and exploitation, exacerbating the gaping chasm between the affluent and the destitute, between developed regions and their underdeveloped counterparts (Nayak, 2023).

The international debt crises and the entrapment they engender in poverty, underdevelopment and inequality are not arbitrary occurrences but rather direct consequences of colonial legacies and neo-colonial policies imposed upon developing nations by their more powerful counterparts (Nayak, 2023). This realisation underscores the urgent need for a paradigm shift in global economic governance – one that prioritises equity, sustainability and genuine empowerment for all nations, irrespective of their economic standing.

The historical context of developed countries' actions towards debt-defaulter nations reveals a persistent pattern of exploitation and control. One notable instance occurred when French and Belgian troops occupied the Ruhr, a region in North Rhine-Westphalia, Germany, to access coal when the nation faltered in repaying its Versailles debts (Schmidt, 2012). This intervention exemplifies how powerful nations have historically leveraged military force to secure economic interests in debtor nations.

Throughout the colonial period, European powers divided territories across Asia, Africa and the Americas among themselves, establishing a pervasive international debt trap in these regions. European colonialism not only extracted resources but also imposed economic structures that perpetuated dependency and indebtedness among colonised nations. Following the devastation of the First World War, the United States Congress notably rebuffed calls for European debt cancellation. However, in the aftermath of the Second World War, European nations took a different approach, opting to forgive each other's debts (Debt Justice, 2015). This cooperative gesture culminated in the Bretton Woods Conference, where nations convened under US leadership to establish a new international financial system.

The Bretton Woods Conference birthed institutions such as the IMF and the World Bank, which ostensibly aimed to foster global economic stability and development. However, in practice, these institutions institutionalised the international debt trap, particularly for postcolonial developing countries (Nayak, 2023). By exerting influence over borrowing conditions and economic policies, they perpetuated a cycle of indebtedness that hindered the autonomy and prosperity of vulnerable nations.

This historical narrative underscores the enduring legacy of colonialism and imperialism in shaping global economic dynamics. It underscores the need for critical reflection on the power dynamics embedded within international financial institutions and calls for a reimagining of economic governance that prioritises equity, sovereignty and sustainable development for all nations. In the 1990s, the G7 developed nations orchestrated a regime promoting a free-market economy, characterised by neo-colonial economic policies. Spearheaded by the World Bank and IMF, these policies imposed structural adjustments, liberalisation, privatisation and globalisation measures on debtor nations unable to meet their financial obligations. Ostensibly aimed at fostering economic stability and growth, these policies served as instruments of indirect control over the natural resources, domestic consumer markets, labour forces and investment landscapes of debtor nations.

The international debt trap emerges as the linchpin of all economic crises plaguing developing countries, perpetuating a cycle of dependency that reinforces the economic and political hegemony of Western European nations and the United States. By leveraging their dominant position within international financial institutions, developed countries assert influence over the economic trajectories of debtor nations, dictating terms that serve their own interests while exacerbating the vulnerabilities of the global South. This systemic exploitation underscores the unequal power dynamics entrenched within the global economic order, where the interests of wealthy nations often take precedence over the well-being and self-determination of marginalised populations. Addressing the root causes of the international debt trap requires a concerted effort to dismantle entrenched systems of exploitation and empower developing nations to chart their own paths towards sustainable development and prosperity.

The resurgence of the international debt trap since 2020 can be traced back to the publication of *The Elements of the China Challenge* by the Policy Planning Staff of the Office of the Secretary of State in the United States. This unclassified paper focuses on what it terms China's 'predatory development programme and debt-trap diplomacy'. It asserts that Beijing's actions are driven by authoritarian goals and hegemonic ambitions, accusing the Chinese Communist Party (CCP) of engaging in debt-trap diplomacy and predatory economic practices worldwide to reshape the global order. However, it's important to critically assess these claims. Many argue that such assertions lack a factual basis and are instead part of a broader anti-Chinese propaganda campaign. There is scepticism regarding the ideological motivations behind these allegations, with critics highlighting the absence of concrete evidence to support the portrayal of China's actions as predatory or hegemonic. It is argued that characterising China's infrastructure and investment projects as 'debt-trap diplomacy' oversimplifies complex economic relationships and overlooks the mutual benefits that can arise from international cooperation. While concerns about debt sustainability and transparency in China's lending practices are legitimate, they should be addressed through constructive dialogue and engagement rather than sensationalised rhetoric (Nayak, 2023).

In essence, while it's essential to scrutinise China's actions and policies, it's equally crucial to approach the discourse surrounding the international debt trap with nuance and objectivity, avoiding the pitfalls of ideological bias and unsubstantiated claims. Constructive dialogue and collaboration remain essential for addressing global challenges and fostering a more equitable and sustainable international economic order. The emergence of China as a global player, driven by principles of peace and development, poses a challenge to the traditional hegemony of the debt-driven international financial system, largely led by Western European nations and the United States. China's approach to international engagement with developing countries is characterised by its emphasis on mutual benefit and cooperation, particularly evident in its efforts to assist nations in Asia and Africa in developing their infrastructure and mobilising their own resources for economic advancement.

Unlike the conditionalities often attached to financial assistance from Western institutions, China's engagement typically comes with fewer strings attached, allowing recipient countries greater flexibility in pursuing their own development agendas. This approach not only fosters a sense of empowerment and self-reliance but also challenges the established norms of debt dependency and Western influence that have long characterised international relations. However, this shifting dynamic has provoked apprehension and resistance from certain quarters in the Western democratic world. As China's influence grows, it is increasingly portrayed as a threat to the existing order by some Western nations and institutions. This portrayal often overlooks the potential benefits of China's engagement, instead framing it as antagonistic to Western interests and values.

In reality, the situation is more complex. While China's rise does challenge the established power structures, it also presents opportunities for collaboration and innovation in addressing global challenges. By fostering a more multipolar world order, China's internationalism opens up avenues for a greater diversity of perspectives and approaches to addressing common concerns such as poverty, climate change and infrastructure development. Ultimately, the portrayal of China as a 'devil of debt trap diplomacy' by Eurocentric scholarship reflects broader geopolitical tensions and anxieties about shifts in global power dynamics. However, a more constructive approach would involve recognising and engaging with the nuances of China's role in the international system, with a focus on finding common ground and pursuing shared goals for the benefit of all nations.

The reality of China's engagement with the African continent tells a different story from the narrative of a 'Chinese debt trap' propagated by some. In fact, the Chinese government has taken concrete steps to strengthen its relationship with African nations by implementing measures aimed at debt relief and restructuring. For instance, Beijing has forgiven 23 interest-free loans for 17 African countries and cancelled over $3.4 billion in debt while restructuring approximately $15 billion in debt between 2000 and 2019 alone. Additionally, China is actively renegotiating 26 other loans and refinancing around $15 billion of debt across Africa. These actions underscore China's commitment to fostering mutual development and cooperation with African nations. Rather than viewing Chinese engagement through a lens of debt dependency, it is important to recognise China's alternative approach to international debt, bilateral and multilateral trade and infrastructure development. Unlike Western counterparts that often attach stringent conditions to investments, China's assistance focuses on providing resources for infrastructural development, thereby supporting the emergence of economically independent states in Africa.

Moreover, China's approach contrasts sharply with Western demands for structural adjustments that often undermine the welfare state and exploit local populations and environments. By prioritising mutually beneficial development projects, China seeks to promote sustainable growth and prosperity in African countries, challenging the traditional hegemony of Western-dominated international financial institutions. Ultimately, characterising China's engagement as a 'debt trap' overlooks the nuances of its approach and the tangible benefits it brings to African nations. Rather than succumbing to ideological biases, a more nuanced understanding of China's role in Africa necessitates a recognition of its contributions to fostering economic development and self-reliance on the continent.

The contrasting narratives surrounding China's engagement with Africa and the Western model of international economic governance highlight the profound implications of debt-driven capitalism on democracy, livelihoods and the environment. While China's approach emphasises mutual development and infrastructure investment, the Western model often prioritises profit over people, leading to exploitation and environmental degradation. The prevalence of debt-driven capitalism perpetuates a cycle of poverty and vulnerability, particularly for the working poor around the world. Under the leadership of Western states and governments, this system prioritises market forces at the expense of democratic principles, often sacrificing the well-being of individuals and communities for the sake of profit.

Furthermore, the environmental consequences of debt-driven capitalism are dire, with ecosystems and communities bearing the brunt of unsustainable resource extraction and pollution. The pursuit of profit-driven growth undermines efforts to address climate change and biodiversity loss, exacerbating the risks of environmental disasters for future generations.

In light of these challenges, there is a growing call to dismantle capitalism and its debt-driven financial architectures in favour of alternative models that prioritise humanity, peace, prosperity and planetary well-being. This requires reimagining economic systems based on principles of equity, sustainability and social justice and fostering cooperation and solidarity on a global scale. By challenging the hegemony of debt-driven capitalism and advocating for transformative change, we can work towards a more just and sustainable future for all. This entails addressing the root causes of inequality, exploitation, environmental degradation and embracing models of economic governance that prioritise the common good over private profit. Only then can we truly build a world that is equitable, prosperous and in harmony with the planet.

The COVID-19 pandemic has served as a stark reminder of the deepening grip of debt-driven capitalism, exacerbating economic inequalities and widening the gap between the haves and have-nots. Even in advanced capitalist economies, where wealth is ostensibly abundant, the burden of debt weighs heavily on ordinary people. As the pandemic rages on, international debt has surged, reaching twenty percent of GDP in many countries, further straining already fragile economic systems. The design of debt policies, rules, regulations and institutions predominantly favours the interests of developed capitalist nations, often at the expense of people and the planet. Despite calls for reform, the international debt architecture remains fundamentally skewed, perpetuating systems of exploitation and inequality.

Even institutions like the IMF have acknowledged the urgent need for reform, albeit with proposals that some deem minimalist. While initiatives like the G20 DSSI may provide temporary relief, they fail to address the underlying colonial and imperialist foundations of international debt. True progress towards a more just and equitable global economy requires radical reform that prioritises the interests of people over profit. This necessitates democratising the international debt system, empowering marginalised voices and dismantling the structures that perpetuate debt-driven capitalism.

By challenging the status quo and advocating for systemic change, we can move towards an egalitarian world economy where the burdens of debt are shared equitably and the well-being of people and the planet takes precedence over corporate interests. Democratisation of international debt is not just a step but a crucial leap towards realising this vision of a fairer and more sustainable future.

In this way, different trajectories of international debt trap diplomacy, which use debt as a tool to control resources, undermine states and governments in countries outside the Westphalian outlook. The debt is not only an economic tool but also a weapon of political leverage. Developed countries use debt as a tool of their economic and political agendas to dominate world economy and politics in order to pursue the project of debt-led capitalist dependency as a dominant global system. The paper argues that it is time to democratise the rules, regulations and institutions that govern international debt to ensure an egalitarian political economy of development focusing on people and the planet. It engages with the alternative Chinese debt-based engagement with Africa.

Peer-to-Peer (P2P) Banking or Monetisation of Interpersonal Relationships

The Sumerian civilisation, one of the earliest known societies, had sophisticated systems of lending, borrowing, credit and debt. These systems were based on mutual trust and social currency, allowing individuals to engage in economic transactions without the need for physical money or barter. Instead, social bonds and communal trust underpinned these interactions, facilitating trade and the distribution of resources. This foundation of trust was crucial for the development of early markets and the overall growth of human civilisation. Social currency operated on the principle that individuals could rely on each other within their communities, creating a network of reciprocal obligations and support. These informal financial systems were essential for maintaining social cohesion and enabling economic activities.

As human societies evolved, the rise of feudalism and capitalism introduced significant changes to these trust-based systems. Economic relationships that were once informal and personal became formalised, legalised and institutionalised. The establishment of legal frameworks and banking institutions standardised lending and borrowing practices, providing a more structured and reliable system for managing credit and debt. This formalisation helped to support larger-scale economic activities and fostered the growth of global trade. In the modern era, technological advancements and the digital revolution are once again transforming the landscape of lending and borrowing. The development of peer-to-peer (P2P) lending platforms represents a significant shift in how financial transactions are conducted. The history of lending and borrowing reveals a continuous evolution from informal, trust-based systems to formalised, institutionalised practices and now to digitally enabled P2P platforms.

The advent of the digital revolution has played a pivotal role in the expansion of P2P lending. As a result of technological innovations and the growth of the platform economy, the P2P lending market has experienced substantial growth over the past decade. Analysts predict that this trend will continue, with the volume of P2P lending expected to reach an astounding one trillion US dollars by 2050. Online platforms and digital tools have streamlined the lending process, offering greater accessibility, convenience and efficiency. These platforms use sophisticated algorithms to match lenders with borrowers, assess creditworthiness and manage transactions, thereby reducing the time and costs associated with traditional lending methods. It is argued that the digital revolution has not only expanded the reach and capabilities of P2P lending but has also positioned it as a major player in the future of global finance.

The proponents of capitalism often assert that it fosters innovation. The priest of finance capital claims that P2P lending represents a groundbreaking idea within finance capital that addresses the institutional lending crisis by creating online marketplace platforms. These platforms enable lenders to directly lend money to individuals or small businesses, bypassing traditional financial institutions. The P2P lending solves the institutional lending crisis by developing online marketplace platforms. It is argued further that P2P lending promotes alternative financing methods. By eliminating the need for traditional financial institutions in the lending process, P2P platforms not only provide more accessible funding options for borrowers but also offer attractive investment opportunities for lenders. This innovative approach helps to democratise finance, making it more inclusive and efficient.

P2P lending, commonly branded as 'social lending' or 'crowd lending', is often categorised under the umbrella of the 'sharing economy' for the sake of mass appeal. This designation suggests a system where resources are shared among individuals, fostering a sense of community and collective benefit. However, the actual mechanics of P2P lending diverge significantly from these idealistic claims.

In practice, P2P lending involves individuals or businesses borrowing money directly from other individuals through online platforms, bypassing traditional financial institutions. While this might seem to align with the principles of a sharing economy – where goods and services are distributed among a community – P2P lending lacks the communal and altruistic aspects typically associated with such economies. The primary motivation behind P2P lending is financial gain rather than social good. Lenders participate to earn interest on their money, and borrowers seek loans often because they can obtain more favourable terms than those offered by traditional banks. This transactional nature emphasises profit over community welfare, contrasting sharply with the sharing economy's ethos of mutual benefit and resource sharing.

Moreover, the risk involved in P2P lending is borne individually by the lenders, who may face significant financial loss if borrowers default on their loans. This individual risk further underscores the lack of collective support and communal risk-sharing that would be present in a true sharing economy model. P2P lending is marketed under the appealing labels of 'social lending' and 'crowd lending' and is positioned within the sharing economy framework, its operational realities reveal a system that is fundamentally profit-driven and individualistic, lacking the community-oriented principles that define a genuine sharing economy.

There is no doubt that the P2P lending and borrowing system fundamentally transforms traditional financial interactions. Unlike conventional banking, which relies heavily on institutional trust and regulatory frameworks, P2P platforms leverage personal trust and social networks to facilitate financial transactions. This shift allows individuals to directly lend and borrow money

from each other without intermediaries, thus monetising the informal processes that have historically existed in many communities. By commodifying
these social foundations, P2P lending alters the dynamics of economic interactions. It turns personal relationships and trust into marketable assets, creating
new opportunities for individuals who might be underserved by traditional
banking systems. However, it also introduces new risks and challenges, as the
absence of formal regulatory oversight can lead to issues related to trustworthi-
ness, repayment and legal recourse.

Despite its innovative approach, P2P lending should not be seen as a
replacement for the cooperative banking system. Cooperative banks are mem-
ber-owned financial institutions that operate based on principles of shared
ownership and democratic decision-making. They are designed to serve the
financial needs of their members, often focusing on community development
and social goals alongside profitability. In contrast, P2P platforms are primarily market-driven and profit-oriented, focusing on facilitating transactions
between individual lenders and borrowers.

In conclusion, it can be said that while P2P lending provides an intrigu-
ing alternative to traditional banking by leveraging social trust and personal
networks, it does not fulfil the same role as cooperative banks. P2P lending and
borrowing systems are not sustainable alternatives like the cooperative banking system.

American Shock Therapy on European Social Democracy

The NATO-led, imperialist-imposed ongoing Russian war on Ukraine is
not only creating a daily human catastrophe but also reshaping the present
and future of Western Europe through American shock therapy. This unjust
war has led to deaths, destitution, significant civilian suffering, with countless
lives disrupted, communities devastated and families ruined. This completely
avoidable war is pushing the entire European continent into a state of nuclear
war and turmoil. The everyday escalation has resulted in widespread instability, economic hardship, political unrest and human tragedy. The ripple effects
of this war are being felt in countries far removed from the front lines, exacerbating existing tensions and creating new challenges for the safety and security
of European people and their livelihoods.

Who cares about human lives and families when war is a profitable business? The grim reality is that the war economy benefits a select few, with

European and American defence contractors, arms manufacturers and other industries profiting immensely from this war. This profit-driven aspect of war often overshadows the human cost, with policymakers and corporations prioritising financial gains over the well-being of individuals and families caught in the crossfires and wars in the name of national sovereignty, for which the most courageous, idealistic young and working-class people sacrifice their lives.

The war in Ukraine is more than just a profitable war; it aims to fundamentally transform the nature of the welfare state, society and social democracy in Western Europe. Despite the capitalist framework, Western Europe remains a relatively prosperous society that offers health care, education, unemployment, housing and childcare benefits, old age care and other welfare benefits to its population, extending beyond the profit-driven logic of the market. This war-led strategic transformation is not merely about economic gain but about reshaping the very fabric of society.

Western European countries have long been characterised by their robust welfare systems, which provide a safety net for all citizens and ensure a higher quality of life. These systems are designed to mitigate the harsher aspects of capitalism, ensuring that even the most vulnerable members of society are cared for. The Russian war in Ukraine disrupts this balance. The redirection of resources towards military efforts and defence spending leads to austerity measures, which weaken these social safety nets. Additionally, the influx of refugees and the broader geopolitical instability strain public services and social cohesion. So, the implications of the war in Ukraine extend far beyond its borders, potentially impacting the welfare states and social democracies of Western Europe. It is a pivotal moment that may redefine the relationship between the state, the market and the individual in Europe.

The welfare states and policies in Western Europe present significant challenges for American health, pharmaceutical and insurance corporations seeking to expand their profitable businesses in the region. These robust welfare systems provide comprehensive health care, education and social security benefits, reducing the market potential for private American companies in these sectors. The extensive public provision of services means there is less demand for the private, profit-driven health and educational alternatives that dominate the American market.

Similarly, the availability of relatively cheaper Russian oil and natural gas has been instrumental in maintaining the high quality of life in Western Europe. This affordability in energy costs is a key factor in sustaining the economic stability and prosperity of the region. Such a situation creates problems for American oil and gas companies, as it limits their ability to penetrate and profit from European markets. The reliance on Russian energy sources reduces the demand for more expensive American alternatives. The geopolitical and economic dynamics surrounding the war in Ukraine could potentially alter these circumstances.

As Western Europe has reduced its dependence on Russian energy, American oil and gas companies find new opportunities to enter the market and profit hugely. However, this shift led to a rising cost of living due to the cost of higher energy prices and economic strain for European consumers and industries, potentially impacting the overall quality of life. In this way, the Russian war in Ukraine has transformed the welfare policies and energy dependencies in Western Europe and removed significant barriers for American corporations to expand their market presence in the region with the help of war shock.

American imperialism has effectively employed its doctrine of shock therapy across various regions, including post-communist Eastern Europe, Latin America, the Middle East, Africa, Asia and even within its own borders over its own people, all in the pursuit of corporate profit. Yankee imperialism, led by the United States, supported by its European allies, continues to fund the Ukrainian war, driven by strategic corporate objectives of making super profits at the cost of their people. Meanwhile, the Russian government persists in its aggressive actions, prolonging a senseless war that brings suffering to countless people.

For American imperialism, wars and conflicts serve as long-term tools of shock therapy, rapidly and drastically transforming societies, states and governments in defence of its corporate interests. This prioritisation of war-inflicted crisis management over addressing the welfare needs of the people is evident, particularly in Europe today. The ongoing imperialist war in Ukraine, coupled with tensions with Russia, serves as American shock therapy intended to reshape the nature of welfare states, governments and social democracies in Western Europe. The underlying aim is to advance corporate interests and consolidate power, even at the expense of human lives and stability in the region.

The challenge facing the European people is clear: to unequivocally oppose warfare both within and beyond Europe's borders and to dismantle the imperialist and military apparatus known as NATO to cultivate enduring peace and stability in the region. The pursuit of a world free from conflict cannot entertain the racist notions of European and American exceptionalism and supremacy. The struggle against war, capitalism and imperialism is a shared endeavour, transcending borders and ideologies. Peace and prosperity are not mere aspirations but essential and inherent rights for all humanity, irrespective of nationality or creed. This vision of peace is universal and indivisible, requiring collective action and solidarity to confront the forces that perpetuate the shock therapy of war, violence and injustice.

Conclusion

Profit-seeking capitalism and its rent-seeking proponents persist in employing strategies of conflict, contradictions and collaboration with China, all the while undermining the Chinese development models that diverge from capitalism. The Chinese alternatives are anathema to ideologues of capitalism. This inseparable capitalist contradiction persists as Western capitalism and its governments collaborate with China, benefiting from its skilled labour and abundance of production of essential, high-quality goods and services at low costs. These products are indispensable for daily life in advanced capitalist countries across America and Europe.

The American and European stance on the Russian war in Ukraine and Israel's war in Palestine exposes the contradictory nature of capitalist states and governments. These contradictions are intrinsic to capitalism, evident in the political positions of capitalist countries in Europe and America that thrive on conflicts to control natural and human resources. The unending conflicts and crises also serve to conceal the failures of capitalism and its democratic deficits (Amin, 2010).

CHAPTER 6

RESISTANCE AND CAPITALISM

Introduction

Despite relentless efforts by capitalist forces to destroy, delegitimise and diminish all progressive ideas and movements, resistance endures. This resistance to capitalism remains vibrant and persistent, continually adapting and finding new forms of expression. As capitalism advances, it forms alliances with various institutions and cultures to promote reactionary elements, ranging from meditation to education and from schools to marketplaces, to undermine egalitarian and progressive society.

The resilience of resistance lies in its ability to adapt and evolve. In educational settings, for instance, progressive movements advocate for critical thinking and inclusive, decolonised and decarbonised curriculums that challenge the status quo. In marketplaces, ethical consumerism and fair-trade practices gain traction as more people seek alternatives to exploitative capitalist models.

Cultural domains such as art, music and literatures have become battlegrounds where progressive ideas flourish and challenge the dominant capitalist narratives. The integration of mindfulness and meditation in resistance movements showcases a holistic approach, emphasising mental well-being and collective consciousness as vital components of social change.

In this way, resistance to capitalism is multifaceted and dynamic, continually finding new avenues and alliances to sustain its momentum against the ever-evolving capitalist structures. This enduring spirit of resistance signifies a profound commitment to envisioning and striving for a just world free from all forms of exploitations and inequalities.

Meditation and Capitalism

The working masses have been practising meditation for centuries to survive the ever-alienating ordeals of various forms of patriarchy, feudalism and capitalism. Meditation has become a coping mechanism to confront the challenges of capitalism, which breeds various forms of alienation, inequalities and exploitation on a daily basis. However, meditation has been co-opted by the consumeristic and therapeutic cultures of capitalism, where the disciplining of body and mind is central to domesticating and controlling the working masses.

The meditation centers, which have been commercialised and medicalised, serve as instruments of a social system where individuals self-discipline in the name of self-help under the guidance of experts (gurus) to ensure a social, spiritual and cultural order that aligns with the requirements of capitalism. Such monetised processes of homogeneous institutionalisation, standardisation of practice and marketisation have destroyed the collective foundations of meditation as a social and spiritual practice. Despite this, many European scholars still promote meditation as unabashedly anti-capitalist (Scherer & Waistell, 2018). Such an uncritical justification promotes neo-traditionalist values in the name of meditation.

Meditation serves capitalism in different ways. Firstly, the atomisation of the individual self and consciousness is crucial for capitalism to expand by dismantling the shared foundations of individual lives and collective consciousness, promoting a profit-seeking commodity market. Meditation, as a tool of atomisation of the 'individual self', aids in the processes of deconditioning individual experiences and consciousness from their social and shared experiences of collective consciousness. It helps in the normalisation of capitalist alienation. Meditation supports the conditions that reconcile people with the unnatural, abnormal and exploitative capitalist system. Meditation training for mindfulness is a tool of governance in the name of self-optimisation in the service of capitalism (Carvalho, 2021).

Meditation, in the name of building resilience, individualises sufferings and silences the conditions of collective and radical consciousness by domesticating individuals to face their challenges alone. Meditation under capitalism functions as a mode of self-governance, empowering individuals to attribute their own miseries to themselves and to independently overcome them with their meditative power alone. This conditioning grants carte blanche to capitalist institutions, structures and processes, allowing them to persist in their unchecked exploitation of both human beings and nature. Capitalism produces loneliness, mental health issues and various other forms of vulnerabilities. In response, it promotes meditation as a means for individuals to address and reconcile these issues on a personal level.

Global, regional, national and local celebrities promote meditation as a mindful revolution, suggesting it can spark a universal renaissance and serve as a panacea for all contemporary societal ailments. However, this culture of naive ethos merely promotes capitalism by individualising alternatives and eroding the radical consciousness people derive from their own labour and working conditions. Individual alienation is not solely a result of individual actions; rather, it is an inherent outcome and integral aspect of capitalism as a system. No amount of meditation can resolve the issues of alienation within capitalism. Therefore, promoting meditation as an alternative is merely a naive diversionary strategy.

The commodification and standardisation of meditation practices have led to the exponential growth of the mindfulness market. This industry is rapidly expanding as a low-investment, high-return service sector where profit is based on individual alienation. In this way, capitalism and the meditation industry complement each other: one produces alienation and the other offers temporary relief from it. Meditation has become a lucrative and burgeoning business. In this cycle of profit-driven therapeutic religiosity between capitalism and meditation, alienated individuals endure false hopes in life. Neither capitalism nor meditation provides any permanent solutions to the issues of alienation and other forms of vulnerabilities within capitalist societies.

The missionaries of meditation and the messiahs of capitalism work together to normalise and naturalise the ravages of capitalism, while working people search for elusive happiness within. It is like seeking salvation only after death. Therefore, it is time for working people to reclaim their collective practice of meditation beyond the market-driven logic of therapeutic culture within capitalism.

Education and Consciousness under Technofeudalism

Education stands on the twin pillars of essentialist and emancipatory consciousness. Education, in terms of skills, qualifications, grades, marks and employability, reflects the essentialist criteria of consciousness, which are crucial for meeting the everyday requirements of human life and ensuring a dignified living. It plays a vital role in helping individuals recover from poverty, homelessness, hunger and illiteracy.

The emancipatory consciousness within education addresses these essential needs while also aspiring to higher goals. It aims to create a society free from all forms of exploitation, inequality and discrimination, including those based on gender, race, caste and other social divisions. By fostering critical thinking and promoting values of justice and equality, emancipatory education empowers individuals to challenge oppressive structures and work towards a more just and equitable world. This dual focus ensures that education not only equips people with the tools needed for personal survival and success but also nurtures a commitment to collective well-being and social transformation (De Lissovoy, 2010).

Mere qualifications defined by certificates do not foster emancipatory and egalitarian consciousness. While individuals may be educated in terms of formal credentials, their social and moral consciousness often falls to a low point in their everyday practice. Education, in many cases, breeds hypocrites of various kinds. Many educated and well-qualified individuals are reactionary and uncivilised in their behaviours, celebrating and upholding regressive values.

The number of such individuals and the prevalence of an essentialist trend within education are growing. Educational institutions, curriculum developers and teachers have largely failed to instil emancipatory ideals within their learning and teaching practices. The focus on the essentialist aspects of education, such as skills development for employability, has been prioritised to meet the demands of the burgeoning techno-feudal markets and their idle capitalist masters. These masters live off rent without producing any real social value or meaningful commodities for society.

As a result, the educational system increasingly caters to the needs of a techno-feudal economy, emphasising practical skills for economic survival while neglecting the development of critical thinking and social consciousness. This shift has contributed to a society where educational attainment does not necessarily translate to enlightened or progressive thought, but rather to the perpetuation of existing power structures and inequalities based on reactionary and immoral ideals.

In the age of technofeudalism, the rent-seeking nature of various political, social and cultural institutions, systems and processes has become pervasive. This has fostered a culture where individuals, families and religious denominations operate like rent-extracting machines in their most brutal form, devoid of accountability, responsibility and human concern. In these processes, relationships between and among individuals and various interpersonal interactions have become transactional, dominated by self-pleasure and self-preservation at every step of human life. This phenomenon has been accelerated by digital media, social media and traditional celebrity culture, where an individual's success and failure are determined by the power of money.

Many of these celebrities are school dropouts or have never attended an educational institution, yet they serve as brand ambassadors of technofeudalism and its ideals in everyday consumerism, defined by both tangible and intangible commodity consumption. These celebrities, as purveyors of techno-feudal dreams, often celebrate low grades or failure in their school or college examinations as if they were achievements. In doing so, they leverage their celebrity status to undermine education and human consciousness grounded in science, reason, rationality and secularism. This celebration of ignorance perpetuates a cycle where education and critical thinking are devalued, further entrenching the power of techno-feudal systems.

In such a context, it is crucial to revive the radical promises of education that can cultivate higher consciousness and skills for the progressive transformation of individuals and society based on solidarity, peace and prosperity. Education must go beyond the mere acquisition of certificates and qualifications, striving instead to develop individuals who are not only skilled but also deeply aware of social justice and committed to positive change.

To achieve this, educational institutions, curriculum developers and teachers need to integrate emancipatory ideals into their teaching practices. This means fostering critical thinking, encouraging empathy and promoting values of equality and justice. Education should aim to empower students to challenge oppressive structures and work towards creating a more equitable and inclusive society.

Moreover, the curriculum should include diverse and decolonial perspectives and histories, teaching students to appreciate and respect differences while working together for common goals. Collaborative projects, community engagement and service learning can be effective in instilling these values. By connecting theoretical knowledge with practical action, students can see the impact of their learning on real-world issues.

Ultimately, the goal is to create a holistic educational experience that prepares individuals not just for economic survival but for active and meaningful participation in society. This approach can help rebuild a sense of collective responsibility and foster a culture of solidarity, peace and prosperity. By reviving the radical promises of education, people can work towards a future where learning is a powerful tool for social transformation and the betterment of all.

Predicaments of All Forms of Lazy Emotions and Idealisms

Emotion and idealism, in their dual manifestations of utopian aspirations and real-world expressions, serve as the twin pillars underpinning the existence of human life. These elements intricately shape not only the present circumstances but also the future trajectories of individuals and families. Moreover, they exert a profound influence on the broader fabric of society, informing the dynamics of social, political, economic, cultural and religious institutions and processes.

Emotion, with its kaleidoscope of feelings ranging from love and empathy to anger and fear, provides the emotional resonance that colours human interactions and relationships. It infuses our daily experiences with meaning, guiding our decisions and actions in both personal and communal contexts. It is emotion that defines life in all its forms. Emotion without material manifestations are utopian self-defeats and often create an environment of hypocrisy.

Idealism, on the other hand, represents the lofty emotional aspirations and visions that propel individuals and societies to move forward on a progressive path. It inspires innovation, drives social progress and fuels the pursuit of justice and equality. Whether in the form of personal dreams or collective movements, idealism serves as a catalyst for change, challenging the status quo and envisioning a better future. In its utopian guise, idealism dares to imagine a world free from conflict, inequality and suffering – a realm where harmony reigns supreme and human potential knows no bounds. While such utopian visions may seem distant or unattainable, they serve as guiding stars, illuminating the path towards a more just and equitable society. However, idealism without material manifestations creates a culture of timeless stagnancy and uncreative laziness in both individual and family lives. Revolution dies in lazy virtues without their material and non-material manifestations.

Both emotion and idealism play a vital role in both radical revolutionary situations and in all relationships beyond blood and defined boundaries.

In times of radical revolution, emotion serves as the fuel that ignites the flames of social, political and cultural transformations. It stirs the passions of individuals, driving them to challenge oppressive systems and envision alternative futures. Emotion fuels the fervour of rebellion, uniting diverse voices under the banner of collective liberation. It fosters solidarity among disparate groups, forging bonds of empathy and resilience in the face of adversity. Moreover, emotion imbues revolutionary movements with a sense of urgency and purpose, compelling individuals to take bold action in pursuit of justice and freedom. Simultaneously, idealism acts as the guiding light that illuminates the path towards transformative change. It inspires revolutionaries to envision a world liberated from tyranny and inequality, daring to imagine possibilities beyond the constraints of the status quo. Idealism infuses revolutionary movements with a sense of hope and possibility, motivating individuals to persist in the face of seemingly insurmountable odds. It fosters a vision of collective empowerment, encouraging communities to reclaim agency over their own destinies and shape a future grounded in principles of equality and justice.

Beyond the realm of revolution, both emotion and idealism continue to play a pivotal role in shaping relationships that transcend conventional boundaries. Emotion forms the bedrock of human connection, fostering bonds of empathy, compassion and understanding. It underpins the intimacy shared between partners, the camaraderie among friends and families and the solidarity among allies. Emotion enables individuals to navigate the complexities of interpersonal dynamics, fostering trust and mutual support in the face of adversity.

Similarly, idealism infuses relationships with a sense of purpose and shared vision. It encourages individuals to aspire towards common goals and values, uniting them in the pursuit of collective flourishing. Idealism inspires acts of generosity, altruism and selflessness, as individuals strive to create a more just and equitable world for themselves and future generations. It fosters a sense of belonging and community, inviting individuals to contribute their unique talents and perspectives towards a shared vision of a better tomorrow, both within the context of family lives and social and political situations.

In both radical revolutionary situations and interpersonal relationships, emotion and idealism intertwine to shape the fabric of human experience. These twin qualities remind us of our daily existence and human capacity for empathy, resilience and collective action, urging us to envision possibilities beyond the confines of the present moment. Together, they inspire us to strive towards a world grounded in principles of justice, equality and human dignity, where every individual could thrive and flourish.

Yet, idealism also confronts the harsh realities of the world, grappling with the complexities of power dynamics, historical injustices and human fallibility. In its real-world manifestations, idealism contends with the practical constraints and trade-offs inherent in effecting change within existing systems and structures. Despite these challenges, however, it persists as a driving force for progress, advocating for reform, challenging injustice and striving towards a more inclusive and compassionate world. Together, emotion and idealism constitute the beating heart of human existence, shaping our individual journeys and collective destinies. They remind us of our capacity for empathy, imagination and resilience, urging us to aspire towards a future guided by compassion, justice and human dignity.

However, lazy idealism devoid of accountability and emotions lacking material and non-material manifestations generate reactionary values that domesticate individuals, stifle creativity, disrupt families and propel society into a dark abyss of traditional and neo-traditional frameworks where feudalism thrives, eroding human emotions, idealism and their inherent values for a progressive, peaceful and prosperous life.

Therefore, science, reason and rational analysis, grounded in empathy and understanding, can steer emotions and idealism towards a path of accountability, rooted in tangible manifestations. Providing unconditional support to unproductive laziness is a destructive course that undermines progressive human potential, emotions and idealism.

Laziness as a Form of Resistance

The productivist ideology lies at the core of the profit-making pyramid of capitalism. It perpetuates a relentless cycle characterised by busy schedules, workplace tension, an imbalance in work-life equilibrium and a pervasive sense of alienation. These challenges afflict individuals across various professions, all of whom contribute their labour for wages in exchange for the creation of value (the core of profit for capitalists). However, rather than fostering prosperity for all, the productivist ideology serves to enrich capitalism while perpetuating poverty among the masses (Butko, 2018).

Capitalism as a system thrives on the perpetual cycle of production and reproduction, sustained by the necessities and desires of everyday life within the framework of capitalist structures. Regardless of the stage of development, these structures persist in our society, ensnaring individuals in a web of risks, insecurities, low wages and exploitation. The pillars of the free market economic project, intertwined with the meritocratic political spectrum, further exacerbate these inequalities. They uphold a system where profit accumulation and individual success are prioritised over the well-being of the collective. Thus, the productivist ideology not only sustains the capitalist machinery but also perpetuates a cycle of inequality and hardship for the masses (Lefebvre, 1976).

The May Day promise of an equitable capital-labour accord, advocating for eight hours of work, eight hours of leisure and eight hours of rest, has withered away in the face of evolving forms of capitalism, especially with the advent of the digital revolution. The traditional collective wage bargaining, once championed by trade union movements, is losing its efficacy as platform economies emerge within the capitalist framework. These platforms further segment the workforce based on various criteria such as skill levels, education and geographic location, creating hierarchies of labour that exacerbate existing inequalities.

In the contemporary landscape, work under capitalism serves not only as a means of survival but also as the root cause of myriad social, economic, cultural and political woes. It perpetuates and amplifies various forms of inequality and exploitative relationships, casting a shadow over the promise of prosperity for all. The seemingly innate drive for work, often fuelled by the commitment and morality of the working class, paradoxically reinforces its own subjugation to capital. This passion for work, while admirable in its dedication, unwittingly perpetuates the bondage to capital in the daily lives of working people, entrenching them deeper within the system.

The technological and digital revolution was anticipated to liberate working people, affording them more leisure time to pursue socially meaningful activities by enhancing productivity. However, this vision has been overshadowed by the reality of technology infiltrating even the most private spaces of people's lives. In today's job landscape, workers in sectors such as information technology find themselves toiling long hours, often without job security or autonomy over their labour. The rise of technology-led work has blurred the boundaries between professional and personal life, with tasks encroaching into people's bedrooms and bathrooms. This intrusion disrupts the traditional notion of work-life balance, leaving workers feeling tethered to their jobs around the clock.

Moreover, the principles of bureaucratic Taylorism, emphasising efficiency and standardisation, have become even more deeply entrenched in contemporary workplaces. This trend serves to intensify the exploitation of workers by imposing greater pressure to accelerate the pace of work, often at the expense of their well-being. These challenges are diminishing the influence of trade union movements, which historically served as a bulwark against worker exploitation. In the current landscape, workers find themselves more vulnerable than ever, lacking the collective bargaining power that characterised the industrial era. This vulnerability exposes them to exploitation and precarious working conditions, highlighting the urgent need for renewed efforts to protect workers' rights in the digital age.

The capitalist work regime ensnares workers within its productivist culture, wherein true emancipation for workers lies in liberation from work itself. There is little merit in fervently dedicating oneself to work and employers when the fruits of labour produced by the working classes are siphoned off by a privileged few bourgeois. Engaging with capitalism as a system of social, political, cultural and economic organisation only serves to perpetuate the organised plunder sanctioned by authority.

Consider the implications if working people were to collectively cease their labour and defy the productivist ideology of capitalism. What would be the future of capitalist work if workers exclusively pursued socially meaningful endeavours aligned with genuine needs and desires? And what might become of the working population if they were to embrace laziness as a political choice? While imagining a world devoid of work in the midst of the technological revolution may seem utopian, it raises profound questions about the nature of labour and its role in society. Could 'No to work', disengagement and non-cooperation be the only viable responses to these fundamental inquiries?

In contemplating these notions, it becomes evident that the current structure of capitalism perpetuates a cycle of exploitation and alienation for the working class. Embracing alternatives that prioritise human well-being over relentless productivity may hold the key to unlocking a future where individuals are liberated from the shackles of labour and empowered to pursue lives socially rich in meaning and fulfilment.

In a society steeped in the decadence of capitalism, laziness takes on a new significance – it becomes a virtue. Choosing to disengage from the relentless pursuit of profit within the confines of the capitalist market is not merely an act of idleness but a potent form of political, social and cultural resistance against an increasingly antisocial culture that commodifies human labour. In the face of a system devoid of humanity, where individuals are reduced to mere cogs in the machinery of production, the concept of 'working for wages' loses its appeal. Capitalism, with its relentless pursuit of profit at the expense of human dignity, offers no semblance of compassion or empathy. In such a system, the only respite from suffering comes with death, highlighting the inherent exploitation embedded within its framework of price and value.

Let us envision a society where the essence of life transcends the constraints of monetised time, where individuals are liberated to explore the richness of existence beyond the dictates of the market. By embracing laziness as a means of tapping into inherent happiness and unleashing the creative potential inherent within every human being that paves the way for social progress, cooperation, solidarity, peace and prosperity. In this vision, the celebration of living labour extends beyond the confines of economic productivity, fostering a culture of genuine fulfilment and collective well-being. Let us dare to be lazy in the pursuit of a world where the true essence of humanity flourishes, unencumbered by the chains of capitalist exploitation. It is imperative to create a society where living labour can celebrate life beyond the capitalist framework of monetising time, people, place and environment. Let laziness be a form of resistance to capitalism. Let's be lazy to explore the inherent happiness within every human being and their creative abilities for social progress, cooperation, solidarity, peace and prosperity.

Global Voices: Progressive Idealism among Students and Youths Across Borders

The geriatric ideology of feudalism, patriarchy, nationalism, religious culture, market-led consumerism, monetised society and capitalism continues to propagate the notion that contemporary youths and students are deviants, lazy, unproductive and useless idiots. They are depicted as being addicted to the digital world, lacking direction and commitment to their own lives, as well as to the state and society. They are also portrayed as lacking a moral compass and any sense of idealism. These propagandas persist in shaping mainstream public discourse without facing scrutiny, serving the interests of the geriatric ruling and non-ruling elites by maintaining their hegemonic power over the masses without challenge. There are consistent efforts by gerontological elites, both in minor forms within families and major forms at local, regional, national and international levels, to undermine the progressive commitments of students and youths. These elites seek to suppress their idealism for radical social, political and cultural transformation on a global scale. However, these geriatric, elitist and ruling class propagandas against students and youths are far from the truth.

Throughout history, the dynamism and fervour of students and young people have consistently positioned them as vanguards in the fight against entrenched systems of oppression. From the shackles of feudalism to the chains of colonialism and imperialism, students and youths have steadfastly confronted and challenged structures and processes that perpetuate inequality and exploitation. Their unwavering commitment to justice and equality has propelled them to the forefront of countless movements aimed at dismantling systems of power that perpetuate injustice. Whether rallying against the subjugation of colonial rule, resisting the rise of fascist regimes, or challenging the insidious grip of capitalism, students and youths have fearlessly stood on the front lines, often at great personal risk. Their collective struggle, etched in the annals of progressive history, serves as a testament to the profound impact of youthful idealism and activism in shaping the course of social and political transformation. Through their sacrifices, resilience,and unwavering dedication, students and youths have not only inspired change in their own time but have also paved the way for future generations to continue the fight for a more just and equitable world.

Contemporary struggles for peace, environmental preservation, justice, equality, the advancement of science and the promotion of secularism remain primarily driven by students and youths worldwide. The transnational character of today's students and youths is defined by the anti-war movements spanning from Vietnam, Iraq, Afghanistan, Yemen and Ukraine to the ongoing struggles in Palestine against Israeli genocide and occupation. The youths and students cannot be held responsible for climate change, warfare, commodification and the alienation of life in society today. Instead, they are victims of patriarchy, feudalism, capitalism and imperialist systems that perpetuate exploitation, inequality, unemployment, poverty, hunger, homelessness and widespread suffering on a global scale. University and college campuses are teeming with anti-war protests, climate action groups and various socially committed organisations dedicated to creating a better world. They are actively engaged in striving for a future that is sustainable, egalitarian and just.

Labelling students and young people as deviants, amoral and fickle undermines their dedication to fostering progressive social change. Such derogatory categorisations not only disparage their potential but also serve to weaken their resolve in challenging the entrenched power structures maintained by older generations. These hegemonic systems perpetuate exploitation, hierarchy and inequality across society, politics, the economy and culture, ultimately benefiting only a select few while marginalising the masses. By dismissing the agency and commitment of the youth, these derogatory labels perpetuate a cycle of disempowerment, hindering the collective efforts towards meaningful societal transformation. Embracing the diverse perspectives and passionate activism of young people is essential for dismantling oppressive systems and forging a more just and equitable future for all.

Students and youths serve as catalysts for social and political transformation, wielding their energy, passion and idealism to challenge the status quo and push for positive change. Therefore, it is not just important but imperative to champion and defend the rights and voices of students and youths in our society. They represent the vanguard of progress, tirelessly advocating for justice, equality and human rights. By empowering and supporting them, we invest in a better tomorrow, one where the aspirations of the younger generation are nurtured and realised. Upholding their rights and amplifying their voices ensures that our societies evolve towards greater inclusivity, equity and opportunity for all. In essence, by safeguarding the agency and dignity of students and youths, we pave the way for a brighter and more promising future for generations to come.

The initial stride towards actualising these aspirations necessitates the cessation of the incessant propagation of false, derogatory and defamatory narratives directed at students and youths by the entrenched geriatric power structures. These unfounded attacks not only malign the character and intentions of the younger generation but also serve to suppress their influence and hinder their efforts towards positive change. It is imperative to dismantle the pervasive narrative constructed by the geriatric ideology of power, which seeks to delegitimise the voices and actions of youth by portraying them as unreliable, reckless and unworthy of meaningful participation in societal discourse. By challenging and debunking these baseless stereotypes, we can foster an environment where the agency and contributions of students and youths are valued and respected. This entails promoting narratives that highlight the resilience, creativity and potential for leadership within the younger demographic. Embracing the diversity of perspectives and experiences offered by students and youths enriches our collective understanding of social issues and strengthens our capacity for innovative problem-solving. In essence, by rejecting the false narratives perpetuated by geriatric power structures and instead affirming the agency and potential of the younger generation, we lay the groundwork for a more inclusive and equitable society. This shift in perspective not only paves the way for meaningful collaboration across generations but also ensures that the voices of students and youths are integral to shaping the future direction of our communities and institutions for a better future.

Reclaim Free Market

Historically, markets were established by working people to serve their everyday needs and desires. These markets were grounded in the local communities they served, reflecting the economic and social realities of the time. People would come together in these markets to trade goods and services, fostering a sense of community and mutual dependence. The primary focus was on meeting the essential needs of the population, ensuring access to food, clothing, tools and other necessities. In these early markets, transactions were straight-forward, often based on barter or simple currency systems and were charac-terised by direct interactions between producers and consumers. This setup allowed for greater transparency and trust, as buyers could directly engage with sellers, understand the origins and quality of the products and negotiate fair prices. The primary aim was to facilitate the exchange of goods and ser-vices in a manner that benefited all parties involved, enhancing the well-being of the entire community.

The markets have historically played a crucial role in transforming the economic activities of producers into social activities, thereby establishing and nurturing relationships between producers and consumers. In its earliest forms, the market was more than just a venue for buying and selling goods; it was a vibrant social and cultural institution where people interacted, exchanged ideas and built community ties. By facilitating direct interactions between pro-ducers and consumers, markets enabled a deeper understanding and apprecia-tion of the goods being traded. Consumers could meet the people who grew their food, made their clothes or crafted their tools, creating a sense of trust and mutual respect. This direct relationship fostered a sense of accountability among producers, who took pride in the quality of their work, knowing they were serving their neighbours and community members.

The market, both as an institution and as a process, was originally intended to facilitate life, making it easier for people to obtain the goods and services they needed. It was designed to serve the community, providing a space where people could exchange resources efficiently and equitably. The core idea was to enhance the quality of life for everyone involved by ensuring the availabil-ity and accessibility of essential products and services and fostering economic and social interdependence. The market was an institution of solidarity and a process of cooperation for a meaningful life and mutual existence. As socie-ties grew more complex and interdependent economies expanded, the nature of markets evolved. However, the foundational principles of the market were changed in the name of promoting the free market.

However, the so-called free market in its current form has deviated signifi-cantly from this original purpose. Today, it often controls everyday lives, func-tioning primarily as a tool for profit-making for a select few capitalists. Instead of serving the broader community, the modern market prioritises the interests of large corporations and wealthy individuals. These entities have the power to influence market dynamics to their advantage, often at the expense of the average consumer and small producer. This shift has led to a situation where the market dictates the terms of economic, social and cultural life, influencing everything from job availability and wages to the prices of essential goods and services. The focus on maximising profit has resulted in practices that undermine the well-being of the broader population, such as monopolistic behaviours, exploitation of labour and environmental degradation.

In essence, the market has transformed from a community-oriented institution into a profit-driven mechanism that primarily benefits a small elite, often leaving the majority of people with little control over their economic, social, political and cultural purposes of their everyday lives. This distortion of the market's original purpose highlights the need for a re-evaluation of how economic systems are structured and governed to ensure they truly serve the needs and desires of all people, not just a privileged few.

The concept of a free market in all its forms within a capitalist system is often touted as being both free and fair. However, this notion is far from reality. The free market is intended to provide freedom to both consumers and producers, yet in practice, neither group truly experiences this freedom. In a so-called free market, consumers and producers are not provided with sufficient information about the products, their producers or the costs involved in production. This lack of transparency leaves consumers in the dark about the reasoning behind pricing decisions. Instead of being a truly open and fair system, the free market operates as a controlled mechanism of global capitalism.

Large corporations dominate this landscape, enhancing their profits by creating a disconnect between consumers and producers. They manipulate the market to establish independent pricing mechanisms that prioritise their interests, often leading to super-profits at the expense of fairness and transparency. Moreover, these corporations often engage in practices that stifle competition, such as forming monopolies or oligopolies, which further undermines the principles of a truly free market. As a result, consumers face higher prices and limited choices, while smaller producers struggle to survive in an environment skewed heavily in favour of big business. In essence, the so-called free market is less about freedom and fairness and more about the strategic manipulation of economic systems to benefit a select few, exacerbating inequality and reducing the agency of both consumers and producers.

Over time, as markets grew and became more complex, these direct relationships were often replaced by more impersonal transactions. However, the fundamental role of the market in linking economic and social activities remains evident. Modern movements such as farmers' markets, local artisanal fairs and community-supported agriculture (CSA) programmes are efforts to rekindle these direct connections, emphasising the social dimensions of economic exchange. Technology and digital market platforms can facilitate these objectives if these digital infrastructures are controlled by the communities.

The market has historically been instrumental in converting economic activities into social ones, establishing meaningful relationships between producers and consumers. This legacy underscores the potential of markets to not only drive economic prosperity but also to build strong, connected communities. It is time to reclaim free and fair markets that serve as community hubs, where people gather not just to trade, but to socialise, share news and engage in cultural activities. These interactions helped to weave the economic fabric into the social fabric of the community, making economic activities a vital part of daily life and social cohesion. It is time to struggle to reclaim free market from free marketers of capitalism and defeat its market-driven culture of mass consumerism and alienation.

Reclaim Free Trade

Right-wing reactionaries assert that they uphold the concept of free trade under the banner of individual liberty, often referred to as consumer liberty. The Hayekian forces argue that free trade under capitalism enables consumers to have the freedom to choose from a variety of products and services, thus fostering a competitive market that benefits everyone. According to their perspective, minimal government intervention in the marketplace is essential for preserving personal freedoms and ensuring that individuals can make their own economic choices without undue restrictions. By advocating for free trade, they believe they are promoting a system where the consumer's power to decide drives innovation, quality and efficiency in the economy.

In reality, free trade under capitalism is neither free nor fair. It disrupts the natural relationship between producers and consumers, preventing the development of independent pricing mechanisms. Instead, it integrates both producers and consumers into a profit-driven system that prioritises corporate interests. Free trade under capitalism manipulates demand and supply to maximise profits, exerting both direct and indirect control over the processes of production, distribution and consumption. By doing so, it creates an economic environment where market forces are heavily influenced by those with the greatest financial power, often at the expense of smaller producers and consumers.

Such a system of free trade means trade is free for producers and consumers. It results in the growth of a system where real free trade between producers and consumers suffers. Consequently, economic inequalities are exacerbated and the autonomy of individual economic agents is significantly diminished. By manipulating market dynamics, free trade often benefits those with the greatest financial power, undermining the principles of fair competition and equitable economic participation of producers and consumers.

Free trade under capitalism destroys the social foundations of free trade. In this system, only consumers with purchasing power can participate in the trading process, which creates a fundamentally unfair economic and social environment. This approach dismantles the concept of trade as a social relationship built on mutual needs, trust and the interaction of free producers and free consumers.

Under capitalism, the dubious ideals of free trade – where all participants have equal opportunity and freedom to trade based on their needs and capabilities – are compromised. The focus shifts to profit maximisation and market dominance, often marginalising those without significant financial resources. As a result, the social aspects of trade, such as community building, equitable exchange and cooperative relationships, are eroded by the unfree trade under capitalism. In a fair trading system, trade acts as a form of social interaction where producers and consumers engage with each other based on mutual trust and shared needs. However, in a capitalist framework, the emphasis on profit and competition leads to exploitation, where powerful entities dictate terms and conditions that serve their interests rather than fostering genuine, trust-based relationships.

Moreover, the exclusion of individuals without purchasing power perpetuates inequality and social division. It prevents the creation of a truly inclusive economic system where everyone has an equal opportunity and access to benefit from trade. By focusing solely on economic gain, capitalism overlooks the broader social implications of trade and its potential to promote social cohesion and collective well-being.

In this way, capitalism promotes unfree trade and simultaneously destroys the social and collective foundations that make trade a meaningful and equitable social relationship. Therefore, it is important to reclaim the social foundations of free trade where producers and consumers are truly free. The reclamation process needs to shift towards an economic system that prioritises social equity, mutual trust and the inclusion of all participants, regardless of their purchasing power. Free access to trading commodities and services based on needs can help create an egalitarian economic order without the exploitation of producers and consumers under capitalism. It is time to reclaim free trade for the freedom of consumers and producers.

Conclusion

The history of human and social progress intertwines with the narrative of resistance. Throughout the ages, the evolution of humanity and its societies has been deeply rooted in acts of resistance. The power of resistance serves as the nucleus from which all forms of progressive transformation emanate. It is through resistance that individuals and communities challenge the status quo, advocate for change and strive for a better future. From the anti-feudal, anti-colonial, anti-capitalist, anti-imperialist and civil rights movements to the fight for gender equality, history is replete with examples of resistance driving significant societal advancements. Importantly, resistance embodies the resilience and determination inherent in human nature, illustrating that no force can entirely suppress the resistance in the quest of peace and progress.

As the rent-seeking technofeudalism by tech giants like Meta, Facebook, Google, Amazon, Apple, Microsoft and Alphabet expands its influence, it increasingly seeks to ensnare individuals, states, governments, communities and entire societies within the confines of its digital platforms. Within this landscape, the algorithms of resistance emerge as a crucial force, manifesting in the daily struggles of ordinary people against the dominance of these technological behemoths. Despite facing legal barriers and biased regulations that often favour the techno overlords, individuals persist in their efforts to push back and reclaim their democratic and digital rights as well as their very way of life. These acts of resistance represent a vital counterforce against the encroachment of corporate power into the fabric of society, serving as a reminder that the battle for autonomy and self-determination in the digital age is far from over.

The pervasive culture of hire-and-fire within the shadow employment environment of the gig economy serves to undermine the stability of social foundations, thereby weakening the collective power of the working masses and eroding their confidence. This strategy is not merely a by-product of economic trends but a deliberate tactic aimed at crippling the potential of the workforce to mobilise and assert their rights. By perpetuating an environment of uncertainty and insecurity, this model of employment not only diminishes the resilience of the resistance movement but also dismantles the conducive environments necessary for fostering progressive change within society. The constant threat of job instability and financial insecurity leaves workers vulnerable and hesitant to organise or challenge the status quo. Moreover, it hampers their ability to envision and pursue long-term goals for societal advancement. As a result, the very fabric of democratic principles and social progress is compromised, as individuals are preoccupied with navigating the precarious nature of their employment rather than engaging in meaningful collective action.

In essence, the culture of hire-and-fire within the digital economy not only undermines the immediate livelihoods of workers but also undermines the broader struggle for democracy and social change. By dismantling stable employment structures and fostering an atmosphere of precarity, it impedes the potential for organised resistance movements to flourish, thereby perpetuating the status quo of inequality and injustice. Addressing these systemic issues is crucial not only for the well-being of workers but also for the preservation and deepening of democratic principles and social harmony.

The formidable power wielded by digital platforms extends far beyond mere convenience or connectivity; it encompasses the ability to capture, control and domesticate individuals within a complex web of surveillance and security measures. Through the securitisation of everyday life, characterised by access controls, password requirements and multi-step verifications, these platforms normalise and institutionalise a pervasive state of surveillance. In doing so, they cultivate an environment where constant monitoring becomes accepted as the norm, effectively blurring the lines between personal autonomy and external control.

This normalisation of surveillance not only serves the interests of technofeudalism but also aligns with the broader agenda of creating a society compliant with its requirements. Under the guise of enhancing security and streamlining processes, individuals are gradually conditioned to relinquish aspects of their privacy and personal agency. In essence, while users may believe they maintain control over their own lives, they are, in fact, indirectly subject to the whims of the platforms they interact with. This phenomenon underscores the intricate power dynamics at play within the digital landscape, where seemingly innocuous interactions serve to reinforce the dominance of techno-feudalistic structures. By fostering a sense of dependency and reliance on their services, digital platforms effectively entrench their influence over individuals, perpetuating a cycle of control and domestication.

To challenge this paradigm, it is imperative to recognise and resist the normalisation of surveillance within society. By advocating for transparency, accountability and the protection of individual rights, it becomes possible to confront the encroachment of technofeudalism and reclaim autonomy over our digital lives. Only through collective awareness and concerted action can we hope to dismantle the mechanisms of control and forge a path towards a more equitable and liberated digital future. Through grassroots movements, advocacy and collective action, people around the world continue to resist the commodification of their data, the erosion of privacy and the erosion of democratic principles, forging a path towards a more equitable and just digital future. Thus, while reactionary opposition may arise, the spirit of resistance remains indomitable, persistently pushing boundaries and shaping the course of history.

Despite relentless efforts to domesticate and control the consciousness of individuals, the flame of progressive consciousness persists, fuelled by the collective labour and resistance against oppressive power structures. Throughout history, resistance has proven to be an indomitable force, challenging all forms of oppression and exploitation. There is no doubt that it is through the resilience of resistance movements that meaningful social change is realised. In the context of today's data-driven digital society, the algorithm of resistance remains integral. Despite the encroachment of technofeudalism, the spirit of resistance endures, transcending barriers and asserting the rights and agency of individuals. Digital subcultures, from piracy to open-source software movements, exemplify this ongoing struggle for the deepening of democracy and citizenship rights within the digital realm. These movements represent more than just acts of defiance; they embody a fundamental commitment to democratising access to information and technology. By challenging monopolistic control and advocating for open, transparent systems, they pave the way for a more equitable and inclusive digital landscape. Moreover, they serve as a potent reminder that, regardless of the obstacles imposed by techno-feudalistic structures, the spirit of resistance remains alive and thriving.

BIBLIOGRAPHY

Adams, M. (2014). Narcissism, overview. In T. Teo (Ed.), *Encyclopedia of critical psychology*. Springer.

Adams, T. V. (2016). *The psychopath factory: How capitalism organises empathy*. Duncan Baird Publishers.

Ahmad, A. (1993). Fascism and national culture: Reading Gramsci in the days of Hindutva. *Social Scientist, 21*(3–4), 32–68.

Alamad, S. (2024). *Beyond profit: The humanisation of economics through the theory of equitable optimality* (1st edition) (Contributions to Economics). Springer. https://doi.org/10.1007/978-3-031-49748-3.

Allchorn, W. (2024). Right-wing threat landscape and far-right threat groups of the greatest concern in the United Kingdom. In *A research agenda for far-right violence and extremism* (pp. 75–110). Edward Elgar Publishing.

Alcoff, L. M. (2018). *Rape and resistance*. John Wiley & Sons.

Alex-Assensoh, Y. M. (2005). *Democracy at risk: How political choices undermine citizen participation and what we can do about it*. Brookings Institution Press.

Alur, M. (2007). Forgotten millions: A case of cultural and systemic bias. *Support for Learning, 22*(4), 174–180.

Anthias, P. (2021). Rethinking territory and property in indigenous land claims. *Geoforum, 119*, 268–278.

Amin, S. (2010). *Ending the crisis of capitalism or ending capitalism?* Fahamu/Pambazuka.

Argun, B. E. (1999). Universal citizenship rights and Turkey's Kurdish question. *Journal of Muslim Minority Affairs, 19*(1), 85–103.

Armitstead, W. D. (2020). *Capitalism perverted: Exposing the sources of income inequality*. FriesenPress.

Bachrach, P. (Ed.). (2017). *Political elites in a democracy*. Routledge.

Backiel, L. (2015). Puerto Rico: The crisis is about colonialism, not debt. *Monthly Review, 67*(5), 11–18.

Bakan, J. (2012). *The corporation: The pathological pursuit of profit and power*. Hachette UK.

Bancroft, A. (2009). *Drugs, intoxication and society*. Polity.

Bannerji, H. (2016). Patriarchy in the era of neoliberalism: The case of India. *Social Scientist, 44*(3–4), 3–27.

Basu, A. (2016). Women, dynasties, and democracy in India. In K. Chandra (Ed.), *Democratic dynasties: State, party and family in contemporary Indian politics* (pp. 136–172). Cambridge University Press, UK.

Behl, N. (2022). India's farmers' protest: An inclusive vision of Indian democracy. *American Political Science Review*, *116*(3), 1141–1146.

Bell, D. (1972). The cultural contradictions of capitalism. *Journal of Aesthetic Education*, *6*(1–2), 11–38.

Benedict, H. (1993). *Virgin or vamp: How the press covers sex crimes*. Oxford University Press.

Benson, B. L. (1998). *To serve and protect: Privatization and community in criminal justice*. New York University Press.

Beteille, A. (2012). *Caste, class and power: Changing patterns of stratification in a Tanjore village*. Oxford University Press.

Betz, H. G. (2003). Xenophobia, identity politics and exclusionary populism in Western Europe. *Socialist Register*, *39*.

Bhambra, G. K. (2014). Introduction: Knowledge production in global context: Power and coloniality. *Current Sociology*, *62*(4), 451–456.

Blomley, N. (2007). Making private property: Enclosure, common right and the work of hedges. *Rural History*, *18*(1), 1–21.

Blomley, N. (2019). The territorialization of property in land: Space, power and practice. *Territory, Politics, Governance*, *7*(2), 233–249.

Bohrer, A. (2018). Intersectionality and Marxism: A critical historiography. *Historical Materialism*, *26*(2), 46–74.

Brautigam, D., & Rithmire, M. (2021). The Chinese 'Debt Trap' is a myth. *The Atlantic*, 6 February 2021.

Brown, N. W. (2006). *Coping with infuriating, mean, critical people: The destructive narcissistic pattern*. Bloomsbury Publishing.

Bruff, I. (2014). The rise of authoritarian neoliberalism. *Rethinking Marxism*, *26*(1), 113–129.

Buchowski, M. (2004). Hierarchies of knowledge in Central-Eastern European anthropology. *Anthropology of East Europe Review*, *22*(2), 5–14.

Burris, C. T. (2022). *Evil in mind: The psychology of harming others*. Oxford University Press.

Butko, S. (2018). *Crises, profit, and exploitation: A structural-Marxist interpretation of the 2007–08 global financial crisis* (Doctoral dissertation, Université d'Ottawa/University of Ottawa).

Callaghan, J. (2024). The left: The ideology of the labour party. In L. Tivey & A. Wright (Eds.), *Party ideology in Britain* (pp. 23–48). Routledge.

Capezza, N. M., & Arriaga, X. B. (2008). Why do people blame victims of abuse? The role of stereotypes of women on perceptions of blame. *Sex Roles*, *59*, 839–850.

Carvalho, A. (2021). Rethinking the politics of meditation: Practice, affect and ontology. *The Sociological Review*, *69*(6), 1260–1276.

Chacko, P. (2019). Marketizing Hindutva: The state, society, and markets in Hindu nationalism. *Modern Asian Studies*, *53*(2), 377–410.

Chandra, P. (2011). Corruption, ethics and politics: The reproduction of capitalism and a ruse of history, radical notes. https://radicalnotes.org/category/commentaries/page/5/?ref=driverlayer.com%2Fimage (accessed on 23 August 2024).

Charitsis, V., Zwick, D., & Bradshaw, A. (2018). Creating worlds that create audiences: Theorising personal data markets in the age of communicative capitalism. *tripleC: Communication, Capitalism & Critique. Open Access Journal for a Global Sustainable Information Society*, *16*(2), 820–834.

Charron, N., & Rothstein, B. (2018). Regions of trust and distrust: How good institutions can foster social cohesion. In U. Bernitz, M. Mårtensson, L. Oxelheim, & T. Persson (Eds.), *Bridging the prosperity gap in the EU* (pp. 220–242). Edward Elgar Publishing.

Chellaney, B. (2017). China's Debt-Trap Diplomacy. Project Syndicate. https://www .project-syndicate.org/commentary/china-one-belt-one-road-loans-debt-by -brahma-chellaney-2017-01.

Cocco, G. (2007). The labor of territories between deterritorialization and reterritorialization. *Rethinking Marxism, 19*(3), 306–318.

Cockburn, P. J. (2018). *The politics of dependence: Economic parasites and vulnerable lives.* Springer.

Cook, J. (2016). Mindful in Westminster: The politics of meditation and the limits of neoliberal critique. *HAU: Journal of Ethnographic Theory, 6*(1), 141–161.

Colley, L. K., & Head, B. (2013). Changing patterns of privatization: Ideology, economic necessity, or political opportunism. *International Journal of Public Administration, 36*(12), 865–875.

Cooper, F. (2005). *Colonialism in question: Theory, knowledge, history.* University of California Press.

Croly, H. (2017). *Progressive democracy.* Routledge.

Crompton, R. (2008). *Class and stratification.* Polity.

Cox, K. R. (2024). States and their territorializations: Class, local dependence, and how geohistory matters. *Human Geography, 17*(1), 15–27.

Debt Justice. (2015). How Europe cancelled Germany's debt in 1953, 26 February 2015. https://debtjustice.org.uk/report/europe-cancelled-germanys-debt-1953 (Accessed on 18 February 2024).

Dejuán, Ó. (2013). 4 The debt trap. In Ó. Dejuán, E. F. Paños, & J. U. Gonzalez (Eds.), *Post-Keynesian Views of the Crisis and its Remedies* (p. 87). Routledge, Oxon.

De Lissovoy, N. (2010). Rethinking education and emancipation: Being, teaching, and power. *Harvard Educational Review, 80*(2), 203–221.

Deleuze, G., & Guattari, F. (2009). *Anti-Oedipus: Capitalism and schizophrenia.* Penguin.

De Mul, J. (2014). *Destiny domesticated: The rebirth of tragedy out of the spirit of technology.* State University of New York Press.

Desai, R. (2011). Gujarat's Hindutva of capitalist development. *South Asia: Journal of South Asian Studies, 34*(3), 354–381.

Desai, R. (2016). Hindutva and fascism [Review of *fascism: Essays on Europe and India*, by J. Banaji]. *Economic and Political Weekly, 51*(53), 20–24. http://www.jstor.org/stable /44166046

De Souza, R., & Hussain, S. A. (2023). 'Howdy Modi!': Mediatization, Hindutva, and long distance ethnonationalism. *Journal of International and Intercultural Communication, 16*(2), 138–161.

Dirlik, A. (2003). Global modernity? Modernity in an age of global capitalism. *European Journal of Social Theory, 6*(3), 275–292.

Doshi, S., & Ranganathan, M. (2019). Towards a critical geography of corruption and power in late capitalism. *Progress in Human Geography, 43*(3), 436–457.

Douglas, H. (2021). *Women, intimate partner violence, and the law.* Oxford University Press.

Dube, S. (2002). Introduction: Colonialism, modernity, colonial modernities. *Nepantla: Views from South, 3*(2), 197–219.

Ehsan, B. (2024). Beyond boundaries: A feminist critique of oppression in the age of anthropocene. *Integrated Journal for Research in Arts and Humanities, 4*(3), 73–77.

Elden, S. (2022). The state of territory under globalization: Empire and the politics of reterritorialization. In A. M. Brighenti & M. Kärrholm (Eds.), *Territories, Environments, Politics* (pp. 15–36). Routledge.

Elhefnawy, N. (2021). 'What is Centrism?': An examination of centrism as a conservative political philosophy. *An examination of centrism as a conservative political philosophy* (15 June 2021).

Elhefnawy, N. (2024). Keir Starmer's ten pledges and the Labour Party's 2024 general election manifesto. *Available at SSRN 4874036.*

Elias, A. (Ed.). (2024). Racism, class and inequality. In *Racism and anti-racism today* (pp. 119–136). Emerald Publishing Limited.

Escobar, A., de Souza Filho, C. F. M., Nunes, J. A., Coelho, J. P. B., dos Santos, L. G., de Oliveira Neves, L. J., . . . Ghai, Y. (2020). *Another knowledge is possible: Beyond northern epistemologies.* Verso Books.

Fabbrini, S. (2010). *Compound democracies: Why the United States and Europe are becoming similar.* Oxford University Press.

Farkas, J., & Schou, J. (2018). Fake news as a floating signifier: Hegemony, antagonism and the politics of falsehood. *Javnost-the Public, 25*(3), 298–314.

Featherstone, M. (1990). Global culture: An introduction. *Theory, Culture & Society, 7*(2–3), 1–14.

Fernandez, J. L. (1995). Family relationship as basis for disqualification to hold public office: A framework for a law prohibiting political dynasties. *Ateneo LJ, 40,* 96.

Fernandez, C. (2008). 'Capitalism, consumerism and individualism: Investigating the rhetoric of *The Secret*'. *USF Tampa Graduate Theses and Dissertations.* https://digitalcommons.usf.edu/etd/237 (accessed on 22 August 2024).

Fitzpatrick, S. (2006). Social parasites: How tramps, idle youth, and busy entrepreneurs impeded the Soviet march to communism. *Cahiers du monde russe, 47*(1–2), 377–408.

Friedrich, D. (2014). *Democratic education as a curricular problem: Historical consciousness and the moralizing limits of the present.* Routledge.

Gardner, L. (2017). Colonialism or super sanctions: Sovereignty and debt in West Africa, 1871–1914. *European Review of Economic History, 21*(2), 236–257.

Geddes, K. (2019). Meet your new overlords: How digital platforms develop and sustain technofeudalism. *The Columbia Journal of Law & the Arts, 43,* 455.

Gianoncelli, E. (2021). The unification of the 'New Right'? On Europe, identity politics and reactionary ideologies. *New Perspectives, 29*(4), 364–375.

Gibbs, D. N. (2012). The military–industrial complex in a globalized context. In R. Cox (Ed.), *Corporate Power and Globalization in US Foreign Policy* (pp. 95–113). Routledge.

Gibson-Graham, J. K. (1995). Identity and economic plurality: Rethinking capitalism and 'capitalist hegemony'. *Environment and Planning D: Society and Space, 13*(3), 275–282.

Gilbert, J. (2024). Techno-feudalism or platform capitalism? Conceptualising the digital society. *European Journal of Social Theory, 27*(4), 561–578. https://doi.org/10.1177/13684310241276474.

Giles, K. (2020). *The headship of men and the abuse of women: Are they related in any way?* Wipf and Stock Publishers.

Giroux, H. (2014). Neoliberalism's war on democracy. *Truthout*, 26 April 2014.

Glasbeek, H. (2018). Capitalism: A crime story (0 ed.). Between the lines. Retrieved from https://www.perlego.com/book/666650/capitalism-a-crime-story-pdf (Original work published 2018).

Goldberg, B. S. (2015). *Queering the violences of men: Deconstructing how neoliberalism, patriarchy, and hegemonic masculinity intersect to foster violent masculinities and perpetuate a rape culture in the United States* (Master's thesis, University for Peace).

Golec de Zavala, A., & Lantos, D. (2020). Collective narcissism and its social consequences: The bad and the ugly. *Current Directions in Psychological Science, 29*(3), 273–278.

Graeber, D. (2011). *Debt: The first 5000 years.* Melville House Brooklyn.

Grant, Z., & Evans, G. (2024). A new dilemma of social democracy? The British Labour Party, the White working class and ethnic minority representation. *British Journal of Political Science, 54*(3), 793–815.

Gualini, E. (2016). Multilevel governance and multiscalar forms of territorialisation. In *Handbook on cohesion policy in the EU.* Cheltenham, UK: Edward Elgar Publishing. Retrieved Dec 19, 2024, from https://doi.org/10.4337/9781784715670.00049.

Halikiopoulou, D. (2018). A right-wing populist momentum: A review of 2017 elections across Europe. *Journal of Common Market Studies, 56*, 63.

Haller, R. (2015). *The narcissist in the mirror: A field guide to our selves and other people.* ecoWing.

Hancké, B., Rhodes, M., & Thatcher, M. (Eds.). (2007). *Beyond varieties of capitalism: Conflict, contradictions, and complementarities in the European economy.* Oxford University Press.

Hanlon, P., & Carlisle, S. (2009). Is 'modern culture' bad for our health and well-being? *Global Health Promotion, 16*(4), 27–34.

Harnecker, C. (2007). Workplace democracy and collective consciousness. *Monthly Review, 59*(6), 27–40.

Harvey, D. (2014). *Seventeen contradictions and the end of capitalism.* Oxford University Press.

Herbst, J. (2014). *States and power in Africa: Comparative lessons in authority and control* (Vol. 149). Princeton University Press.

Hirst, M. (2017). Towards a political economy of fake news. *The Political Economy of Communication, 5*(2).

Hillier, J. (2023). Deleuze, Guattari and power. In *Handbook on Planning and Power* (pp. 74–89). Edward Elgar Publishing.

Himmer, M., & Rod, Z. (2022). Chinese debt trap diplomacy: Reality or myth? *Journal of the Indian Ocean Region, 18*(3), 250–272. https://doi.org/10.1080/19480881.2023.2195280

Holmwood, J. (2014). From social rights to the market: Neoliberalism and the knowledge economy. *International Journal of Lifelong Education, 33*(1), 62–76.

Howard, A. (1995). Global capital and labor internationalism in comparative historical perspective: A Marxist analysis. *Sociological Inquiry, 65*(3–4), 365–394.

IMF. (2020). *Reform of the international debt architecture is urgently needed* by Kristalina Georgieva, Ceyla Pazarbasioglu and Rhoda Weeks-Brown. https://www.imf

.org/en/Blogs/Articles/2020/10/01/blog-reform-of-the-international-debt
-architecture-is-urgently-needed (accessed on 10 November 2022).

Ince, A. (2012). In the shell of the old: Anarchist geographies of territorialisation. *Antipode, 44*(5), 1645–1666.

Inglehart, R., & Norris, P. (2017). Trump and the populist authoritarian parties: The silent revolution in reverse. *Perspectives on Politics, 15*(2), 443–454.

Iqbal, M., Gul, S., & Rashid, A. (2023). Marxist analysis of capitalistic trauma and its impact on moral degeneration after Industrial Revolution. *Journal of Asian Development Studies, 12*(4), 991–1004.

Issar, S. (2023). Historicizing real estate: The East India Company in early colonial Bombay. *Enterprise & Society*, 1–23. https://doi.org/10.1017/eso.2023.40.

Jack, C. (2019). Wicked content. *Communication, Culture & Critique, 12*(4), 435–454.

Jackson, T. (2021). *Post growth: Life after capitalism.* John Wiley & Sons.

Jansson, H. (2024). Fences are like ghosts are like monuments: Ephemeral social agreements under the neoliberal rule. https://www.diva-portal.org/smash/get/diva2:1837636/FULLTEXT01.pdf (accessed on 21 August 2024).

Johansen, E. (2008). *Territorialized cosmopolitanism: Space, place and cosmopolitan identity* (PhD diss., McMaster University).

John, O. I., Messina, G. M., & Odumegwu, A. C. (2023). The effects of neocolonialism on Africa's development. *PanAfrican Journal of Governance and Development (PJGD), 4*(2), 3–35.

Johnston, J., Laxer, G. (2003). Solidarity in the age of globalization: Lessons from the anti-MAI and Zapatista struggles. *Theory and Society, 32*, 39–91. https://doi.org/10.1023/A:1023025130342.

Jones, L., & Hameiri, S. (2020). *Debunking the myth of 'Debt-trap diplomacy' How recipient countries shape China's belt and road initiative*, Asia-Pacific Programme | August 2020, Chatham House, London.

Jordan, B. (2008). *Welfare and well-being: Social value in public policy.* Policy Press.

Jubilee Debt Campaign. (2015). The new debt trap. https://jubileedebt.org.uk/wp-content/uploads/2015/07/The-new-debt-trap_07.15.pdf (accessed on 20 February 2024).

Kabeer, N. (Ed.). (2005). *Inclusive citizenship: Meanings and expressions* (Vol. 1). Zed Books.

Kanungo, P. (2003). Hindutva's entry into a 'Hindu Province': Early years of RSS in Orissa. *Economic and Political Weekly, 38*(31), 3293–3303.

Karelse, C. M. (2019). *White mindfulness in the US and UK: The impact of racial neoliberalism* (Doctoral dissertation, SOAS University of London).

Kaul, N. (2017). Rise of the political right in India: Hindutva-development mix, Modi myth, and dualities. *Journal of Labor and Society, 20*(4), 523–548.

Kenny, M. (2024). *Fractured union: Politics, sovereignty and the fight to save the UK.* Oxford University Press.

King, U., & Parrish, L. (2007). Springing the debt trap. Center for Responsible Lending, Durham, North Carolina, United State.

Kitschelt, H. P., Marks, G., & Stephens, J. (1998). Conclusion: Convergence and divergence of advanced capitalist democracies. In H. Kitschelt, P. Lange, G. Marks, & J. Stephens (Eds.), *The politics and political economy of advanced industrial societies* (pp. 427–460). Cambridge: Cambridge University Press.

Klein, L. E. (1995). Gender and the public/private distinction in the eighteenth century: Some questions about evidence and analytic procedure. *Eighteenth-Century Studies, 29*(1), 97–109.

Kochegurov, D. A. (2022). Formation of an anti-Chinese consensus among US 'Think Tanks': From D. Trump to J. Biden. *Herald Russian Academy of Sciences, 92*(Suppl 7), S601–S611. https://doi.org/10.1134/S1019331622130044

Kothari, A. (2019). Radical well-being alternatives to development. In P. Cullet & S. Koonan (Eds.), *Research handbook on law, environment and the Global South* (pp. 64–84). Edward Elgar Publishing.

Kramer, J. M. (2021). From predator to parasite: On private property and our ecological disaster. *Journal of Economic Issues, 55*(2), 416–422.

Kumral, Ş. (2023). Globalization, crisis and right-wing populists in the Global South: The cases of India and Turkey. *Globalizations, 20*(5), 752–781.

Kwet, M. (2022). Digital colonialism and infrastructure-as-debt. *Kwet, Michael. Digital colonialism and infrastructure-as-debt.* University of Bayreuth African Studies Online.

Lall, M., & Anand, K. (2022). Higher education, neoliberalism, and Hindu nationalism. In M. Lall & K. Anand (Eds.), *Bridging neoliberalism and Hindu nationalism* (pp. 154–186). Bristol University Press.

Leal, L. S. (2018). Ideology, alienation and reification: Concepts for a radical theory of communication in contemporary capitalism. *tripleC: Communication, Capitalism & Critique. Open Access Journal for a Global Sustainable Information Society, 16*(2), 687–695.

Lebowitz, M. A. (2021). *Between capitalism and community.* Monthly Review Press.

Lee, G. B. (2007). Consuming cultures: Translating the global, homogenizing the local. *Discourse and International Relations.* U. Dagmar Scheu Lottgen & José Saura Sanchez, eds., Peter Lang, pp. 205–219, 2007, Available at SSRN: https://ssrn.com/abstract=1112224.

Lefebvre, H. (1976). *The survival of capitalism.* Allison and Busby.

Leidig, E. (2020). Hindutva as a variant of right-wing extremism. *Patterns of Prejudice, 54*(3), 215–237.

Lelo, T., & Fígaro, R. (2021). A materialist approach to fake news. In G. Lopez-Garcia, D. Palau-Sampio, B. Palomo, E. C. Domínguez, Masip, & Pere (Eds.), *Politics of disinformation: The influence of fake news on the public sphere* (pp. 23–34). Wiley-Blackwell.

Leong, N. (2021). When diversity is not enough: A reflection on identity capitalists. *New England Law Review, 56,* 185.

Levine, P. (1999). *The new progressive era: Toward a fair and deliberative democracy.* Rowman & Littlefield Publishers.

Lewin, H. (2011). *Stones against the mirror: Friendship in the time of the South African struggle.* Penguin Random House South Africa.

Leys, C. (2001). *Market-driven politics: Neoliberal democracy and the public interest.* Verso.

Leys, C. (2010). Health, health care and capitalism. *Socialist Register, 46,* 1–28.

Lind, M. (2020). *The new class war: Saving democracy from the managerial elite.* Penguin.

Looney, S. (2017). Breaking point? An examination of the politics of othering in Brexit Britain. *An Examination of the Politics of Othering in Brexit Britain (28 April 2017).* TLI Think.

Lunt, P. K., & Livingstone, S. (1992). *Mass consumption and personal identity: Everyday Economic Experience.* Buckingham, UK: Open University Press.

Maistry, S. (2008). *Community development education: The integration of individual and collective consciousness for community well-being within a social development paradigm in South Africa* (Doctoral dissertation, University of Fort Hare).

Malesza, M., & Kaczmarek, M. C. (2018). Grandiose narcissism versus vulnerable narcissism and impulsivity. *Personality and Individual Differences, 126*, 61–65.

Maseland, R. (2013). Parasitical cultures? The cultural origins of institutions and development. *Journal of Economic Growth, 18*, 109–136.

Matlin, D. (2018). Harlem: The making of a ghetto discourse. In A. M. Fearnley & D. Matlin (Eds.), *Race capital? Harlem as setting and symbol* (pp. 71–90). Columbia University Press.

Matthews, D. (2019). Capitalism and mental health. *Monthly Review, 70*(8), 49–62.

Mayal, T. (2021). Pluralism and secularism in India: Sustainability and challenges of pluralism in a democratic set-up. *International Journal of Law Management & Humanities, 4*(3), 2646–2653.

McKay, S., & Tenove, C. (2021). Disinformation as a threat to deliberative democracy. *Political Research Quarterly, 74*(3), 703–717.

McKean, L. (1996). *Divine enterprise: Gurus and the Hindu nationalist movement.* University of Chicago Press.

Melamed, J. (2015). Racial capitalism. *Critical Ethnic Studies, 1*(1), 76–85.

Meyers, M. (1996). *News coverage of violence against women: Engendering blame.* Sage Publications.

Mohanty, T. R. (2024). Majoritarianism: Contextualizing populism in India. In J. C. Chennattuserry, M. Deshpande, & P. Hong (Eds.), *Encyclopedia of new populism and responses in the 21st century* (pp. 1–6). Springer Nature Singapore.

Mondon, A., & Winter, A. (2020). *Reactionary democracy: How racism and the populist far right became mainstream.* Verso Books.

Mount, F. (2012). *The new few: Or a very British oligarchy.* Simon and Schuster.

Navarro, V. (2017). The worldwide class struggle. In Kevin B. Anderson and Bertell Ollman (Eds.), *Karl Marx* (pp. 273–288). Routledge.

Nayak, B. S. (2017). *Hindu fundamentalism and the spirit of capitalism in India: Hinduisation of tribals in kalahandi during the new economic reforms.* Rowman & Littlefield.

Nayak, B. S. (2021a). Colonial world of postcolonial historians: Reification, theoreticism, and the neoliberal reinvention of tribal identity in India. *Journal of Asian and African Studies, 56*(3), 511–532.

Nayak, B. S. (2021b). *Disenchanted India and beyond: Musings on the lockdown alternatives.* Rowman & Littlefield.

Nayak, B. S. (Ed.). (2023). Introduction: China—Challenges of the great transition. In *China: The great transition: From Agrarian economy to technological powerhouse* (pp. 1–7). Springer Nature Singapore.

Nehring, D., Madsen, O. J., Cabanas, E., Mills, C., & Kerrigan, D. (Eds.). (2020). *The Routledge international handbook of global therapeutic cultures.* Routledge.

Nilges, M. (2019). *Right-wing culture in contemporary capitalism: Regression and hope in a time without future.* Bloomsbury Academic.

Nine, C. (2012). *Global justice and territory.* Oxford University Press.

Nitin Kumar Bharti, Lucas Chancel, Thomas Piketty, & Anmol Somanchi. (2024). *Income and Wealth Inequality in India, 1922–2023: The Rise of the Billionaire Raj.* Working Papers halshs-04563836, HAL.

Otero, G., & Gürcan, E. C. (2024). *Collective empowerment in Latin America: Indigenous peasant movements and political transformation.* Taylor & Francis.

Panda, A. (2019). Mike Pompeo also criticized China's 'debt trap' diplomacy. *The Diplomat.* https://thediplomat.com/2019/03/us-secretary-of-state-criticizes-chinas-south-chinasea-practices/, 14th March (accessed on 22 February 2024).

Patel, S. (2022). Colonialism and its knowledges. In McCallum, D. (Ed.), *The Palgrave handbook of the history of human sciences* (pp. 1–24). Palgrave Macmillan, Singapore. https://doi.org/10.1007/978-981-15-4106-3_68-1.

Payer, C. (1975). *The debt trap: The international monetary fund and the third world.* Monthly Review Press.

Peluso, N. L., & Lund, C. (2011). New frontiers of land control: Introduction. *Journal of Peasant Studies, 38*(4), 667–681.

Pfohl, S. (1993). Twilight of the parasites: Ultramodern capital and the new world order. *Social Problems, 40*(2), 125–151.

Piff, P. K. (2014). Wealth and the inflated self: Class, entitlement, and narcissism. *Personality and Social Psychology Bulletin, 40*(1), 34–43.

Pinatih, I. D. S. (2024). Identity politics and political parties in India. *Nation State: Journal of International Studies, 7*(1), 71–85.

Pistono, S. P. (1987). Susan Brownmiller and the history of rape. *Women's Studies: An Interdisciplinary Journal, 14*(3), 265–276.

Pratt, G., Johnston, C., & Johnson, K. (2023). Robots and care of the ageing self: An emerging economy of loneliness. *Environment and Planning A: Economy and Space, 55*(8), 2051–2066.

Radhakrishnan, P. (2004). Religion under globalisation. *Economic and Political Weekly, 39*(13), 1403–1411.

Rahman, A. (2013). *Essays on political dynasties: Evidence from empirical investigations* (Doctoral dissertation, London School of Economics and Political Science).

Rana, P. B., & Xianbai, J. J. (2020). *China's belt and road initiative impacts on Asia and policy agenda.* Palgrave Macmillan.

Rasmussen, M. B., & Lund, C. (2018). Reconfiguring frontier spaces: The territorialization of resource control. *World Development, 101*, 388–399.

Reid-Henry, S. (2020). *Empire of democracy: The remaking of the west since the Cold War.* Simon & Schuster.

Reinert, K. A. (2018). *No small hope: Towards the universal provision of basic goods.* Oxford University Press.

Roberts, J. (2021). *Capitalism and the limits of desire.* Bloomsbury.

Roberts, P. (2014). *The impulse society: What's wrong with getting what we want?* Bloomsbury Publishing.

Rogaly, B. (Ed.). (2020). 'If not you, they can get ten different workers in your place': Racial capitalism and workplace resistance. In *Stories from a migrant city* (pp. 72–113). Manchester University Press.

Roy, S. (2005). Indian freedom struggle and Muslims. In A. Ali Engineer (Ed.), *They Too Fought for India's Freedom: The Role of Minorities* (pp. 103–120). Hope India Publications, New Delhi.

Rutherford, J. (2008). The culture of capitalism. *Soundings*. Lawrence & Wishart Ltd (pp. 8–18).

Sassen, S. (2002). Towards post-national and denationalized citizenship. In E. F. Isin, & B. S. Turner (Eds.), *Handbook of citizenship studies* (pp. 277–291). London:Sage. https://doi.org/10.4135/9781848608276.n17.

Sassoon, D. (2021). *Morbid symptoms: An anatomy of a world in crisis.* Verso Books.

Scholz, S. J. (2008). *Political solidarity.* Penn State Press.

Scherer, B., & Waistell, J. (2018). Incorporating mindfulness: Questioning capitalism. *Journal of Management, Spirituality & Religion, 15*(2), 123–140.

Schmidt, R. J. (2012). *Versailles and the ruhr: Seedbed of world war II.* Springer Dordrecht. https://doi.org/10.1007/978-94-015-1081-3

Schuilenburg, M. (2015). *The securitization of society: Crime, risk, and social order* (Vol. 12). New York University Press.

Scott-Villiers, P., Chisholm, N., Wanjiku Kelbert, A., & Hossain, N. (2016). Precarious lives: Food, work and care after the global food crisis. The Institute of Development Studies and Partner Organisations. Report. https://hdl.handle.net/20.500.12413/12190.

Seth, S. (2009). Putting knowledge in its place: Science, colonialism, and the postcolonial. *Postcolonial Studies, 12*(4), 373–388.

Sevilla-Buitrago, A. (2012). Territory and the governmentalisation of social reproduction: Parliamentary enclosure and spatial rationalities in the transition from feudalism to capitalism. *Journal of Historical Geography, 38*(3), 209–219.

Sevilla-Buitrago, A. (2015). Capitalist formations of enclosure: Space and the extinction of the commons. *Antipode, 47*(4), 999–1020.

Shaikh, A. (2016). *Capitalism: Competition, conflict, crises.* Oxford University Press.

Shani, G. (2021). Towards a Hindu Rashtra: Hindutva, religion, and nationalism in India. *Religion, State & Society, 49*(3), 264–280.

Sharma, P. (2014). From India against corruption to the Aam Aadmi Party: Social movements, political parties and citizen engagement in India. In R. Cordenillo & S. van der Staak (Eds.), *Political parties and citizen movements in Asia and Europe* (pp. 39–59). International IDEA, Sweden.

Shelby, T. (2002). Parasites, pimps, and capitalists: A naturalistic conception of exploitation. *Social Theory and Practice, 28*(3), 381–418.

Sibley, M. A. (2021). *A genealogy of 'Rape Culture': Knowing and governing sexual violence* (Doctoral dissertation, Carleton University).

Siddiqui, K. (2017). Hindutva, neoliberalism and the reinventing of India. *Journal of Economic and Social Thought, 4*(2), 142–186.

Silver, J. (2023). *Scoundrels and shirkers: Capitalism and poverty in Britain.* Fernwood Publishing.

Singh, A. (2020): The myth of 'debt-trap diplomacy' and realities of Chinese development finance. *Third World Quarterly, 42*, 239–253. https://doi.org/10.1080/01436597.2020.1807318

Singh, M. P. (2014). New social movements and alternative politics: India in a comparative theoretical perspective. *Journal of Social and Political Studies, 50.* http://socialsciences.in/article/new-social-movements-and-alternative-politics-india-comparative-theoretical-perspective.

Skonieczny, K. (2023). Capitalism and slowness: Resistance or reterritorialization? The case of slow food. In S. Wróbel & K. Skonieczny (Eds.), *Regimes of capital in the post-digital age* (pp. 231–242). Routledge.

Slater, D. (1987). On the wings of the sign: Commodity culture and social practice. *Media, Culture & Society, 9*(4), 457–480.

Smith, C. J. (1974). History of rape and rape laws. *Women Lawyers Journal, 60,* 188.

Soon, C., & Goh, S. (2018). Fake news, false information and more: Countering human biases. *Institute of Policy Studies (IPS) Working Papers, 31.*

Stallings, B. (1992). International influence on economic policy: Debt, stabilization, and structural reform. In S. Haggard & R. R. Kaufman (Eds.), *The politics of economic adjustment: International constraints, distributive conflicts and the state* (pp. 41–88). Princeton: Princeton University Press. https://doi.org/10.1515/9780691188034-005.

Stavrides, S. (Ed.). (2020). Territorialities of emancipation. In *Common spaces of urban emancipation* (pp. 47–63). Manchester University Press.

Steed, C. (2016). *A question of worth: Economy, society and the quantification of human value.* Bloomsbury Publishing.

Steger, M. B. (2008). *The rise of the global imaginary: Political ideologies from the French revolution to the global war on terror.* Oxford University Press.

Stern, A. (2023). Centrist illusions: How not to defend liberalism. *Commonweal, 150*(8), 36–42.

Stoddart, M. C. (2007). Ideology, hegemony, discourse: A critical review of theories of knowledge and power. *Social Thought & Research, 28,* 191–225.

Swan, T. (2018). *The anatomy of loneliness: How to find your way back to connection.* Watkins Media Limited.

Tabassum, N., & Nayak, B. S. (2021). Gender stereotypes and their impact on women's career progressions from a managerial perspective. *IIM Kozhikode Society & Management Review, 10*(2), 192–208.

Taiwo, O. (1993). Colonialism and its aftermath: The crisis of knowledge production. *Callaloo, 16*(4), 891–908.

Taylor, J. (2020). *Why women are blamed for everything: Exposing the culture of victim-blaming.* Hachette UK.

Teune, H. (2009). Citizenship deterritorialized: Global citizenships, In J. V. Ciprut (Ed.), *The Future of Citizenship.* The MIT Press.

Thomas, A. (2024). *The politics and ethics of transhumanism: Techno-human evolution and advanced capitalism.* Policy Press.

Tilley, H., & Gordon, R. (Eds.). (2017). *Ordering Africa: Anthropology, European imperialism and the politics of knowledge* (Vol. 67). Manchester University Press.

Torabian, J. E. (Ed.). (2022). The capitalist Trojan Horse and its tenets. In *Wealth, Values, Culture & Education: Reviving the essentials for equality & sustainability* (pp. 59–90). Springer International Publishing.

Torre, A. (2014). *Myths of capitalism: A guide for the 99%.* Xlibris Corporation.

Tripodi, F. B. (2022). *The propagandists' playbook: How conservative elites manipulate search and threaten democracy.* Yale University Press.

Twenge, J. M., & Campbell, W. K. (2009). *The narcissism epidemic: Living in the age of entitlement.* Simon and Schuster.

Ullman, S. E. (2004). Sexual assault victimization and suicidal behavior in women: A review of the literature. *Aggression and Violent Behavior, 9*(4), 331–351.

Upreti, G. (Ed.). (2023). Power of collective human consciousness. In *Ecosociocentrism: The earth first paradigm for sustainable living* (pp. 287–305). Springer Nature Switzerland.

Usmani, A. (2018). Democracy and the class struggle. *American Journal of Sociology, 124*(3), 664–704.

UwakweJ, I. C., & Onebunne, J. I. (2022). Neo-imperialism and paradox of African dent crisis. *Nnadiebjbe Journal of Philosophy, 2*(2), 58–75.

Varoufakis, Y. (2023). *Technofeudalism: What killed capitalism.* Bodley Head.

van Niekerk, A. J. (2020). Inclusive economic sustainability: SDGs and global inequality. *Sustainability, 12*(13), 5427.

Van Niekerk, D., Peréz-Ortiz, M., Shawe-Taylor, J., Orlic, D., Kay, J., Siegel, N., . . . Aneja, U. (2024). Challenging systematic prejudices: An investigation into bias against women and girls. https://discovery.ucl.ac.uk/id/eprint/10188772/ (accessed on 20 August 2024).

Vighi, F. (2019). Genie out of the bottle: Lacan and the loneliness of global capitalism. *Crisis and Critique, 6*(1), 390–415.

Vincze, E. (2019). Ghettoization: The production of marginal spaces of housing and the reproduction of racialized labour. In E. Vincze, N. Petrovici, C. Raț, & G. Picker (Eds.), *Racialized labour in Romania*. Neighborhoods, Communities, and Urban Marginality. Palgrave Macmillan, Cham. https://doi.org/10.1007/978-3-319-76273-9_3.

Vujnovic, M., & Kruckeberg, D. (2023). Disinformation, misinformation, fake news, and their global impact. In Y. R. Kamalipour & J. V. Pavlik (Eds.), *Communicating global crises: Media, war, climate, and politics*, 97. Rowman and Littlefield, Maryland.

Wang, J. (2018). *Carceral capitalism* (Vol. 21). MIT Press.

Warren, M. O. (2021). *History of the rise, progress, and termination of the American Revolution.* Good Press.

Watson, R., & Levin, M. (2023). The collective intelligence of evolution and development. *Collective Intelligence, 2*(2). https://doi.org/10.1177/26339137231168355.

Webster, C. (Ed.). (2023). Accumulation by dispossession: Land grabs, enclosure and trespass. In *Rich Crime, Poor Crime: Inequality and the Rule of Law* (pp. 35–59). Emerald Publishing Limited.

Weiler, A. M., Otero, G., & Wittman, H. (2016). Rock stars and bad apples: Moral economies of alternative food networks and precarious farm work regimes. *Antipode, 48*(4), 1140–1162.

Williams, B. (2024). The 'New Right' and its legacy for British conservatism. *Journal of Political Ideologies, 29*(1), 121–144.

Wright, C., & Nyberg, D. (2015). *Climate change, capitalism, and corporations.* Cambridge University Press.

Yates, M. D. (2018). *Can the working class change the world?* New York University Press.

Young, C. (1986). Africa's colonial legacy. In R. J. Berg, & J. S. Whitaker (Eds.), *Strategies for African development* (pp. 25–51). University of California Press, London.

Young, R. (2017). *Personal autonomy: Beyond negative and positive liberty.* Routledge.

INDEX

187

www.ingramcontent.com/pod-product-compliance
Lightning Source LLC
Chambersburg PA
CBHW020611270326
41927CB00005B/280